A Guide to
Dublin Bay

A Guide to
Dublin Bay

Mirror to the City

John Givens

The Liffey Press

Published by
The Liffey Press
Ashbrook House
10 Main Street
Raheny, Dublin 5, Ireland
www.theliffeypress.com

© 2006 John Givens

A catalogue record of this book is
available from the British Library.

ISBN 1-905785-08-9

Printed in the UK by MPG Books

Contents

About the Author

John Givens is a writer currently living in Howth. New York Harbour, San Francisco Bay, and Tokyo Bay have all formed important parts of his life, and his writing career has included essays on communications strategy, branding and digital design, as well as travel essays and novels.

Acknowledgements

Any survey of a place as complex and fascinating as Dublin Bay requires a good deal of compression. This book could have been ten times longer, and I would like to thank The Liffey Press for the guidance and good counsel that kept it within bounds. Senior Editor Brian Langan wielded a steady pen with a light hand. I am indebted to his patience, fortitude and good humour.

The Dublin Port Company has been generous with their aid, and in particular I owe a debt of gratitude to the Dublin Port Archives. The Dun Laoghaire Harbour Company got me pointed in the right directions, and I am grateful. Thank you to Stephen McAvoy and Niall Hatch of BirdWatch Ireland for providing information and images. Dublin Bay Watch offered many valuable insights, for which I thank them, Seán Dublin Bay Loftus, in particular. Thank you also to Anita Joyce and Elizabeth Kirwan of the National Library of Ireland, Niamh Stephenson of RNLI Ireland, Graham Smith of the Howth Yacht Club and the many others who provided useful information.

Three books deserve mentioning. *A History of the Port of Dublin* by Henry Gilligan (Gill and Macmillan, Dublin, 1988) was incomparably useful. *Dublin Bay: From Killiney to Howth* by Brian Lalor (The O'Brien Press, Dublin, 1989) is as beautiful as it was inspiring. *The Book of the Liffey: From Source to the Sea*, by Elizabeth Healy, Christopher Moriarty and Gerard O'Flaherty (Wolfhound Press, Dublin, 1988) filled in gaps and answered questions. My debt to all three is hereby acknowledged.

The credit for what went right belongs to the many people involved in this project; the blunders, alas, are my own.

Image Credits

The author and publishers wish to thank the following individuals and organisations for kind permission to reproduce their copyrighted photographs and illustrations: © National Library of Ireland, pages 1, 14, 24, 51, 56; 77, 82, 184, 189; © Andrzej Tokarski, page 5; © Richard Hawkes, page 20; Phoenix Maps (26 Ashington Avenue, Navan Road, Dublin 7), for maps on pages 25, 36, 43, 56, 87, 146, 182; Guinness Archives, pages 28, 31, 32, 33; © Padraig Cronin, pages 48, 160, 173, 197, 200, 207; myhometownsales.ie, page 55; © Aidan O'Rourke (www.aidan.co.uk), front cover, pages 59, 75, 80, 131, 145, 237; © Aiden McCabe (www.irishships.com), pages 60, 62, 64, 68, 148, 157, 235, 239, 240, 241, 242; © istockphoto, page 66; RNLI Ireland, pages 71, 73; © Ronan Shouldice, pages 91, 93; BirdWatch Ireland, pages 115, 116, 119, 120 (Clive Timmons), page 118 (Dick Coombes (top) and Ken Kinsella (bottom)), page 121 (Jerry Cassidy) and page 122 (Oran O'Sullivan); © Matej Krajcovic, page 124; © Shane O'Donnell, page 126; © Graham Smith (Howth Yacht Club), pages 133, 165; © Brian Kelly, pages 134, 164, 201; © Darren Kelly, page 141, 210; dalkeyhomepages.ie, pages 181, 206; © Hall of Pictures (www.hallofpictures.com), pages 203, 209, 243.

In memory of Boyd and Eleanor Givens

Chronology

839 – Major Norse advance on Dublin Bay

841 – Norse over-winter at *Dubh Linn*

902 – Initial Norse settlement driven out of Dublin

914 – Second wave of Viking invaders

1014 – Battle of Clontarf

1154 – Anglo-Norman invasion of Ireland

1288 – Earliest recorded wreck at the Liffey mouth

1429 – Goat Castle at Dalkey constructed

1620 – Essex Quay developed as a wharf

1640 – Customs house established on Essex Quay

1649 – Cromwell lands at Ringsend

1665 – King Charles II orders first lighthouses to be built in Ireland

1676 – Ballast Office created to enforce regulation of ships dredging
      ballast

1715 – Stone wall extended as far as City Quay; work begun on 'The
      Piles'

1728 – Purty Kitchen pub founded in Dunleary Village

1735 – Pigeon House Road completed; Floating Light stationed at Liffey
      mouth

1759 – Guinness Brewery at St James's Gate founded

1761 – South Bull Wall stone version begun; Pigeon House built on South Wall

1762 – John Rocque's chart of the bay with 'bulls'

1767 – First Dun Laoghaire Pier completed (now the Old Pier); coal imports begin

1768 – Poolbeg Lighthouse on South Wall completed

1768 – Ballast Office Committee replaces Ballast Board

1786 – Great South Wall completed

1790 – Pigeon House Harbour becomes station for mail packets

1791 – Custom House opened

1793 – Pigeon House Hotel constructed

1796 – Custom House Dock opened / First Guinness 'extra stout' porter exported across the bay

1797 – Annesley Bridge completed, opening north side to development

1798 – Poolbeg Lighthouse completed

1800 – Captain Bligh's survey of Dublin Bay; Lifeboat service begun

1804 – First Martello towers built as defence against Napoleon

1807 – Ballast Board starts building Howth Harbour

1807 – *Rochdale* and HMS *Prince of Wales* sunk off Blackrock and Seapoint

1810 – Ballast Board takes responsibility for lights and lighthouses

1811 – Kish Bank Lightboat established

1813 – Howth Harbour completed

1814 – Pigeon House sold to British Army, funds used to built North Bull Wall

1814 – Construction of Baily Light at current location completed

1815 – Dun Laoghaire Harbour Commission formed

1817 – Dun Laoghaire Harbour construction begun

1818 – Howth Harbour Lighthouse built; Howth Harbour becomes mail packet station

1820 – Construction on the North Bull Wall begun

1821 – Visit of King George IV; Dunleary renamed Kingstown

1824 – Convict hulk *Essex* placed in Dun Laoghaire Harbour

1824 – North Bull Wall completed

1826 – Mail service transferred from Howth to Dun Laoghaire

1827 – Wharf built on East Pier at Dun Laoghaire for mail packets

1828 – Dublin Regatta held, first major yachting event in Dun Laoghaire Harbour

1833 – Select Committee on Ship Canal chaired by Daniel O'Connell

1834 – Packet station for the Royal Mail shifted to Kingstown; Railway opens

1835 – City of Dublin Steam Packet Company starts Dun Laoghaire passenger service

1836 – Kingstown Harbour becomes independent of Dublin Port

1836 – City of Dublin Steam Packet company wins mail contract for Kingstown/Dun Laoghaire

1837 – Convict hulk *Essex* removed

1837 – Victoria Wharf at Dun Laoghaire built (later called St Michael's Wharf)

1842 – East Pier Lighthouse built, finishing Dun Laoghaire Harbour

1843 – Royal St George Yacht Club clubhouse completed

1844 – Atmospheric Railway opens between Kingstown and Dalkey

1844 – Last bit of Clontarf Island destroyed in a storm

1846 – City of Dublin Steam Packet Company's *Queen Victoria* sunk at Howth Head

1850 – Royal Irish Yacht Club building completed

1853 – Last convict transport from Ireland to Australia leaves Dun Laoghaire

1855 – Traders Wharf and Carlisle Pier completed at Dun Laoghaire

1856 – Railway extended from Dun Laoghaire to Bray

1858 – East Pier Battery built at Dun Laoghaire

1861 – Lifeboat House built at foot of East Pier at Dun Laoghaire

1864 – Clontarf Baths built

1868 – Dublin Corporation proposes converting Bull Island into a sewage dump

1870 – National Yacht Club clubhouse built

1870 – North Wall extension and reconstruction of South Quays begun

1879 – Port gains ownership of north side bay except up to 1,000 feet from Clontarf shore

1880 – North Bull Light and The Muglins Light built

1882 – North Bank Light built and North Wall extension completed

1885 – Royal Dublin Golf Course on Bull Island founded

1885 – Alexandra Basin named in honour of Princess of Wales

1895 – Howth Sailing Club formed

1896 – Trunk-sewer system established to channel wastes to Ringsend

1899 – First oil tanker discharges oil at Anglo-American oil tank farm

1902 – North Wall Quay Light built; Pigeon House Station for electricity generation opens

1904 – Irish Society for the Protection of Birds formed

1905 – First 100-ton electric crane at port; Dun Laoghaire Baths constructed

1912 – First Dublin Bay sea scouts headquarters established on Bull Island

1913 – Guinness Ships begin sailing; reconstruction of South Quays completed

1918 – *RMS Leinster* sunk by German U Boat, worst shipping disaster in Irish waters

1920 – Kingstown reverts to name Dun Laoghaire

1921 – St Anne's Golf Club on Bull Island founded

1941 – Irish Shipping Limited founded as a national flag-carrier

1946 – Harbours Act establishes basics of the current system of port management

1949 – ESB's North Wall Generating Station begins operation

1964 – Construction of causeway to Bull Island

1965 – Kish Light established

1968 – Howth Yacht Club formed

1971 – ESB Poolbeg Generating Station begins operation

1968 – Roll-on/roll-off passenger ferry service inaugurated at Dublin Port

1968 – Irish Wildbird Conservancy formed

1972 – Permission to construct oil refinery on the bay denied

1977 – Dun Laoghaire East Pier Light becomes fully automatic

1982 – New Howth Harbour light built

1986 – Bull Island Interpretive Centre opens

1996 – Harbours Act defines the limits of Dublin Port

1997 – Baily Light converted to automatic operation, last manned lighthouse in Ireland

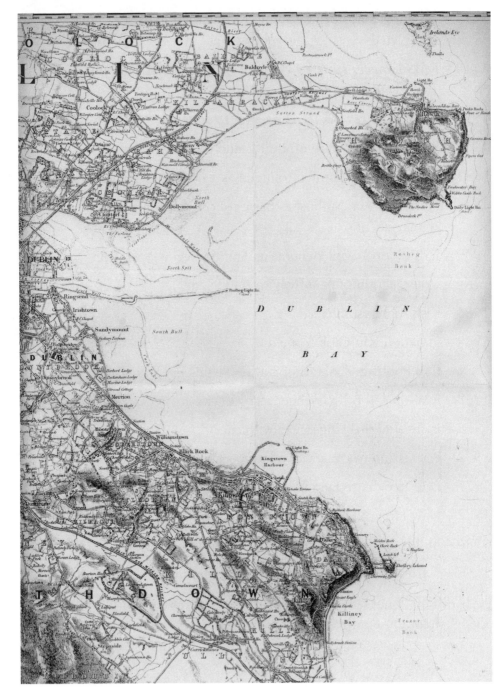

One-inch Ordnance Survey Map of Ireland, 1860
extract from Sheet 112

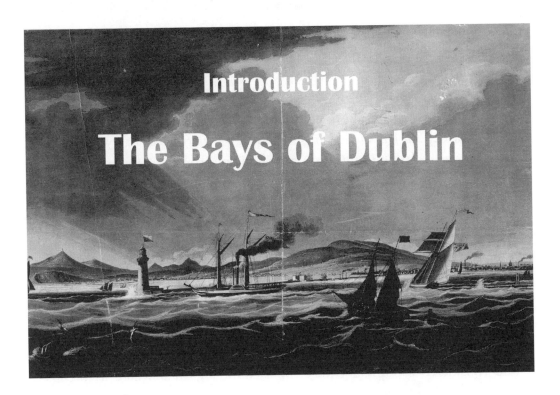

Introduction

The Bays of Dublin

There are as many Dublin Bays as there are people living around it. No two are exactly alike. And although the bay was certainly the single most important factor in determining the location of our city, it has for much of its history seemed a difficulty to be navigated rather than an amenity to be enjoyed, an impediment to be managed – or even a vacancy to be filled with more 'useful' configurations – rather than a place to be celebrated and protected.

But what is this bay – what are these bays?

For some, Dublin Bay is a heaving, rolling surface to be glided over in a Water Wag or a Howth Seventeen-Footer or a kayak or canoe. Others descend into its depths and explore known wrecks such as the *Bolivar* or the *Leinster* or perhaps even hope to stumble across that elusive treasure ship filled with priceless classical antiquities from Rome that allegedly went down in the bay in 1806 and has never been found.

Many use the bay as a place out of which to pull fish – or, failing that, to sit facing placidly while dreaming of the perfect catch. There are those for whom the bay is the channel through which arrives our container-loads of Taiwanese computer parts or cases of the king of American beers, or our bulk phosphates or petroleum or our molasses or tea; or through which we dispatch car ferries to Holyhead or barrels of the black stuff to a thirsty world.

In summer, one bay becomes a 'scene' whereby many of us placidly absorb suntans which, although not as remarkable as those available on the Costa del Sol (or indeed from a bottle), nevertheless carry a certain satisfaction, with the implication that holiday bronzing can happen here too. There are those whose bay provides a venue for watching grey herons stalk the shallows in their summer unsociability or for welcoming the very sociable brent geese as they glide in for their winter visit, murmuring comments to each other as they arrive.

There are many bays here.

Dublin Bay is also a prawn, *Nephrops norvegicus*, also called Norway lobster or langoustine, and not really a 'true' prawn at all since it has small pincer claws. Like a lobster. A Viking lobster.

Dublin Bay is also a tall red shrub rose, usually grown as a climber, and considered a popular choice for a country garden where it spreads itself easily on a fence or fills in a border.

Dublin Bay is the middle name of the man who was Dublin's Lord Mayor between 1995 and 1996, Seán Dublin Bay Rockall Loftus, the Irish barrister, politician and environmentalist who cared so much about preserving the bay that he extended his middle name in order to express his determination.

Dublin Bay is a symmetrically shaped body of water, about seven kilometres in diameter. Howth Head defines its northern point, Dalkey Island has the same role on the south, and the submerged Burford Banks can be thought of as the bay's eastern boundary with the Irish Sea.

About fifty rivers and streams empty directly or indirectly into the bay, with today the Liffey, the Dodder and the Tolka being the only ones we are really aware of.

Dublin Bay is shallow. It has more sand banks and sand bars than any other distinguishing feature although they are submerged so few people pay much attention to them. Mariners have always paid attention to them, however; or, rather, surviving mariners have. Probably a distinguishing characteristic of Dublin Bay is the fact that it is littered with shipwrecks, the oldest perhaps dating back to Roman times. The floor of the bay is mostly sand. The shore is rocky in places such as Howth, Dalkey, parts of Sandycove and Blackrock. Strand or mud flats occur in other areas, with Sandymount, Clontarf and Dollymount the most noticeable.

Ecologically, the bay is comparatively healthy. Marine mammals such as seals and various cetaceans are seen regularly in the bay; the popularity of sea angling demonstrates the continued availability of fish. The shores teem with birds during seasons of migration, and the north side in particular is one of Europe's most significant habitats and certainly the most impressive nature preserve located within a European capital city.

Certainly the bay has been embraced by its residents.

Some find the bay a subject to photograph or paint or write about: Joyce's 'snot-green' and 'scrotum-tightening' sea was the bay, after all. Most Dubliners have at one time or another been drawn to the bay and strolled at low tide along the strands at Sandymount or Dollymount, pondering the meaning of life or the mystery of the cosmos or the source of those little piles of extruded lug worm coils on the wet sand. Some of us jog or cycle or push prams along bay-side promenades that link Fairview to Howth and that may one day extend all the way to Sandycove, creating a single, extravagant opportunity for serious exhaustion if not the early onset of chronic ligament damage. And most of us have at one time or another just stopped on the foreshore and stood and gazed out at it and felt blessed by its existence.

So whatever it is, for each of us, Dublin Bay is an essential part of our lives: both an asset and an amenity. And although it seems like an endless resource that is much too bountiful ever to be harmed, harm has been done to it in the past and may be done again.

Dublin Bay is what we make of it. It is ours to protect for future generations or exploit for our own short-term gratification. We can preserve our wetlands or build apartments on them. We can celebrate the achievement of earning Blue Flag bathing status on our bay. Or we can dump trash in it. We can see the bay as the one of the primary sources for the wonderful quality of life in our city, or as a convenient site for an oil refinery.

Our bay mirrors us. It reflects our lives on it and on its shores. We each have one. And whenever we look out at our bay, we see ourselves.

Chapter 1
The Early Bay

The Vikings' Bay

One fine morning in 839, an ominous sight greeted the small communities arranged along the shoreline of Dublin Bay. A group of about sixty large warships with high, serpent-headed prows, striped sails and multiple oars had arrived. Residents would have known what this meant. The Vikings had been pillaging Ireland for over forty years, launching murderous hit-and-run raids along the coastline. But they had never come in such numbers before; and even though the inhabitants living around the rim of the bay couldn't have known it at the time, their world would be altered forever.

What was that world like? Much of it has been lost to the passage of time and the depredations of development and redevelopment. Very little direct evidence of the first human visitors to Dublin Bay has been found, so that any discussion of pre-Norse Dublin Bay is speculative. Most of what we know is extrapolated from similar locations in other parts of Ireland, and a lot of it is educated guesswork. That the shoreline of the bay was inhabited by the earliest-known humans on this island seems certain since traces of Mesolithic (Middle Stone Age) habitations have been uncovered at Howth and on Dalkey Island. That's hardly surprising. The eastern coast with its wide sandy beaches and many rivers must have been particularly appealing to these early migrants, with the comparatively accessible waters of the bay providing a valuable source of food. Not much is known about these ancient ancestors. Unlike less populous parts of Ireland, the shoreline of Dublin Bay has been altered by those who came after, erasing all evidence of these very first residents.

With the advent of the Neolithic Era, or New Stone Age, things picked up around the bay. The new residents were agriculturalists who domesticated animals and used their stone tools to clear forests and create land which could then be farmed. With them came the advent of settled communities, and the lands surrounding Dublin Bay would have been particularly salubrious. These pre-Dubliners would have organised themselves into communities and shared out tasks. They would have managed their flocks and herds and tilled fields as well as harvested the rich waters of the bay. Their first dwellings may have been covered pits, but archaeological evidence from other parts of Ireland show traces of more substantial buildings appearing in this period, with the remains of the oldest wooden house found in County Tyrone and dating from around 3200 BC. There is every reason to believe that the complex Neolithic culture which was developing at that time in other locations was equally prevalent around Dublin Bay, although little of it remains. The tumulus or cromlech on Howth Head is one of the few such remnants of that age around the bay itself. Perhaps Newgrange in County Meath, one of the most impressive Neolithic sites in Europe and dating from around 2500 BC, can serve as a spectacular indication of the achievements of the culture which was developing in the general area around Dublin Bay.

The bay would have experienced an increase in traffic sometime before 2000 BC. The Early Bronze Age represents a technological breakthrough which gave those who mastered it an advantage over rivals. Although Ireland was geographically on the far outer edge of Europe, there was a sea-borne commerce that brought the more transportable skills and techniques of ancient Greece to these shores. Copper was found in Munster and the fashioning of copper tools and weapons developed there. Around 2000 BC, the discovery of gold in the Wicklow Hills added to the inducements to visit Dublin Bay and a brilliant period of cultural florescence began. Irish gold ornaments reached continental European markets, and products from areas as widely separated as the Baltic region and Portugal were

Tumulus on the Ben of Howth

arriving in ancient Ireland. Dublin Bay was one among several locations for this increased exchange of goods. If the bay previously had been utilised primarily as a source of food, it was now the site for an early form of international commerce.

The second millennium BC also saw the arrival of an entirely new race of people, who are thought to have been Indo-Europeans, and are categorised as proto-Celts. The story of the rise of the Celts is too complex to tell here. They were never a separate race; but they did forge themselves into what can be thought of as a nation of various peoples connected by common religions, customs and languages. And as bronze gave way to iron, the Celts became and remained the dominant force in continental Europe until they were defeated by superior Roman military strategy and bureaucratic organisation. For all their ferocity on the battlefield, the Celts were poor at co-operating in common causes and the dawn of the Christian era saw a Europe under the sway of Rome.

Tucked away on the periphery of Europe, Ireland was not occupied by Rome. (There may have been a Roman outpost on Dublin Bay: a few coins have been found but little else; they could as well have come from traders.) Celtic society survived in Ireland, and the rich cultural heritage of modern Ireland is based on a thousand years of evolutionary development rather than cataclysmic change. Yet Ireland was hardly isolated. Traders still found Dublin Bay and other Irish ports well worth visiting.

The early Irish living around the shoreline of Dublin Bay did venture out in their little hide-covered curraghs, of course; and examples of longing for distant places can be found in songs and poems. But the great journeys made during this period are associated with the wild west coast of the island, from lonely outposts such as Inishmurray in County Sligo to Inishmore on the Aran Islands off Galway and the beehive huts of Skellig Michael in County Kerry. It is the very wildness of such places that has preserved them, so small wonder that nothing similar remains around Dublin Bay.

Arrival of the Northmen

Then we reach Anno Domini 839 and our Viking warships assembling for what at the time must have seemed the onset of yet another horrific orgy of pillage and rapine, differing only in the vastly increased numbers of the forces filling Dublin Bay. The residents around the bay couldn't have known it, but a similar group of Northmen was also sailing up the Boyne, and yet another would shortly arrive on the Shannon. Like our massed invaders on Dublin Bay, they too were following a new strategy. For forty years of seasonal raids, Norse buccaneers had attacked coastal monasteries or sailed upriver in search of rich pickings, stripping away what plunder was easily available and fleeing back to their boats for the triumphant return home. Their numbers had grown as the wealth of the

Irish monasteries became known, and the raids had become more frequent. Now, in addition to the usual slaughter and looting, the Vikings intended to do something they had never before attempted. They intended to stay.

We have evidence of this, both archaeological and documented. The first part of the story of Dublin Bay begins on the banks of the Liffey when the warships of a horde of fair-haired, blood-thirsty invaders were dragged up somewhere near a 'black pool' and beached there.

The arrival of the large Norse fleet at Dublin Bay in 839 represented a major change in strategy. What had been seasonal hit-and-run raids would now become a sustained invasion using established bases. Raiders became invaders. And as the Vikings extended their forays deeper into the interior, they engaged in battles with the resident Irish forces and occasionally suffered catastrophic losses.

The Dubh Linn

Dublin Bay was the primary staging point for these invading forces. The shallowness of the bay was easily managed by the Vikings since their longboats drew little water. Despite a great deal of archaeological work, these early days are still murky. The first Viking *longphort* is thought to have been established at the *Dubh Linn*, the 'dark pool' where the River Poddle joins the Liffey, near where South Great George's Street is today. The site would have been defensible, with rivers on two sides; and it would have had sand beaches or mud banks where boats could have been kept, ready for a quick escape into the bay should that become necessary.

There are references after 843 to a settlement at *Áth Cliath*, the 'ford-of-the-hurdles', and evidence of Viking habitation can be found as far upriver as Islandbridge and at Kilmainham which contain Viking burial sites. Precise dating of these establishments along the river estuary is difficult. But it seems clear that the banks of the Liffey as far as Islandbridge and the river's estuary on the bay made up the initial Norse settlement that grew into the city of Dublin. The Liffey becomes tidal at about Islandbridge, and as it flows down between the narrow constraints of the modern quays, it passes sites of historical relevance that describe over a thousand years of change. Some historians believe the original ford-of-the-hurdles was located at Islandbridge just above the reach of the tides but most have settled on an area close to where the Four Courts are today.

By 841, there is evidence that the Vikings had sufficiently established themselves to risk wintering at the defensible position they had established at the confluence of the Poddle and the Liffey. Another large Viking fleet arrived on Dublin Bay in 842, and it is around this time that the first evidence of Norse-Irish alliances can be found although there may very well have been earlier instances of co-operation. The new Viking

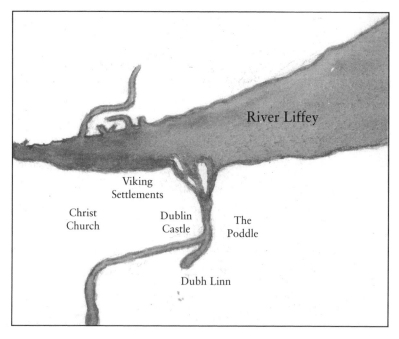

Sketch of early Dublin

settlement on Dublin Bay soon became crammed with warriors, and written evidence suggests that in addition to the usual buccaneering, they were also beginning to function as mercenaries for various Irish kings. Dublin Bay was no longer just a landing site for hit-and-run attacks. It had become a beachhead for continuous, if intermittent, warfare.

The shoreline of the bay at the Liffey mouth is much altered from what it was during the Viking period. The original northern shore would have been at about where Amiens Street and North Strand Road are today, with what is now Fairview Park once 'sloblands' of mud flats and sand beaches.

The southern shoreline followed along Fleet Street, across Trinity College, and on to a marsh formed where the Dodder emptied into it. As the Liffey neared the estuary, it became a wide shallow river delta separated into channels with mud flats, the southern-most determined by the spit of higher land at Ringsend.

The establishment of fording places over the river can be considered the initial attempts at managing it. The *Áth Cliath*, near where the Four Courts are today, gave its name to the settlement that grew up on the ridge there. A fording place is not a bridge, of course, but a construction making it possible to wade across an otherwise formidable river. Those using it could remain dry only if they were on horseback. Tidal flow would restrict usage as well, but the ford-of-the-hurdles became a significant feature of the settlement there, with major roads passing across it.

Viking incursions increased after the establishment of fortified positions in various parts of the country, with the raiders mounting large attacks that pierced deep into the interior of the country. But this change in Viking tactics also gave the Irish an opportunity to fight back since even a well-defended Viking *longphort* was still vulnerable to a committed assault. The Vikings had in effect begun the transition from sea-borne raiders to participants in domestic Irish politics; and for all their ferocity and superior weaponry, they were vastly outnumbered by the local inhabitants. If mercenary warfare had originally been a way of extending opportunities for plunder, integration and tactical alliance had now become necessary for survival. Dublin Bay was becoming a Scandinavian lake, and the small settlement at *Dubh Linn* would evolve into the primary Norse stronghold in Ireland – and one of the most important Norse trading depots in a wide-spread and well-developed international commercial system. Other bases were established at Waterford, Wexford, Limerick and Cork; and the Viking's integration into existing society took its first tentative steps – even as the buccaneering continued. Old habits die hard.

These initial Northmen were fair-haired Norwegians or Swedes, called the '*Finngaills*', or white strangers by the local Irish, the source of today's Fingal. In the years 849–852, new raiders began appearing on the scene, dark-haired Danes who were labelled the '*Dubhgaills*', or black strangers. The established Dublin Norse fought against these interlopers with the usual carnage resulting, and even as trade in commodities and finished goods continued out of it, Dublin Bay had also evolved into a major slaving centre and launch site for attacks against Britannia.

Excavations at Wood Quay and in the Temple Bar area give us an idea of what this first Dublin-Norse settlement must have been like. It was situated on high ground beside where the river Poddle entered the Liffey, and surrounded by an embankment of earth which was at this time topped by a post-and-wattle palisade. Streets were surfaced with gravel and stones in some cases, or with wattle mats or split logs. Wattle seems to have been the preferred building technique of the time. The 'ford-of-the-hurdles' over the then much wider and shallower Liffey apparently used wattle

Excavation at Wood Quay

platforms on logs linked to stone piles; wattles formed the main walls of Viking homes; and their various garden plots or yards were divided from each other by low post-and-wattle fences. No question about it: it was an age of wattles.

In 853, Olaf the White sailed into Dublin Bay and with Ivar the Boneless assumed joint sovereignty of the Viking stronghold there. Battles continued to rage along the Irish coast, with Viking outposts demolished occasionally by various Norse-Irish configurations. The settlement at Dublin held on until 902 when the kings of Brega and Leinster combined to destroy the Dublin Norse and expel them from Ireland. Recent archaeological evidence suggests some continuity of residence during this period, which is hardly surprising since a good deal of cultural assimilation had already occurred.

Renewed Viking incursions in Ireland came from established Danish bases in Britain, with large fleets of warships setting sail in 914. Munster was attacked in 915. The Vikings returned in force to Dublin Bay in 917; and in 919, the King of Tara was killed in a combined Irish attack on the re-established Dublin Norse. *Áth Cliath* seems to have been the primary settlement on Dublin Bay, or at least that was the name used for what got burned when the tide of battle turned against those living there. The tenth century presents a dreary catalogue of raids on monasteries, the forming and betrayal of alliances, and the unending squabbling of petty kings or would-be kings. Dublin Bay with the Irish Sea beyond was now an important part of a trading network of Norse colonies that had been planted down the western coast of Europe and out onto the many offshore islands, large and small.

Skirmishes sputtered on, however, and the Norse kings of Dublin became more and more confined to the town and its immediate hinterland, with the open waters of Dublin Bay their final fall-back position. In 951, the last great raiding expedition was launched, reaping a rich harvest of cattle, horses, gold and silver, plus a large supply of slaves for the international slave market which was operating out of Dublin Bay. Some historians see this final raid as marking a key point of transition for Dublin. A base for launching raids was being replaced by the more settled activity of running trade out of the bay.

The trading economy that had developed on the Irish Sea began using currency in the latter half of the tenth century, and Dublin minted its own coins bearing variations on the name 'Diflin'. This new economic strength did not stop local assaults from occurring, of course. In 980, the Norse

King of Dublin was defeated at Tara, and the new King of Tara then seized Dublin and released large numbers of hostages. But the age of Norse fighting against Irish was long since past. Which is not to say that people didn't still enjoy a good fight. But what had once been a Viking outpost was now a settled Hiberno-Norse town; and although 'Irish' attacks on the 'strangers' continued throughout the tenth century, the picture was more complicated.

The Battle of Clontarf

As the eleventh century began, Dublin had evolved well beyond being merely a Viking stronghold, and Dublin Bay was now a significant port for international trade. Norse Dublin was a vibrant community, with evidence of the crafts of the age uncovered by recent excavations. Exotic finds such as whalebone and walrus skulls indicate an extensive commerce, as do luxuries such as jet, silk and gold braid. Local craftsmen fashioned imported amber into glass beads, pendants, and rings; smelters created Irish silver and bronze jewellery, examples of which have been found in

The Battle of Clontarf

other parts of Europe. Armlets and brooches were prized, and the native Irish ringed-pin became very popular among the Vikings. Decorated bone pins were used as clothes fasteners and hair ornaments.

There was now a thriving bay-side community involved in the importing and exporting of trade goods. Ships were now being built and repaired in Norse Dublin. Some were smaller vessels used for coastal traffic, but larger ocean-going trading ships were built there too, as were the familiar Viking warships.

Dublin Bay on the eve of the Battle of Clontarf was much more than just the site for one of the most famous battles in Ireland. It was an integral part of a sophisticated, international entrepôt that had melded Irish and Scandinavian cultures into a successful new entity. The Norse 'strangers' were no longer an enemy to be driven back into the sea; they had been transformed into a potential source of wealth and tribute. Claimants to the High Kingship of Ireland would be judged on their ability to control what had become the most valuable port in the country. Dublin Bay was inextricably bound up in local politics. And politics at the end of the tenth century was a blood sport.

Brian Boru has always been considered one of the greatest leaders in the history of Ireland. Although he defeated the Vikings of Munster in a major battle, Brian also made alliances with them; and in 984, the Norse of Waterford attacked Leinster by sea while Brian attacked by land. Brian became king of the southern part of Ireland while his great rival, the King of Tara, ruled the northern half of the country; and in 998, the two kings co-operated in an attack on Dublin. Eventually, the Dublin Norse were defeated and Brian became king of the whole of Ireland, with the Norse King Sitric allowed to retain authority in Dublin under his rule – a tactical error, or a clever ploy leading to a final showdown.

The Norse at this time were well established throughout parts of Northwest Europe. Normandy as a Norse kingdom had been established in France; and in 1017, a Danish prince, Canute, would be crowned king in England. Danish warships continued to appear in Dublin Bay and elsewhere along the eastern coast of Ireland, and inland raids were still launched occasionally although with less success than earlier attacks. In 1012, Leinster and the Norse of Dublin revolted against Brian. An inconclusive blockade of the city led to a temporary truce enabling both sides to gather allies for a major battle. Sitric found willing Danish participants throughout the area. The Vikings hoped to maintain exclusive control of the Irish Sea and retain Dublin as their primary trading post. In April 1014, Dublin Bay filled with black Norse warships in preparation for the final onslaught from this natural staging point; and although local inhabitants had long since become accustomed to heavy ship traffic on the bay, the sight of so many warships must have been astonishing.

The battle itself was joined on Good Friday. Brian's forces included Irish fighters from all over the island, although the Uí Néill of the north refused to participate. Brian also had Norse allies and Scots who hoped to reduced Danish hegemony in the area. The Danes were organised in three large battalions spread around the rim of the northern quarter of the bay with their warships behind them. The central group straddled the Tolka River, the left flank stretched as far as the walls of Dublin city, and the right flank continued around the bay to Clontarf. Danish warships in the bay held positions all along the Clontarf coastline from Howth to the mouth of the Liffey.

Artist's impression of Brian Boru

Brian Boru's army was encamped inland and also separated into three large forces, with the central one in Fairview, the right flank between Drumcondra and the city, and the left flank at Clontarf.

The fighting raged back and forth over a broad area between the Liffey and the Tolka, with some action occurring along the coast at Fairview and extending up into Clontarf. It was a general melee of carnage and destruction with neither side able to gain a decisive advantage. Late in the afternoon, the Irish made a desperate mass attack and the Danes gave way. They tried to retreat to their ships, but the tide was at full and the estuary of the River Tolka was impassable. The Danes were trapped at a fishing weir and butchered, with those not cut down drowning in the flood tide. What had been a battle turned into a rout; and the guards stationed at the tent of the aged King Brian Boru, eager for a taste of the slaughter, left him undefended. He was found by one of the fleeing Danes and killed.

The Battle of Clontarf marked the end of Norse adventuring. Not all the Danes were killed at the battle at the fishing weir. A sizeable contingent fought their way to Howth and took refuge on the peninsula there, defending it against attack until their ships could be organised for a rescue. And of course a great many Vikings had long since become residents of Ireland and were integrated into Irish society.

The Battle of Clontarf was not a simple Irish versus Norse battle. But Brian's victory did result in the end of the martial power of Norse Dublin, and Viking dominance of Dublin Bay which had begun in 839 was now ended forever. Dublin continued to be a highly successful trading emporium, and Dublin Bay remained part of the flourishing sea-borne trade developed by the Northmen. But it was Irish-owned and Irish-managed now – at least until the ships of the next wave of invaders appeared on the horizon.

From Fort to Port

Beginning with tenth-century Norse Dublin, public works were often attempts at making the tidal estuary better suited for water-borne trade, a tradition that has continued to this day. The need has always been for deeper water. The Liffey silts naturally and the bay fills with sand. Even if ships didn't grow larger, without centuries of strenuous human intervention there would have been no port at Dublin.

As far as we know, the only pre-Norse attempt at adjusting the bay-side environment was the construction of fording places. Early residents around the bay seemed to have been content with things as they were. Impressive feats of construction were certainly within the capabilities of even the earliest residents of the region, as Newgrange or the Cromlech at Howth with its immense capstone attest, and the development of monasteries and churches during this period indicates a sophisticated understanding of the planning and organisation that is required for successful civil engineering projects. Before the arrival of the Vikings, Dublin Bay was used mostly as an extension of the land surrounding it, a resource to be exploited directly, much as were the surrounding forests or boglands. There was some sea trade, some coastal travel; but for the most part, the horizon line bounded Dublin Bay.

This attitude changed with the advent of the Northmen. For them, Dublin Bay was part of an expansive system of sea roads: it was a thing to be crossed, as was the Irish Sea and, for that matter, the North Sea. Building a defensive position near an important terminus of that sea road was simple good sense. Dublin Bay became a strategic location from which the Vikings could launch raids on Britain and other strategic targets. But the Vikings eventually wanted more than just a military base. And taking the next step, building a port there, was an act of civic affirmation and a statement of the intent to remain. Dublin as a geographical entity begins with the beaching of Viking warships at the *Dubh Linn*; but it begins as a commercial city with the establishment of its port.

It is interesting that the Vikings never tried to span the Liffey; true seafarers, their concern was always with the river, the bay and the open ocean. Their axis of interest ran along waterways: inwards on the Liffey to the rich plunder-grounds of the interior or outwards across the bay and the Irish Sea. It would take the arrival of a second group of invaders, the Anglo-Normans, to begin bridge-building.

The first Viking attempt at converting the river estuary into a permanent port was the construction of Wood Quay, the original of which was located under Dublin Corporation at about the level of where West Essex Street is today. Wood Quay, dating from around the year 900, was so-named because it was composed of wooden barriers that were built out into the river. The Liffey is tidal here, of course, so it would have been necessary to establish a more consistent interface between the land and water deep enough for the various activities associated with even a primitive port. If the initial idea was to gain access to deep water by building out to it, this would also have suggested a second approach, that of managing the shape of the tidal estuary and deepening the river itself by restricting its flow. These two endeavours – to find deeper water or to create it – configure much of the history of the shoreline of Dublin Bay. Although the addition of bridges would eventually cut off access to upriver landing sites, it was the silting of the river and its estuary that made it impossible for larger ships to reach what had previously been adequate water.

The Viking's Wood Quay, constructed around 900, is long gone, although the somewhat hurried excavations before the construction of the new civic buildings unearthed a wealth of archaeological findings. Viking Dublin, for that matter, is long since buried under succeeding incarnations of the city, with the bold culture of the Norse sea rovers reduced to the farcical imitations of the local splash tours. Traces of important alterations can still be found today in modern names, however. The Normans built a dam near where the Poddle entered the Liffey, giving us Dame Street but also erasing the actual 'black pool' itself due to silting and thus eliminating the key geological feature that had led the original invaders to choose this site for their fort. The dry land formed by the filling in of the old *Dubh Linn* helped to extend the growing Norman settlement, the successful development of which depended upon the ability to manage the river estuary and the bay. But one wonders if at the time there wasn't a slight fluttering of vestigial memory and regret within the hearts of the Hiberno-Norse Dubs who saw in the busybody Norman efforts at land reclamation the loss of a better way, with beached warships maintained within easy access of the pool, the river, the bay, the open ocean and in the far distance the frozen fjords of home.

The Normans Arrive

Dublin Bay in 1154 was a plum ripe for the plucking. And King Henry II was just the man to pluck it.

The bay came with a city attached to it, of course, and a country as well, with rich farmlands and splendid monastic settlements; but what Henry II wanted primarily was the Norse trading centre on Dublin Bay, as well as the other Norse ports along the eastern coast.

The English king – first of the Plantagenets – ruled over a large portion of France as well and was himself essentially French. His kingdom was already large and complex, and Henry was a strategic innovator who recognised an opportunity when one appeared. All he needed was an

Dublin Castle, built by the Normans

invitation. The fractious twelfth-century Irish were all too willing to oblige.

At the time of Henry II's incursion, Dublin Bay had evolved into one of the world's most important venues for international trade, and Dublin was far and away the predominant Norse city in Ireland. Close commercial relations linked Dublin to Chester and Bristol; and it was the advantages offered by Dublin Bay that determined the location of what was eventually to become Ireland's capital.

The fur trade, in particular, used Dublin Bay as a staging point since its location on the Irish Sea provided convenient access to the major population centres of Scandinavia, England and the Continent. Dublin Bay was critical to this lucrative business. Furs were shipped in from Iceland and Greenland, then moved on to their ultimate destinations. This was, of course, a purely Norse monopoly, and Dublin Bay and the Irish Sea were Norse sea routes. The Irish profited from these new developments; and now that the Vikings had replaced pillage with profits from trading, Ireland enjoyed a brilliant period of sustained economic, artistic and cultural reinvigoration.

In the 150 years that followed the Battle of Clontarf, strong, centralising Irish high kings did emerge. But there were also periods when no single ruler predominated and the great regional barons were able to enforce what they saw as their ancestral prerogatives, usually to the detriment of national unification. Regionalism was not unique to medieval Ireland, of course. All over Europe various kingdoms were created around a hegemonist family and it would be centuries before actual nation-states began forming.

Henry II had long had his eye on the fractious island off his west coast and he seized the opportunity to cut into Scandinavian dominance. Controlling Dublin Bay and the other trading ports on the eastern coastline was his primary objective at the time since by so doing, he could shift much of the lucrative fur trade to his own port at Bristol.

In 1154, Pope Adrian IV (who just happened to be English), seeing the need to save the erring souls of the Irish, gave Ireland to Henry as if it were a gift box he need only go collect. The problem was how to collect it, and Henry would have to wait a dozen years until grasping the gift became a reality. A ready supply of bored Norman knights was available in Wales; an indigent earl, Richard de Clare of Pembroke, aka Strongbow, was ready to assume leadership; and a gullible high king of Ireland was ready to allow a beachhead to be established in Leinster.

Like the Viking invasions three centuries before, the new arrivals had superior weapons – Norman chain mail and the deadly English long bow were new to Ireland – and the results would not have been hard to predict. The Normans inflicted the usual butchery on the inhabitants, slaughtering with alacrity unresisting populations. The Irish fighters were no match for the invaders. But they fell back and adopted a guerrilla strategy, attacking out of the forests and boglands which they knew well so that at the end of this first stage of the conflict, the invaders had managed to secure only their main objective: Dublin Bay, its port city, and the surrounding nearby countryside.

It would take four bloody centuries for the Irish to be conquered finally.

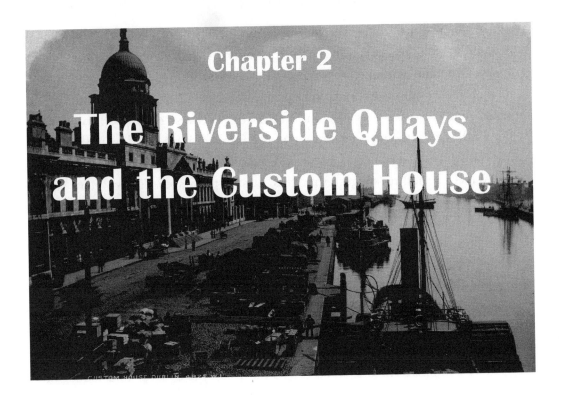

Chapter 2

The Riverside Quays and the Custom House

CUSTOM HOUSE DUBLIN

The Riverside Quays

River estuaries have the unfortunate habit of forming deltas. This matters less when the surrounding real estate is mangrove swamps; but for Dublin Bay, managing the places where the land meets the water has always been a significant issue.

The Normans pushed the banks of the Liffey out toward the channel at Wood Quay and the neighbouring Merchants Quay in order to reach water deep enough for medieval ships to tie up and off-load cargo directly. Wine, fine wool, pottery, exotic spices and other commodities were brought in and sent up the river to the interior. Exports included livestock, hides and food crops. The first customs house was established at or near Winetavern Street – centre of the wine trade during the medieval period and for all its bibulous history, today a street without a pub.

We have seen that the port at Dublin Bay was one of the most important trade depots for Viking and early medieval seafaring. But in the fifteenth century, new shipbuilding technologies and improved navigational instruments radically changed the nature of seafaring. This was the age of the great Portuguese and Spanish explorers; and while Dublin Bay was still viable as a port, it could no longer be included among the pre-eminent marine commercial centres. All of coastal Europe seemed involved in a race to explore and exploit distant lands; and in the sixteenth and seventeenth centuries, as England's seafaring prowess continued to grow, Dublin Bay became just one among many English ports, used primarily for the transportation of goods between England and Ireland.

Which is not to suggest that this wasn't profitable. Essex Quay was developed as a wharf in 1620 and enlarged twenty years later to accommodate the new customs house. It was a time of trade-driven prosperity, with ships crowding the river or riding at anchor in the deep pools near the Liffey mouth, waiting for the tide to rise sufficiently for them to make it up the shallow river. Ships were getting bigger; and by the middle of the seventeenth century, many were already finding it difficult to reach the upstream quays, particularly at low tide; and some of the largest were unable to get any farther than Ringsend.

The combination of a silted river and a bay filled with sand made for treacherous navigation. In stormy weather, the bay was exposed to north-eastern gales and catastrophic wrecks were common. The future seemed distinctly unsettled for the port, and political turmoil added to the general unease of the times.

Then in 1649, the end of the English Civil War gave Oliver Cromwell the opportunity he sought to apply his unique talents to the stalemate that had become Ireland; and in September of that year, the Lord Protector landed at Ringsend with over 10,000 troops. For him, sand banks and silting were no hindrance. Cromwell's determination to be intolerant in all things he disapproved of drove him ashore fizzing with the certainty of those who enjoy a direct and personal relationship with their God, and his New Model Army marched up the coast to Drogheda, overwhelmed the garrison there and slaughtered every male combatant. It would not be his last massacre.

The restoration of Charles II yielded a positive outcome for the future of Irish trade, and Dublin Bay once again became a thriving seaport so that by the end of the seventeenth century, the city of Dublin began a period of growth, with its newly invigorated commerce once again greeting ships from exotic ports – at least those that could make it.

In 1676, the first bridge at Capel Street was built, indicating that no hope remained for using the older upriver quays as a port. That bridge was soon lost to a flood and replaced a couple of times before the present span, Grattan Bridge, was completed in 1875. Wellington Quay, just east of this bridge, had become the primary customs port in 1620, and the river there was constantly filled with ships waiting to offload, lined up six, seven, eight deep. The port struggled to cope for decades, but it was eventually agreed that the customs house was too far upstream; and at the end of the eighteenth century, today's Custom House was established, not without protest from those who wished to retain the original location. Wellington Quay today is where the Poddle River – what's left of it – enters the bay through a grate at Eustace Street near the new Millennium Bridge. It is an undignified end to the little river with the odd name that had played such a key role in the founding of Dublin.

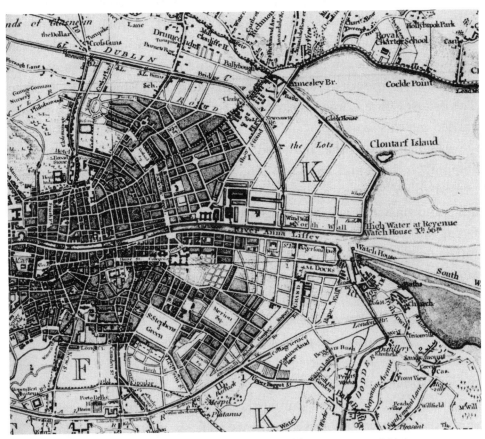

Detail of John Taylor's Map of Dublin Environs, 1816

Dublin Corporation promoted extensive development of the quay-side areas throughout this period. Already by 1700, the Liffey's tributary rivers were converted to underground channels and the Liffey itself had stone quays on the north side extending from Arran Quay to Bachelor's Walk, with similar quays on the south side. Narrowing the river increased its flow and helped reduce silting – or at least sent the suspended particles farther into the bay. Periodic dredging was required then and is still required today. As it flowed through the city, the Liffey was gradually being narrowed and constrained between the stone embankment walls, and the port's riverside wharfs were being steadily forced down river in a process that also still continues. By the end of the seventeenth century, the south side of the river was restricted by established embankments as far down as the mouth of the Dodder River. On the north side, the massive North Wall Quay was begun and reclamation of the shoreline between the Liffey and the Tolka was also underway. By 1715, a stone wall extended as far as City Quay, with the Pigeon House Road completed in 1735. In 1716, work had begun on a bank that would protect the south side of the channel at the mouth of the harbour, extending from Ringsend to Poolbeg. The Ballast Office Committee, recently established by Dublin Corporation, carried out this work.

The bank along the south shore provided only limited protection for shipping; in 1754 and again in 1756, funds for work on a wall that would extend to the eastern end of the 'Piles' were secured and construction advanced on what would eventually become South Bull Wall (see 'The Great Walls of Dublin'). A lightship was stationed at the mouth of the Liffey from 1735 to 1768; known as the 'Floating Light', it had two lanterns placed at either side of a square yard on the mast which were lit at night from half-flood to half-ebb. It was replaced by the Poolbeg Lighthouse at the end of the Great South Wall; passengers and packets of mail were now landed at the wall – or at the Pigeon House – where they made their way into the city on land or on boats that were shallow enough to negotiate upstream.

Dublin Bay prospered during the eighteenth century, and merchants shipped cargos of fine Irish linen, as well as agricultural products, to Britain and beyond. Luxury goods were imported, as was a great deal of

Marine School, Dublin, looking up the Liffey, 1796

coal, with the bulk of it coming from British ports. Most port activity had taken place on the south side of the River Liffey; but the opening of the new Custom House in 1791 shifted the main wharfs to the north bank of the river, where they remain today.

D'Olier Street and Westmoreland Street were laid out by the Wide Streets Commission in 1784, and the famous Ballast Office was housed at the corner of Westmoreland Street and Aston Quay, an area that also became the centre of the second-hand book trade in the nineteenth century. In 1794, with the Custom House now being moved closer to the mouth of the Liffey, construction on the Carlisle Bridge was begun. It was rebuilt in 1880 and widened to align better with Lower O'Connell Street and the juncture of D'Olier and Westmoreland Streets, and the port of Dublin – as well as the heart of the city itself – was once again shifted down river.

The Custom House and its Docks

One of Dublin's finest eighteenth-century buildings, the Custom House was built between 1781 and 1791, and almost destroyed in 1921 when the IRA burned it to eliminate the main tax and local government records.

Unloading Guinness boat at the docks

The building was gutted to an empty shell; and although it has since been restored, it seems staid.

The Custom House Quays were used until fairly recently. Bonded warehouses were located there, and ships importing cargos of dutiable goods such as wine, tobacco, sugar and tea continued to off-load at the nearby quays and manage the customs process there. The original Custom House Dock was opened in 1796 and was joined by George's Dock five years later, with its large warehouses and storage vaults. The area was left behind by the port as it continued advancing into the bay with new reclamation and new, expanded facilities, as we will discuss in the chapter on Dublin Port. New uses have been found for it, thanks to the Dublin Docklands Development Authority, and a bright future seems probable.

The Custom House no doubt was once among the most impressive buildings in Dublin. But today, it does have about it the whiff of a thing preserved for no purpose other than to exist as a memorial to itself. Other recent changes along the docklands are more exciting, as we will see in

'The Future of the Bay', and the Custom House can be allowed to settle into its self-commemorative somnolence.

It was certainly a lively enough place once, and paintings of it inevitably provide a sense of great bustle, with ships being unloaded along the quay and carters hauling away cargo. The presentation inevitably is of a jolly, hectic, urban scene, with all the optimism of outreach and mercantile profit. Until 1978, Custom House Quay was still used by the Guinness ships, and the quayside would be stacked high with barrels of stout. (See 'The Guinneses Boats'.) It is said that a few old fellows used to gather there in odd corners and appropriate the dregs of the returned barrels for their own pleasure and amusement. The barrels are steel not wood now; they are no longer managed there, and the old fellows too are gone, leaving the emptiness in front of the grand old building complete.

On the south side, the Grand Canal Docks have found their reincarnated state more successful than their original purpose as commercial docks. The Dodder River which enters the Liffey estuary here silted badly (as does the bay beyond, of course), and that seems to have been a fatal impediment. Locks there dated 1796 call to mind the possibility of using the area as a terminus for a Dun Laoghaire to Dublin inland canal, an idea that after decades of study and consideration and debate was finally judged impractical in the 1830s, mostly because the Great Walls of Dublin Bay had both been built, canals as a mode of transport were being replaced by the newer technology of the railway, and anyway it would have cost too much.

Today, the docklands and warehouses on both sides of the Liffey have experienced almost inconceivable alterations, and more and greater alterations are on the way to this area where the Liffey finally enters into the bay. Improvements can be found everywhere, and the pace of change seems to be accelerating.

Chapter 3

The Guinness Boats

The Guinness St James's Gate Brewery was founded in Dublin in 1759, and, given that the Liffey at Victoria Quay is still tidal, can be considered a legitimate part of the bay.

Dublin Bay and Guinness go way back. In 1796, the brewery exported six and a half barrels of extra stout porter to England, establishing an export market that has grown into a world-wide phenomenon. (That Guinness is good for you seems globally established although too much of the black stuff can lead to sodden consequences.) From 1875, the Guinness barrels were loaded onto river barges for the short trip from the brewery to the port at the mouth of the Liffey. They could not travel between two hours before and two after high tide because bridge clearance was too low.

Unloading Guinness boat at the docks

The barges were phased out in 1961 due to the development of modern bulk packaging in steel transportable tanks.

Guinness's export shipments of extra stout porter to England was dependent on the conventional shipping of the time, but the business was so well established that in 1913 the brewery bought a repurposed collier to become the first of its dedicated 'Guinness Boats' to make the passage across the Irish Sea. Several others followed, exporting the black stuff to London, Manchester and Liverpool.

There was an interregnum during the First World War when the British government commandeered the Guinness Boats, and one – the SS *William Barkley* – was torpedoed in 1917 by the pilsner-preferring German submarine service.

The world's thirst for Guinness continued to grow throughout the twentieth century. New ships were added as demand rose; and in 1952, the first ships built specifically for the transportation of beer in bulk were launched, to the delight of eager throngs in Manchester and Liverpool. The identically configured MV *The Lady Grania* and MV *The Lady Gwendolen*, both named after members of the Guinness family, were designed to carry Guinness in transportable tanks that could be transferred directly onto platform lorries which then became road tankers. These two maritime pioneers were replaced by another pair of remarkable ships. In 1973, MV *The Lady Patricia* was converted into a dedicated beer tanker with a bulk capacity equal to about 1.87 million pints or about 885,000 litres. She was joined by the MV *Miranda Guinness* in 1976, the world's first purpose-built beer tanker.

In 1987, the Irish Marine Services Ltd. took over the running of the Guinness ships; and in 1993, Guinness discontinued its tanker operations although its product is more popular than ever worldwide.

Guinness boat in front of Custom House

Chapter 4

The Great Walls of Dublin

Much of the story of Dublin Bay pivots around a remarkable engineering achievement: the construction of the two long breakwater walls that extend out on either side of the mouth of the Liffey. To understand why they were needed, visit Sandymount Strand at low tide. The entire inner half of the bay comprised two immense sand banks known as the North Bull and the South Bull, with 'bull' either a variation on 'ball', an old term for sand bank or, more poetically, a reference to the sound the shifting tides made drawing across the shingle with a roar like the bellowing of a bull. Both explanations exist widely and could be considered equally probable. These two extensive sand flats are always included in early maps of the bay, separated by the open channel – or channels – that are formed by the combined estuaries of the Liffey, Tolka and Dodder rivers; and although the coastline of Dublin Bay is easy to recognise, the sand banks look slightly different in each of the early maps, suggesting the danger inherent in such an unstable yet massive entity.

John Rocque's chart of the bay, made in 1762, shows the North Bull sand bank extending to Howth with a major channel formed at what is today Sutton Creek. The South Bull sand bank reached as far as Blackrock. The channel at the Liffey mouth at that time was separated into discrete flows divided by smaller sand banks, and areas of deep water are labelled as 'pools' with Clontarf Pool and Poolbeg both noted. Again, the danger that these massive, shifting, sometimes partially submerged sand banks posed

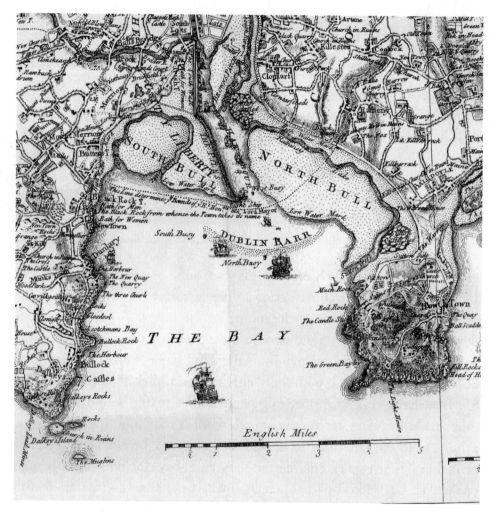

A Map of the County of Dublin by John Rocque, 1762

to ships would be hard to exaggerate. For mariners of the seventeenth and eighteenth centuries in particular, navigating into Dublin Bay was a risky undertaking that threatened the economic viability of the entire island.

The sand banks were no hindrance to the Vikings, however, and probably made Dublin Bay an attractive landing site. Their boats drew very little water and were well able to manage the shallowness of the bay. Before heading off for an inland raid, the Vikings would drag their warships up onto a sand beach from where they could be easily launched back out to the safety of the open sea. The first Norse *longphort* established at the *Dubh Linn* was set at the conjunction of the Liffey and the Poddle rivers, a land spit that offered a defensible site with water on two sides and beaches above the high-tide line that would provide extended storage for their ships without forgoing the option of a quick escape.

For Norman invaders, however, the shallowness of the Liffey and Dublin Bay became more of an obstacle since their ships required deeper water. As noted in 'The Early Bay', one of the main attractions of Ireland to these new invaders was the essential role played by the port at Dublin Bay in the growing international trade of the time. Yet advances in shipbuilding soon resulted in that very port becoming unsuitable. River silting and the 'bulls' were a constant threat. Traces of early attempts at solving the silting problem in the Liffey have been uncovered in the structures built along the river quays during the early middle ages, the idea being to deepen the river channel by narrowing it. Nevertheless, as the European maritime powers continued to advance in the fifteenth and sixteenth centuries, sending larger ships further, Dublin Bay's position as one of the primary ports of Europe was steadily eroded, partly because economic primacy was shifting to the Iberian Peninsula, but also because of the difficulty of access. Since the development of Norse Dublin, riverside quays had been used for loading and unloading cargo even as the silting of the river meant constant dredging was required and new quays constructed. But it was a losing battle, and archaeological evidence tracks the eastward movement of the commercial quays as the upstream river became increasingly unnavigable. Findings at Wood Quay indicate Viking and Norman use, for example; but in later ages, the larger, sea-going ships required to facilitate exploration and trade were no longer capable of manoeuvring that far upstream even in high water and what had been the primary port of Dublin atrophied. The silting of the river and the unpredictability of the channel as it cut through the sand banks had become a serious limitation on the city's commercial growth. (And again, it is worth recalling that the Norse port at Dublin Bay had been one of the primary objects of Henry II's cupidity.) Evidence at Islandbridge suggests that it was one of the earliest and most important Viking settlements. By the seventeenth century, the largest ships then in common service could no longer get up the Liffey at all, and only the quays at Ringsend were being used for offloading.

The problem of the river was compounded by the sand banks in the bay. The growing city of Dublin was not the only place affected. Dublin port had become the chief importing centre for the entire country – as it is today – and the shallow approaches created unacceptable hazards that would have an increasingly negative economic effect on the entire island. Water-borne transportation was essentially choked off at low tide. The very large, deep-draught ships of the late seventeenth century were obliged to anchor in one of the off-shore pools and transfer their cargo onto coastal lighters. Moreover, there was no protection from storms on the open bay so even riding at anchor could become hazardous during foul weather. Periodic dredging of the river and bay channel was never sufficient and the 'bulls' restricted opportunities for shipping on Dublin Bay at a time when the city was dependent on imported coal and other commodities. The requirements were obvious. For the economy to prosper, the sand banks had to be eliminated in order to create a deep-water harbour, a method had to be found to shelter ships in the bay during storms, and the main channel of the Liffey had to be deepened and maintained at a sufficient depth to accommodate shipping.

This was a tall order. But 1676 saw the first of several attempts at a solution, one that today sounds more like wishful thinking than a hard-nosed effort likely to have a major impact. Yet it did set into motion a train of decisions that in the end resulted in a degree of success.

Ships sailing out of the port empty took on sand as ballast. An authority was created – the Ballast Office – whose responsibility it was to compel departing ships to dredge out their ballast-sand from the centre of the river channel rather than from the banks. This would hardly seem to qualify even as a stop-gap measure. But it did result in the establishment of the Ballast Office as an authoritative entity with a mandate to solve the problem; and thirty years later, a project was finally approved that would begin to remedy what had become an increasingly desperate situation.

A study of the bottom of the bay was authorised to gain a better understanding of what could be done, and various suggestions brought forward. One idea – to create a weir and sluice at the river mouth so that the river could be kept at a high level until low tide then released all at once to scour out the channel – although innovative was not adopted. It did, however, indicate an improved understanding of the hydrodynamics of the bay, and one which would soon lead to a decision that would ultimately result in a permanent solution – the Great South Wall and North Bull Wall – a matched pair of elegant engineering achievements that exemplify the kind of big projects the eighteenth century did well.

The Great South Wall

As so often, the name itself is various. From its initiation, the stonework seawall that was extended out into the bay seems to have been known both as the Great South Wall and South Bull Wall. We will go with the 'bull' version, perhaps in an unconsciously vicarious imitation of old Queen Medb's bovine partiality.

Work on the first version of South Bull Wall was begun in 1715 and completed in 1730. This was actually a wooden jetty that extended from Ringsend out to the edge of the low water line, a much more limited attempt than what is there today. One assumes the builders were testing an idea. Oak piles were driven down through the sand and anchored into the floor of the bay. This framework was then knitted together and reinforced with wattles and containers filled with gravel. The 'Piles', as it was called, succeeded in two ways: it helped provide some shelter for ships during storms and it restricted the flow of sand from the sand banks of the South Bull into the navigational channel of the Liffey as it flowed into the bay. Equally importantly, the concept of managing the shape of the bay by extending a wall out into it was proven – or seemed to be. In the 1750s, a double wall was built, then filled in to form what is today

Pigeon House Road. No wooden construction could last long in sea water, however, and the 'Piles' were deteriorating; so by 1761, work was begun on replacing the 'Piles' with a permanent stone breakwater pier. Work on the eastern-most sections was initiated and early work on the platform for a lighthouse at the far end of what would become the South Bull Wall also occurred, although the project was troubled by insufficient funding.

This new wall – the one we have today – was constructed out of immense granite blocks that were quarried and shaped in Dalkey and Blackrock, then transported on barges and fitted together. The same building techniques and source of granite were used to construct Dun Laoghaire Harbour. The core of the wall was filled with sand and gravel dredged from the harbour mouth, deepening the Liffey channel. An actual completion date for South Bull Wall is hard to pin down since it was an ongoing project for a number of years. The Poolbeg Lighthouse went into service in 1768 and a completion date for the long wall itself can be set at 1786. At 18,000 feet (5,486 metres), from Ringsend to Poolbeg, it is one of the longest breakwater walls in Europe.

The Great South Wall – or South Bull Wall – soon had a beneficial effect on the bay. It straightened and restricted the channel of the Liffey, creating

View of South Bull Wall

a stronger flowing action which therefore carried suspended particles farther into the bay and thus helped reduce silting. It also lessened wave surge driven by storms and so created a safer harbour for ships during foul weather. The South Bull Wall was considered a spectacular engineering feat at the time, but it did not finally solve the problem. The river channel was improved yet it was still not deep enough or wide enough for the increasingly large ships of the late eighteenth century. Even after the wall was completed, the deep-water pools at Poolbeg and Clontarf still had to be used for anchorage and offloading of large ships so that the goal of having even very large ships enter the port safely and tie up at the quays was not achieved. Moreover, the sand banks had continued to expand, particularly on the north side now; and it seemed probable that the North Bull would continue to grow, extending from Clontarf farther and farther out into the bay until it posed an even greater hazard to shipping.

Part of the North Bull was also staying dry even during high tides. This now-permanent sand spit on the north side of the bay was the first incarnation of what would become North Bull Island (see 'North Bull Island'). Marine engineers were getting a better understanding of the interrelated forces that formed the sand banks in the bay so the movement of sand carried into Dublin Bay then on around toward Sutton and the island forming off Dollymount suggested a final step in the process of converting Dublin Bay into a viable and sustainable port with sufficient capacity to serve the entire island.

North Bull Wall

It was obvious that the completion of the South Bull Wall had improved the situation but not solved the problem. Sand bars still formed that blocked the mouth of the port, the channel still was not deep enough, and there was no true asylum harbour for shelter in bad weather.

New proposals were submitted, beginning in 1800 – including one by Captain William Bligh of *Mutiny on the Bounty* fame – but the project was not authorised for fifteen years. The solution was predictable enough, and elegant in its simplicity. The Great South Wall had already constricted river flow and tidal action somewhat. By constructing a second wall on the north side of the Liffey mouth, the flow of the river and the outgoing tidal flow would be even more intensely concentrated into a narrow channel. Since the water could then no longer escape to the north side, this would create a powerful natural scouring action which would eliminate the need for dredging and thus deepen the river entryway sufficiently to accommodate the larger ships that were then in use.

Finding sufficient money to fund the project delayed it. But in 1814, the Pigeon House on the South Bull Wall was sold to the British Army to be used as a fort, and those funds were made available for the new project.

North Bull Wall

The official name of this new wall was 'The Great North Wall', matching its earlier cousin; but it became known popularly as the 'Bull Wall' or 'North Bull Wall' and remains so today. Interestingly, Bull Bridge was erected first as a footbridge in 1819, linking the as yet unnamed offshore sand spit to Clontarf so as to facilitate the larger undertaking of building the wall itself. Bull Bridge was later reconstructed to accommodate cars, and the present structure dates from 1907.

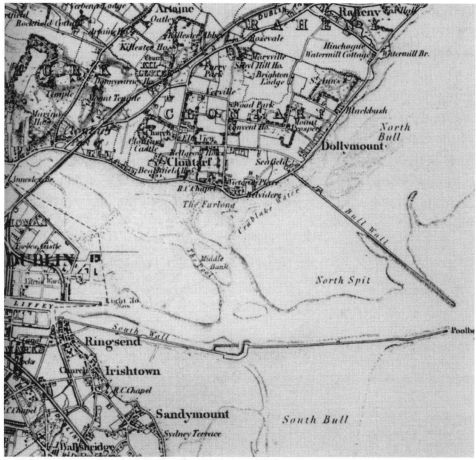

One-inch Ordnance Survey Map of Ireland, 1860
extract from Sheet 112

Construction on the North Bull Wall began in 1820 and was completed three years later, with much of the work being done by convicts. Boulders were brought from Dalkey by barge again, as with the South Bull Wall, and from local quarries by carts, with both granite and limestone used. A short section of closely fitted granite blocks extends and connects the seawall of the Clontarf Promenade to Bull Bridge; but the bulk of the off-shore wall was formed by simply piling roughly hewn boulders in a long straight jetty that extends slightly less than 3,000 metres from the shore at Clontarf to the North Bull Light. The wall itself has three distinct sections: Bull Bridge, a one-lane wooden bridge about 185 metres long; the main 1,680-metre stretch with a walkway that is always well above water even during the highest tides, and a final, inaccessible 'half-tide wall' of 1,070 metres that continues on to the North Bull Light. This final section of wall is exposed at about the half-way point of the ebb tide but wholly covered when the tide is full. This means that for the second half of the out-going tide, water is forced to flow in a narrow channel between the two lighthouses, reinforcing the scouring effect. Yet during the initial stages of the ebb tide, water moves over the half-tide wall as well, reducing the flow of the outward current. This was deemed necessary because the sail-powered vessels of that era would not be able sail into a stronger current and thus would have difficulty even making it into the port at the Liffey mouth.

Bull Bridge

Silting on the Bull Island side of the wall is quite extensive, while on the Clontarf side, the water is deeper. Moreover, the decision to erect a bridge over the channel stream flowing between the Bull Island and Clontarf preserved the natural current of the bay along the shore, allowing the lagoon formed between Bull Island and Dollymount to flush itself, a beneficial effect that has since been terminated by the construction of the causeway in 1964. (For more, see 'North Bull Island'.)

Building the North Bull Wall narrowed the channel formed by the Liffey as it empties into the bay, compelling the current to flow with greater force; this restricted channel also increases the force of the ebb tide retreating out of the river mouth, resulting in a heavy natural tidal scour that helps to keep the shipping lanes open into Dublin Port and prevents the build-up of sandbars that had proven such problems over the centuries.

That is the story. And the 'great walls of Dublin Bay' were certainly a remarkable marine engineering achievement.

But sand isn't so easily dealt with. The bay continues to fill with silt and dredging is still necessary. The river scour did deepen the channel – it is at its deepest in the open water between the Poolbeg Light and the North Bull Light. But suspended matter was just carried farther out into the bay and then deposited so a sand bar formed beyond that deep pool, and it has to be dredged even today, as do various parts of the port facilities.

The water in the channel today has a depth of up to nine metres at low tide so with a little help from the dredgers, the 'scouring' action can be considered a success of self-management. An open navigational channel 1,000 feet (305 metres) wide is maintained.

Chapter 5
Martello Towers

In February 1794, two British warships attacked a round, heavily fortified tower at Mortella Point in Corsica. The two warships launched a fierce cannonade that continued for almost three hours but made not the slightest impression on the tower, and return fire finally forced the British ships to withdraw. Two days later, the intact tower fell to an intensive assault by land-based forces, and the British were so impressed by the effectiveness of the tower against their most modern warships that they copied the design, misspelling the name 'Mortella' as 'Martello'. The term now is a universal term for any round defensive tower.

Between 1804 and 1812, fearing a possible invasion attempt from France, the British established a chain of similar structures to defend the south and east coast of England, Ireland, Jersey and Guernsey. Each one was built the same, and was positioned within firing distance of the next. Although they look round, the towers are slightly elliptical, with the walls

Martello Tower at Seapoint

thicker on the side facing the sea since that was where enemy fire was expected to come from. The roundness was intentional since the curved surface would deflect cannon balls. A round brick pillar rose through the centre of each tower to support the roof.

Most of the Irish Martello towers were built along the east coast of Ireland, especially around Dublin Bay, and Cork Harbour on the south coast. The interior of each was divided into a ground floor where ammunition, stores and provisions were kept; a middle floor with quarters for the garrison; and the roof, which was mounted with one or two cannon riding on a circular rail and so capable of turning through 360 degrees. The living quarters were divided into separate rooms and had fireplaces for heating and cooking. A well or cistern provided the garrison with fresh water.

Probably the most famous Martello is the one at Sandycove where James Joyce stayed briefly and where the opening chapter of *Ulysses* is set. Known as the 'James Joyce Tower', it is now a museum dedicated to Joyce and his work. A Martello tower in Cork Harbour was briefly captured and held during the nineteenth-century Fenian uprising, making it the only one in Ireland ever defeated.

Over one hundred towers were built in England, set at intervals along the coast from Seaford, Sussex, to Aldeburgh, Suffolk. None was ever tested in battle. The Martello tower design was exported to many colonies of the British Empire, with several in South Africa, Australia, and Canada; and France built similar towers along its own coastline, which they used as platforms for communication by optical telegraphs. The United States government also built Martello towers along the east coast of the US, copying the British design with some modifications.

Chapter 6
Famous Shipwrecks

Travellers along the coastline of Georgian Dublin reported seeing masts sticking up here and there in the bay, some providing convenient roosting places for seabirds, others still draped with the wispy ends of lines or the shreds of the sails which had been unable to save them.

Until the advent of steam power, Dublin Bay was a ship's graveyard feared by mariners for its shifting sand banks, strong tidal draw and treacherous winds. Dublin Port was sited at a particularly dangerous place, and ships were obliged to make their way up a narrow channel to reach the docks where they could unload cargo and passengers. (It is instructive that VIPs sometimes disembarked at Dalkey or Dun Laoghaire, letting the ship then continue on to the port without them.) Marine traffic was heavy in Dublin Bay as the city developed through the centuries, and the berthing facilities were limited so that ships were often obliged to ride at anchor in the deep pools offshore – one at Clontarf, another at Poolbeg – and this left them vulnerable to storms. Even when the weather was clement, larger vessels could only manage the channel during flood tides, so delays were inevitable.

Wind power on the Irish Sea and in Dublin Bay made travel and trade possible and was reliable because windless days were rare, unlike southern seas where great extended periods of calm could become life-threatening to mariners. The risk obviously was too much wind, and in particular gales from the north-east were feared on Dublin Bay since they would drive ships onto the sand banks of the shallow bay or even onto shoreline rocks.

Strollers on the East Pier of Dun Laoghaire Harbour are familiar with the monument to Captain Boyd and his crew. *The Times* of 12 February 1861 gives a vivid depiction of this one, violent storm:

MELANCHOLY CATASTROPHE AT KINGSTOWN.

Intelligence reached town this afternoon that Captain Boyd, of Her Majesty's ship *Ajax*, and 14 men of his crew, were unfortunately drowned about 12 o'clock to-day outside Kingstown Harbour. A telegram received states that:

"Captain Boyd with his men were standing on the Eastern Pier, endeavouring to save the crew of a vessel which had gone ashore at the back of the pier, when a wave swept them all into the sea. Mr. John Mulvany, architect, was with them, but was saved. As far as can be ascertained, 16 vessels have gone ashore in or about Kingstown Harbour. Many lives have been lost in addition to those of Captain Boyd and boat's crew."

Last night, about 9 o'clock, one of the severest gales remembered in Dublin for many years set in from the south-east, and continued to rage up to an advanced hour to-day, accompanied by heavy rain and sleet. In addition to the sad disasters at Kingstown already detailed, numerous shipwrecks have occurred along the eastern coast, in the neighbourhood of Dublin, and it is much feared that the destruction of life and property has been considerable.

Shipwrecks fill the bay and beyond, which is hardly surprising given the importance of trade throughout the history of Ireland. The numbers would be impossible to estimate – anecdotal evidence recounts 'hundreds' of wrecks a year throughout the eighteenth century, and with the loss of 'thousands' of lives. A great many of these would have been small boats with small crews, most of whom would have been unable to swim.

But even a review of the major wrecks which were newsworthy enough to have been recorded as occurring in Dublin Bay runs into the many hundreds of vessels, some of which where recovered and their crews saved while others were lost, with crew and even passengers drowning, often within view of their would-be rescuers. Comprehensive lists of the most important or largest wrecks exist; and a number of shipwrecks in the bay are popular dive sites. Keeping in mind that smaller boats would have gone down without leaving any lasting record, and that a great many large ships that were lost near or in the bay are still categorised as 'unknown', some sense of the risk and scale of the suffering endured by mariners over the centuries can be gained by the following overview.

The North Bay

Major wrecks on the north side of the bay can be separated into those that occurred around Howth and those that are inside the bay proper, usually associated with the North Bull sand bank. Early records of sea disasters at Howth are not reliable, with only a dozen named ships reported before the nineteenth century when the actual number would have been vastly larger. In the last two hundred years, however, eleven large ships are recorded as lost on the rocks at Baily Lighthouse, with another fifty wrecked along the headlands of Howth, including the *Queen Victoria*, a paddle steamer that was lost in February 1853. The *Queen Victoria* was owned by The City of Dublin Steam Packet Company and was powered by a two-cylinder steam engine. She was returning from Liverpool with general cargo and passengers in a snowstorm when she struck Howth Head in the middle of the night. The captain decided to try to save the ship by backing off, but the damage was extensive and she struck again under the Baily Lighthouse and went down just offshore. Conditions were awful, and over eighty people died trying to make it to shore. A subsequent enquiry blamed the captain, first mate and those responsible for the lighthouse.

Attempts to raise the vessel failed and the *Queen Victoria* was broken open and salvaged in situ. The wreck still exists just under the Baily Light in about twenty metres of water, with the boilers and remains of the engine visible, along with her anchors and paddle wheels. The site is protected by The National Monuments Act, and is occasionally visited by scuba divers, although the rocks and strong currents make it a risky site.

Improvements in marine technology bring down the totals in the twentieth century yet tragedies still occurred. A number of fishing trawlers operating out of Howth have been lost, including the *Geraldine* and the *St Michan*, both sunk gratuitously on the same day in 1918 by the German submarine U-96.

The waters towards Ireland's Eye and Lambay Island add another fifty significant shipwrecks, including what is believed to be the oldest in the Dublin Bay area, a Roman sailing vessel dating from 672. (A wreck off Malahide is said to date from the year 500 but little seems to be known about it.)

Recorded losses inside the bay on the north side begin in the seventeenth century, with about ten major ships lost off Sutton or Clontarf. Obviously, the North Bull became a more formidable obstacle as ships grew larger and more numerous. In the eighteenth century, about fifty ships were lost to the sand banks on the north side of the Liffey Channel, including the *Friendship*, the *Hope*, the *Happy Return*, the *Blessing*, the *Speculation*, the *Hope* (again), the *Resolution*, the *Active*, and the *Good Intent*. Clontarf was also a busy fishing village so that the loss of small fishing boats on the bay would have been substantial, although today no evidence remains.

Ringsend and Poolbeg

The Dublin Port area of Ringsend and Poolbeg is the area of greatest losses, not surprisingly since historically most of the major vessels crossing Dublin Bay were trying to reach the Liffey mouth. The earliest known wreck is dated 1288, when the *Thomas Petley* foundered on the sand bar at Ringsend Basin and was lost. In the sixteenth and seventeenth centuries, fourteen shipping disasters were considered sufficiently noteworthy for recording, with the various cargoes listed as 'unknown' – most commonly

Stormy Sea in Clontarf, c. 1914

– or as 'passengers', 'soldiers' or 'wine'. About 155 vessels were recorded as lost at the port entry or directly off-shore from it in the eighteenth century, reflecting both the huge growth in trade and improvements in record-keeping. Many of these ships were reported as salvaged and with their cargoes retrieved, with 'unknown' again heading the list, followed by wine, brandy, gin, porter and hops. The loss of soldiers and other passengers is also often recorded.

In the nineteenth century, the shipwrecks around the port area grew in number, with about 175 substantial ships lost – an average of almost two a year although some were 're-floated'. The brig *Sally* was wrecked in the harbour in 1800 but successfully salvaged and returned to service in time to go down at more or less the same location a year later, with no record of her being salvaged a second time. Despite all the improvements to the shipping channel and the port itself, fifteen ships were lost there in the twentieth century.

The South Bay

The sand banks of the South Bull claimed twenty-one large ships in the eighteenth century and the same number again in the nineteenth century. Kingstown/Dun Laoghaire Harbour was the site of many horrific catastrophes, as *The Times* report above indicates. In the period before the eighteenth century, a few major wrecks are recorded in Dalkey and old Dunleary, as it was then known, another twenty or so occurring at Dalkey, and off Dalkey Island and the Muglins during the eighteenth and nineteenth centuries. One of the worst happened in one of the most benign-looking locations, Blackrock. In November, 1807, the *HMS Prince of Wales* and the *Rochdale*, both loaded with passengers, including around 500 soldiers and their families, were caught by a fierce storm, driven onto the rocks and wrecked. The *Prince of Wales* broke up near where Blackrock Park is today while the *Rochdale* hit the shore at Seapoint. All the passengers and crew were lost, and only the captain and some of the crew of the *Prince of Wales* escaped, abandoning their ship and leaving passengers and other

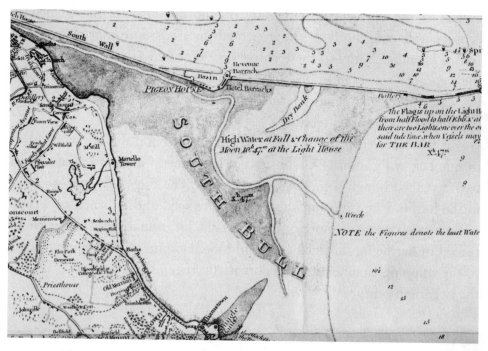

The Dangerous South Bull – Detail from John Taylor's Map of Dublin Environs, 1816

crew members to their fate. The corpses of the drowned washed ashore for days afterwards; and the disaster, added to the many others that had occurred on the bay, led to the demand for the construction of an asylum harbour at Dun Laoghaire.

Even an 'asylum harbour' was no guarantee of safety, as some mariners making for Kingstown/Dun Laoghaire Harbour discovered. In the eighteenth century, seven were wrecked by being driven ashore at the old pier, a number that ballooned to sixty-three in the nineteenth century, with some of the worst disasters at the harbour entrance. Twenty ships were lost in the twentieth century, the lesser number again reflecting improvements in marine technology. Smaller fishing boats, as well as yachts and other pleasure boats, are not categorised as shipwrecks when they go down although the trauma involved can easily be imagined.

The Eastern Edge

The Kish Bank is at the eastern edge of Dublin Bay, and it has seen its share of maritime disasters. Over forty substantial wrecks are to be found there, dating from the seventeenth through the nineteenth centuries. The Kish Bank has always been a hazard. The *Success* became stuck on the bank in 1783 while carrying what is listed as 'general' cargo; the ship was salvaged, got stuck again in 1790, then did it for a third time in 1800, loaded with convicts bound from Liverpool to Dublin. No further records of the *Success* or its mishaps seem to exist. In the twentieth century, fifteen ships have been lost at the Kish Bank, including seven torpedoed by German U-boats in 1917–18, with another two torpedoed in the same area during World War II.

The most notorious sinking at the Kish Bank was the torpedoing of the *RMS Leinster*. The *Leinster* served as the Kingstown–Holyhead mail boat during World War I, carrying passengers and mail between Ireland and Wales. There was a lot of U-boat activity in the Irish Sea during the war as the Germans tried to cut off seaborne supplies to Britain, and the *Leinster* was attacked by German submarine UB 123 on 10 October 1918. She was carrying over 700 passengers, of which about 300 were soldiers. The *Leinster* was torpedoed twice in quick succession and began sinking immediately. Only 256 passengers were rescued, while almost 500 drowned. The loss was one of Dublin Bay's greatest tragedies. The wreck of the *Leinster* still exists. It lies in about thirty metres of water and has badly deteriorated.

The *Vanguard* is another famous wreck on the Kish Bank. In September, 1915, the *HMS Vanguard* steamed out of Kingstown (Dun Laoghaire) to join a squadron of full-rigged ironclads that had just completed a summer season of training cruises to test the efficiency of the gun crews at gunnery practice. The ships had passed the Kish Light only to run into a dense fog bank, giving visibility of less than a ship's length. The outline of a sailing ship emerged in the fog; the helm was thrown hard to starboard and the engines stopped. The ship then returned to its original course but this put her in the path of another battleship in the squadron, *The Iron Duke*. The fog was so thick that neither ship saw the other until they were about forty yards apart. *The Iron Duke* struck the *Vanguard* full amidships, tearing a gaping hole in her flank which quickly flooded the engine and boiler rooms. The crew was ferried safely to *The Iron Duke*, and the *Vanguard* sank with no loss of life although her captain was severely reprimanded and dismissed from his ship.

The above lists don't fully capture the number of losses on the bay and surrounding seas during the nineteenth century. What may well have been the worst storm – the one mentioned above by *The Times* – saw 135 ships recorded as missing in the waters around Britain and Ireland, with fifteen ships wrecked in Dublin Bay and another eight off Howth.

Melancholy indeed.

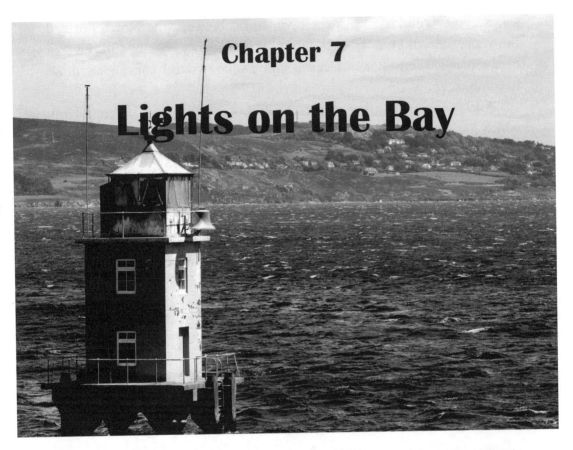

Chapter 7
Lights on the Bay

About ten kilometres offshore in the Irish Sea, a series of sand-banks runs roughly parallel to the coast. Standing in twenty to thirty metres of water and rising to within a few metres of the surface, they imperilled coastal shipping before modern technologies reduced the threat. The Kish Bank is the largest of these offshore hazards and is marked today by the Kish Lighthouse. It is also littered with the wrecks of ships which have foundered there.

About five kilometres inside the Kish Bank is the Burford Bank, and it effectively forms the eastern boundary of Dublin Bay. If a straight line were drawn from the Baily Light to the Muglins Beacon off Dalkey Island, the Burford Bank would lie just outside it. Although it is always submerged, the Burford Bank is a prominent feature of Dublin Bay. It influences tidal and current flows, and it also somewhat suppresses wave action in the bay. Two radar-beacon buoys – the North Burford Buoy and the South Burford Buoy – mark the longitudinal extent of this bank and also indicate safe shipping channels, with the open water between the North Burford Buoy and Howth Head used by ships on a northerly course; and the area between the South Burford Buoy and Dalkey Island chosen by those heading south.

Also in the bay is what mariners call the 'bar'. The bar is a sand bank which has formed just beyond the deepest pool at the Liffey mouth. It is the result of the scouring effect created by the two Bull Walls. The sand and silt was carried farther, thanks to the increased tidal flow, but it still got deposited. Today, the bar is one part of Dublin Bay that still requires regular dredging.

Various surveys of the Dublin Bay seabed have been carried out over the years in order to understand the results of human interventions in the bay such as channel dredging, the scouring effect resulting from the

Poolbeg Lighthouse

construction of the Great South Wall and the North Bull Wall, or, for that matter, the impact of the release of sewage into the bay over the years. One result of these efforts has been the confirmation that the sea floor is largely covered with rippled fine sand. Studies have also confirmed the remarkable number of shipwrecks in Dublin Bay. The highest concentration of shipwrecks in Irish waters is found in conjunction with the offshore sand banks, reminders both that Dublin Port traffic has always been heavy, and that attempting to enter into the bay has always been perilous.

Comparison of data collected from between the middle of the eighteenth century until well into the twentieth century also seems to indicate that little alteration has occurred in the Burford Bank, and the Kish Bank out beyond it seems equally stable. This could of course change due to global warming. If the sea level rises, the increased energy of winds and waves could lead to a diminution of the banks. Were the sand banks to be significantly degraded or removed, the configuration of tidal currents inside the bay would change – perhaps drastically – and the shoreline would receive much stronger wave energy, resulting in serious damage to coastal facilities such as docks, seawalls and jetties, winter flooding at coastal areas such as Clontarf, and even new threats to shipping.

The radar beacon buoys that mark the Burford Banks are called 'Racons', an example of the modern technologies that ships rely on to enter Dublin Bay safely. Racons receive signals from ships' radars which trigger the Racon to emit a characteristic series of response pulses which is then received by the ship's radar. This unique response signal allows easy identification of the particular Racon being interrogated. Other technologies, such as GPS, the satellite position-fixing system operated by the US Department of Defence, are also used for general navigation. Yet classic lighthouses are still required, and the bay's lights are among its most historically significant and technologically beautiful amenities – working amenities, that is.

Lighthouses have changed over the years. Early lighthouses were erected by private individuals who acted under letters of authorisation granted by the Crown. The lighthouses were meant to be commercial affairs and their owners were granted the right to collect tolls from any ship benefiting from the light. Collecting tolls proved difficult, apparently, since it would have been impossible to prove that a ship had in fact relied on a light.

Originally, the lighthouse keeper's family lived with him at the lighthouse. Then manned lighthouses were converted to a 'relieving' status in which crews worked and bunked there on a rotating schedule but their families lived elsewhere. Finally, lighthouses were converted to a fully automated operation, in Dublin Bay's case, controlled from the Commissioners of Irish Lights facilities at Dun Laoghaire Harbour. Today, a variety of navigational aids are found at the lighthouse sites, including Racons and GPS navigation aides. But for all that, an arriving vessel would still find some comfort in the patterns of flashing lights they encounter as they navigate into Dublin Bay.

Kish Lighthouse

The Kish Light

In 1810, the body that was later to become the Commissioners of Irish Lights decided to purchase a ship and fit it out as a 'floating light' to be stationed on the Kish Bank. In foggy weather a gong was sounded, but when the Holyhead Packet was expected, the ship's crew fired a cannon to warn of the danger. In 1842, an attempt was made to erect a lighthouse on the Kish Bank using screw piles but the structure was destroyed by a severe gale and the project abandoned. Over the years, various other light vessels with fog signals were employed on the Kish Banks; then in 1960, the Commissioners of Irish Lights became interested in the possibility of using a platform similar to deep-sea oil rigs for lighthouse purposes. The design they selected was not for a steel platform like an oil rig but for a concrete lighthouse similar to one in Sweden. In order to withstand the fierce weather conditions on the Irish Sea, the structure had to be more than twice as big as the largest of similar lighthouses built by the Swedish Board of Shipping and Navigation.

The lighthouse was constructed of reinforced concrete in the form of a circular caisson. The whole thing was floated out to the Kish Bank. Inside the caisson was the actual light tower which was telescoped up to its full height once it reached the site. The tower had the lantern, the keepers' quarters, and all the equipment and stores needed to maintain it. Construction work commenced at Dun Laoghaire in 1963, and after some mishaps, the bottom portion of the lighthouse was built as a caisson with an outside diameter of 31.5 metres riding on a base slab one metre thick. Three concentric walls with twelve interlocking radial walls formed sections which would be flooded as required during the sinking operation. The light tower itself is a self-contained unit of twelve floors built within the caisson, thirty metres high when extended and surmounted by a helicopter landing platform.

In June 1965, the immense caisson was towed out of Dun Laoghaire Harbour to the Kish Bank and sunk onto a level platform of stones which had previously been prepared. The tower was raised by flooding the lower caisson with water, causing the tower portion to rise up to the surface. After adjusting the base structure to ensure that the tower was vertical, the water was then pumped out of the caissons and replaced by 18,000 tons of sand that was topped with concrete, sealing the space between the tower and the caisson.

The light operates as a two-million candlepower beam with a range of twenty-seven nautical miles, and it can be increased to three million in fog. A Racon, added in 1968, shows on the radar screens of vessels as an unmistakable and identifiable blip; and a modern radio beacon adds another form of warning.

The lighthouse was manned by a crew until 1992 when it was converted to fully automatic operation and the last keepers of the Kish Light were withdrawn from the station. The light and other aids to navigation are all monitored by the Commissioners of Irish Lights at Dun Laoghaire via a telemetry link, and the lighthouse itself is easily visible from Howth Head, a lonely sentinel on the edge of the Irish Sea.

The Baily Light

In 1665, Charles II ordered the construction of six lighthouses around the coast of Ireland, and among them was a cottage-type lighthouse which had a coal-burning beacon on top of a square tower at the eastern gable end of the cottage. Horses and carts transported fuel from a quay specially built for the lighthouse at the village of Howth. In 1790, the coal burning light was replaced by a lantern composed of six oil lamps with silvered copper parabolic reflectors directing the light through six bulls-eye glass panes which acted as crude lenses. The light was set too high on the hill and was therefore often obscured by mist or low clouds; so in 1811 it was decided to move the light to a new location lower down on the headland at the Little Baily and construction was completed in 1814.

Baily Lighthouse

The new lighthouse had a fixed white catoptric light comprising twenty-four oil lamps and reflectors, and it was positioned in a cut-granite tower that rose forty-one metres above the high water level. A fog bell was added to the tower in 1853, partially in response to some of the horrific shipwrecks in the area. In 1846, the City of Dublin Steam Packet Company's paddle steamer *Prince* struck the cliffs in thick fog near the Nose of Howth, just north of the Baily. Then in February 1853, another of the Steam Packet Company's ships, the *Queen Victoria*, was caught in a night snowstorm while on the way to Liverpool. She struck Howth Head, backed off, but then foundered on the rocks off the Baily and broke up with the loss of over eighty lives. No one could know if a fog bell would have prevented these accidents, but all agreed it was worth attempting. (See 'Famous Shipwrecks'.)

In 1865, the Baily's light was improved 'to a first-order dioptric', and experiments were also begun to convert the light source to a gas that could be made at the site, at first from oil, then shale, and finally rich cannel coal. The idea proved successful and nine other Irish lighthouses were converted to either oil gas or coal gas.

The need for fog warnings did not diminish, and an 'air trumpet' foghorn was installed; a device which used a small coal-fired hot air engine to compress air in a cylinder on top of which was a mounted reed horn. This air trumpet was replaced by a siren in 1879; and the siren yielded to a compressed-air diaphone in 1926, creating the familiar low-pitched 'grunt' that ends each note.

The light beam was altered to a flashing mode in 1902, and after operating for over forty years on gas, the light source was converted to incandescent vaporised paraffin. The optics received another upgrade in 1972, with a new 375mm lens and an even more powerful light source.

The Baily Light was the last light in Ireland to be operated by a lighthouse keeper and crew. During 1996–7, the Baily Light was converted to automatic operation and the lighthouse keepers were withdrawn, ending the era of the manned lighthouse in Ireland. Aids to navigation today are controlled and monitored via a telemetry link from Commissioners of Irish Lights in Dun Laoghaire. The Baily Light with its attractive keeper's house and other facilities is easily viewed from the cliff walk in Howth, and reached by an access road off Old Thormanby Road.

The Harbour Lights at Howth and Dun Laoghaire

There is a fine old Regency lighthouse at the end of the Eastern Pier at Howth Harbour. (We look at the harbour in more detail in the chapter on Howth.) Today, it is strictly decorative but well in keeping with the harbour itself. It was built in 1818, and like much of the formal public stone work in that era, the finish is very fine and impressive. The lighthouse is a round granite tower ten metres tall and with deep-set windows facing out over the sea. The lantern at the top still contains its element although it is no longer used; the lantern is a pleasantly old-fashioned chamber with panes of glass riding in an iron frame surmounted by a white, cupola-like roof bearing a large arrow-shaped weathervane, a lighting rod and a flag pole. The iron gallery that surrounds the lantern is painted red.

The rectangular keeper's house is attached directly to the light itself and is also built of granite and the workmanship is excellent. The curved planes of stone of the lighthouse contrast nicely with the flat walls of the two-storey keeper's house. Lace curtains are in the windows, flower boxes are planted with petunias and the front door is painted a bright orange-red.

Howth Lighthouse

The light itself is no longer used. Like the the East Pier Light at Dun Laoghaire, the original lighthouse at Howth also had a defensive purpose, and the curved wall wrapping around it on the seaward side once defended a gun position, with a similar wall on the opposite pier to the west. (And also at Dun Laoghaire, as we shall see.)

The present Howth Harbour light was built in 1982 on a new jetty that extends about fifty metres farther out towards Ireland's Eye. It is elegantly functional, with the light mounted atop a white concrete pillar and surrounded by a red iron gallery railing which echoes the similar railing atop the older light. A set of green channel buoys extending out further east guide ships to the harbour mouth. The light emits two flashes every eight seconds, and they appear white or red, depending on the viewer's orientation. Access to the light comes from an interior ladder, which qualifies it – barely – as a lighthouse.

Harbour lights mounted at the ends of sea-piers have a slightly different function to warning beacons such as the Baily or the Kish. One warns of danger while the other marks the entry of an asylum harbour, a very reassuring sight, particularly in fog or a storm.

There are two lights at the mouth of Dun Laoghaire Harbour, built at about the same time, with the East Pier Light finished in the 1840s and the West Pier Light five years later. (For more on the construction of the harbour, see the chapter Dun Laoghaire.) Both lights are mounted on stone towers and were built primarily to mark the harbour entrance for ships that were unable to get into the Port of Dublin, either due to weather or occasionally even crowding. The lantern on the East Pier Light was painted white with a red dome; it emits two red flashes every ten seconds. The West Pier Light emits three green flashes every eight seconds, and the lantern was painted green in 1996. (There is also a small light on the derelict Carlisle Pier that emits a red flash every three seconds.)

In 1909 a fog horn was added to the West Pier Light at the request of the London North-Western Railway; and in 1949, the principal keeper from the East Pier Light moved into the dwelling on the West Pier, apparently because the facilities on the East Pier Light had become too crowded when the light gained the status of a 'three-keeper' station. Before this, the West Pier Light was unmanned. The two assistant-keepers and their families continued to live in the dwellings at the base of the East Pier Light.

In 1955, the East Pier Light was converted to 'relieving' status and the keepers' families ceased living there. The keepers themselves continued to occupy the dwellings inside the East Pier Battery walls while on duty, working a shift system of six weeks' on-duty followed by two weeks off. The lighthouse was fully automated in 1977.

The Commissioners of Irish Lights maintain their highly sophisticated control station at Dun Laoghaire Harbour, centrally located slightly east of Trader's Wharf.

The Poolbeg Light and the North Bull Light

Two very similar lights mark the entrance to Dublin Port, with the red Poolbeg Light at the end of the South Bull Wall and the green North Bull

Light at the end of North Bull Wall, although it appears to be alone in the water during high tides because the end of Bull Wall is submerged other than from mid to low tides. A

Poolbeg Lighthouse

lightship was stationed at the harbour mouth of the Liffey channel from 1735 to 1768. It was known as the Floating Light, and is usually referred to as the Dublin Lightship although the term lightship was not used at the time. The vessel had two lanterns placed at either side of a square yard on the mast which were lit at night from half-flood to half-ebb. The original light tower at the end of the Great South Wall was built in 1768 and redesigned into its present form in 1820. The colour of the tower changed over the years from white to black to its present red. The light emitted is red, and alternates on and off in sustained flashes

North Bull Light

of eight or four second duration. The North Bull Light was built in 1880. A green conical stone tower, it emits three green flashes every ten seconds. As with the light at Poolbeg, the Dublin Port Company manages the North Bull Light as a key feature ensuring safe navigation into the port.

Also operated by the Dublin Port Company are the North Bank Light from 1882 – a green flashing light on a green tower with white lantern and gallery, mounted on concrete piles and located west of North Bull Light on the north side of the Liffey entrance channel – and the light at the end of the North Wall Quay, built in 1902 and emitting a quick white flash every two seconds. It is a cylindrical cast iron tower with lantern and gallery, painted black with two white horizontal bands. A fog bell, hanging from the gallery, is no longer used.

The Muglins Light

The warning lights on the bay mark its boundaries. The Kish Light and the two radio-beacons on the Burford Banks define the eastern edge where the Irish Sea begins. The centre is characterised by the red and green lights at the ends of the Great South Wall and the North Bull Wall; and at the southern extremity of Dublin Bay, there is no better candidate for border-status than the squat little oddity on The Muglins.

Dalkey Sound – the Dalkey 'Roads' – has been a haven since Viking times. The deep water found there offered shelter, particularly when compared to the shallowness of Dublin Bay with its two huge sand banks. Dalkey was a Danish trading centre, and the Normans continued the practice and built seven castles there which also functioned as fortified warehouses. Two still exist. (We discuss this more in 'Sandycove to Dalkey'.)

Muglins Light

Dalkey lost some of its commercial importance early in the seventeenth century, but the need for a safe refuge from storms continued, and the Dalkey Roads were considered a good candidate until the construction of the asylum harbour at Dun Laoghaire. Dalkey Island with its Martello tower protected the southern entry of the sound and the bay beyond, but a series of rocks north-west of Dalkey Island were a threat to shipping; and even more dangerous was The Muglins, located some five hundred metres north-east of Dalkey Island.

The Muglins is a single oval granite island about one hundred metres long. The resident population is limited to seagulls, shags, cormorants and other sea birds. A small quay on the side facing Dalkey Island gives access to visitors, and the waters around The Muglins are popular with scuba divers, with various shipwrecks to explore and a rich marine habitat.

The Muglins Light, a nine-metre high conical solid stone tower painted white with one red horizontal band, is classified as a lighthouse. But strictly speaking, it isn't one since it lacks interior space – there's no 'house' there. (The term is applied in order to distinguish it from the system of buoys in operation around the bay.) It dates from 1880, and has been lighted since 1906. In 1997, the Muglins Light was converted to electric power and its range was increased to eleven nautical miles. It emits a white flash every five seconds.

Chapter 8
Lifeboats on the Bay

The Irish Lifeboat Service

One of the most attractive old buildings at Dun Laoghaire Harbour is the fine granite boathouse that was erected in 1861 at the base of the East Pier. A pair of long stone skids leads out of it down the slip and into the harbour water, with a second pair connecting the top of the open shed to the land above. Undeniably a beautiful example of nineteenth-century stone work, the original lifeboat shed is also historically significant, for the difficulties of crossing Dublin Bay have often meant that ships foundered on the sand bar and were blown into rocks and it was only the courage of lifeboat crews that prevented even more lives from being lost.

There is a second, more sombre reminder farther out on the East Pier. The memorial is to Captain McNeil-Boyd and members of his crew on the *Ajax* lifeboat who died while trying to rescue sailors from two large brigs that were drifting onto the rocks at the back of the East Pier during a fierce storm (see 'Famous Shipwrecks' for more on this storm.)

In 1800, Dublin Port decided to set up Europe's first co-ordinated lifeboat service. Dublin Bay already had the reputation of being one of the most dangerous ports in Europe so the decision was certainly warranted. The first boat was built at Ringsend and stationed at the 'Sheds' in Clontarf in 1801 since, before the construction of North Bull Wall, the north side of the bay was the site of the majority of shipwrecks. Additional boats were stationed at Sandycove, Sutton and the Pigeon House at Poolbeg. In 1816, the Ballast Board also stationed a lifeboat at Howth. Each of the lifeboats was placed under the authority of a board employee living locally. Lifeboats changed their locations occasionally, and eventually only three remained, one each at Kingstown, Howth and Poolbeg.

In 1824, the 'National Institution for the Preservation of Life from Shipwrecks' was established in the United Kingdom but that somewhat ungainly name was changed to the 'Royal National Lifeboat Institution' – RNLI – in 1854, the name it bears today. In 1861, the port authority transferred responsibility for the lifeboat stations at Kingstown, Poolbeg and Howth to the RNLI which then became the primary marine rescue organisation on Dublin Bay although the port's pilot boats and tugs have continued to play a role in emergencies.

Nineteenth-century lifeboats were open vessels propelled by oars, very much at the mercy of storms and rough seas. It was harrowing duty, and even today with the modern technology that the RNLI has available, the courage of the lifeboat crews is impressive – as is the fact that they are mostly volunteers who come from all walks of life and give up their time and comfort to carry out rescues and save lives at sea on the lifeboats.

There are 233 RNLI lifeboat stations in the UK and the Republic of Ireland. Two serve Dublin Bay, one at Dun Laoghaire and the other at Howth. Their lifesaving work is essential, often difficult and sometimes very dangerous. In addition to the crews that manned the lifeboats, there are voluntary shore helpers who manage RNLI stations and assist with the launch and recovery of the lifeboats. There are also volunteer fund raisers, trustees who carry financial and operational responsibility, and an executive team that does the day-to-day running of the RNLI.

The first lifeboat was placed at the Dun Laoghaire station in 1817 and a second lifeboat was placed on station there in 1890. The first inshore lifeboat arrived at the station in 1986. The station at Dun Laoghaire is one of the busiest in Ireland, being situated at a major yachting centre and near a shipping zone. Throughout the station's history, two Gold, ten Silver and one Bronze Medals for Gallantry have been awarded.

The Howth station has operated a motor lifeboat since 1930 and, in April 1967, an inshore lifeboat station was established. The Howth station's new boathouse for the inshore boat was completed in 1984, and new moorings for the all-weather lifeboat were provided nearby. Howth has a proud record of service. A total of eleven Medals for Gallantry have been awarded, seven Silver and four Bronze, the last being in 1976.

Because the RNLI is a volunteer service, it can allocate a high proportion of its funds on first-class lifeboats and equipment. The RNLI facilities at Dun Laoghaire has a visitor centre onshore near the East Pier where the public can learn more about this important volunteer organisation. The Dun Laoghaire and Howth lifeboat stations are similarly equipped; each has a Trent class all-weather lifeboat and a D-class inflatable lifeboat.

The Trent class lifeboat is always moored in open water, the one in Dun Laoghaire near the Carlisle Pier while the one at Howth is inside the West Pier. Trent class boats can operate far out at sea and in very harsh conditions; yet they can also work in close to rocks or jetties or distressed ships. A small XP boat is carried deflated on board. Having an inflatable keel and powered by an outboard motor, it can be launched when needed to assist in rescuing casualties at locations that would be otherwise inaccessible to the larger lifeboat.

The D-class is the most common of the inshore fleet. Introduced in 1963, it is the first inflatable lifeboat. D-class lifeboats are fast, light and have a very shallow draught, making it possible for them to respond rapidly and to work in very shallow and confined waters. The D-class is the ideal lifeboat for rescue operations close to shore in fair-to-moderate conditions, and it operates in both daylight and darkness. D-class lifeboats are fitted with a single outboard engine and can be launched from special trolleys or, as in Dun Laoghaire Harbour, down the elegant stone slip that has been serving marine rescuers since 1862.

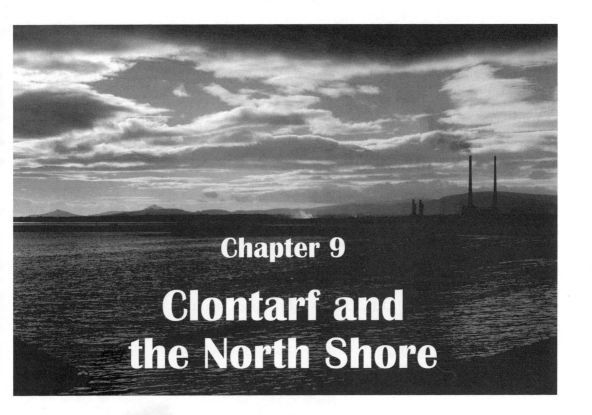

Chapter 9

Clontarf and the North Shore

From Fairview to Sutton

Clontarf – *Cluain Tarbh*: 'Meadow of the Bull' – is a pleasant suburb that stretches along the north-western rim of Dublin Bay from Fairview to Dollymount, with St Anne's Park, Raheny, Kilbarrack and Sutton continuing on around to Howth. Although it extends inland and contains substantial neighbourhoods with appealing characteristics all their own, visitors travelling along the shore road view Clontarf as a series of residential terraces separated from the bay by a broad green with a promenade that runs the length of it. East of Bull Wall, the promenade narrows to a bike path that continues along the sea front all the way to Sutton Cross – the narrow isthmus linking Howth to the mainland – where it divides, the bay-side path following Sutton Strand around to Shielmartin and access to the southern cliff walk at the Red Rock Martello while the northern route leads directly into Howth Village. This bike path is among the bay's great amenities, and it continues intermittently along the south side of the bay too, particularly at Sandymount Strand and again between Blackrock and Booterstown. But nowhere is it more inviting than from Clontarf to Sutton. Fresh air and sea breezes, an expansive sky with a spectacular view of Howth in the near distance; even the most sedentary of visitors soon feels the urge to engage in physical activity – biking or jogging or at least walking more vigorously than usual.

Fairview Park

Fairview Park precedes Clontarf. It functions as a kind of sylvan filter, making the transition from the gritty urban charms of Amiens Street/North Strand Road (with the East Wall Road and the East Point Business Park more properly considered as part of the port facilities) to coastal Clontarf less jarring. The ordered walkways of Fairview Park with seasonal flower beds and masses of mature trees – maples and sycamores and chestnuts in neat rows, plus the occasional uncommon specimen such as silver fir or weeping birch – all serve to ease the soul, soften the psyche and prepare the spirit for the benign vistas that lie ahead. The bay, which due to the sprawl of the port facilities has been out of sight, reappears all at once as one arrives by DART at the Clontarf Road Station or passes by bus or car or bike or on foot under the Skew Bridge, an entry-way gate which looks as if it had

The cycle lane in Fairview Park

been grasped at each end by gigantic hands and wrenched violently twenty degrees off true so that, as you gaze up at the interior brickwork, the results of that awesome torsion are there to see. You emerge into an expansiveness of open sky, broad green lawns, sparkling water (or sparkling mud, given the tidal draw) and an absence of pretentiousness or faux grandeur that announces a neighbourhood sustained by what it has preserved – and aware of what could still be lost.

Vistas matter. And although it is certainly true that bay views add a good twenty-five per cent or more to house prices anywhere around the rim of the city, what they bring to the soul would be harder to quantify. Clontarf faces its bay intensely. One could almost wonder if a vestigial memory of Norse invaders lingers, making residents alert to the possible depredations of other, more immediate would-be despoilers. Certainly the burden that a large-scale industrial development places on residential neighbourhoods would be hard to miss here. An attempt has been made to mask the massed fuel storage tanks and pyramids of shipping containers with a screen of evergreens. Clontarf residents are not always reassured, however, and they take the occasional protruding smokestack as a cautionary warning that all is not bucolic over there; and as one continues on into Clontarf, the unappealing enterprises on the 'reclaimed' southern shore become increasingly visible. ('Land reclamation' always sounds as if something thought lost has been fortunately found. Now where did I put that fifty-acre oil refinery? Ah! There it is!)

This north-western vista at Fairview was greatly prized by Lord Charlemont, whose demesne occupied much of this corner of north Dublin and who built his spectacular Marino House on an elevation in order to

The 'Fair View' across Dublin Bay

enjoy the sweep of the bay with the Wicklow Hills beyond. All that remains of his grand pile is the Casino, one of Dublin's architectural jewels; and, in an oddly ironic gesture of survival, the Marino Crescent, now a somewhat reduced structure that straddles the boundary between Fairview and Clontarf, with cars parked in what should have been gardens and one end disfigured (or improved) by its renovation into modern apartments designed to fit the 'street-scape' of that lower section of Howth Road. A couple of the units in the crescent have been restored, but most of it looks unloved and a little sad, despite the well-maintained garden fronting the curve of the terrace. At one time, the Marino Crescent was Dublin's first and finest example of that particular style of Georgian architecture. Now it is the only one. Story has it that the developer intentionally sited Marino Crescent at its location to block Lord Charlemont's 'fair view' in an act of architectural spite. The grandee and his developer-bogey are both long gone, as is his view, for that matter, filled in by the port's land reclamation. Marino Crescent deserves a better future than its current state seems to promise. It was an early example of a shift in the use of suburban land, with mass-residential housing complexes replacing the single, stand-alone manor house surrounded by parkland that had existed to that point. And if that isn't reason enough to promote the crescent, Bram Stoker, author of *Dracula*, was born there in what is today one of the better-maintained houses.

This north-west corner of Dublin Bay feels like something of a backwater (it isn't: the tides flush it nicely); and there are those who detect a whiff of the disreputable still clinging to Fairview, with the park itself deemed unsafe late at night. Fairview does have its history, however. Before the South and North Bull Walls were constructed, Dublin Bay silted badly. Ships at low tide were required to anchor in deep pools, one at Poolbeg and another – the Clontarf Pool – near the mouth of the Tolka River. Passengers and cargo were offloaded onto coastal lighters that could manage the shallow waters of the port. In the eighteenth century, locals residing along the underdeveloped northern shore of Dublin Bay prided themselves on their ability to recognise entrepreneurial extensions to the legitimate livelihoods they scraped out by ferrying people and goods to and from the shore. These unconventional activities did oblige them to evade the Crown's constabulary, using the cover of darkness or foul weather to minimise unpleasant confrontations. The improved supply of crates of tea and casks of wine or brandy would have been much appreciated locally since the addition of import duties and other charges priced such commodities beyond the reach of those north-side consumers who might otherwise have been considered part of their natural demographic. Discretion yielded positive results. The shoreline at Fairview Strand was an expanse of mud flats at that time, with a stretch of shingle and sand beach that curved around toward Clontarf; and these 'sloblands' were used as a clandestine storage facility for those unauthorised appropriations which required a quiet period of non-availability before they could be safely dispersed and enjoyed.

Residents at the time would not have had many illusions as to the need for prudence. A gallows had been erected near Ballybough Bridge, and hanged miscreants were left dangling for days as an improving example to others, albeit one that seems to have been little heeded. There was also a cemetery for suicides nearby, adding to the morbid atmosphere at that corner of the bay (appropriate for Bram Stoker's nativity), and perhaps some traces of local dolefulness can still be found there today, particularly at Gaffney's on those Sundays when the Dubs fall a little short at Croker.

But waterside Fairview wasn't just thuggery and gloom. The building of the Annesley Bridge in 1797 made the north shore of the bay more accessible, and the shingle beach at Fairview had already become a popular venue in the eighteenth century where the city's great and good came to parade and admire each other's horses and carriages. Dean Swift was said to have been fond of riding there, particularly in winter, apparently, perhaps because fewer humans would be around.

Fairview Park was developed by the Corporation in the late 1920s; it is in every measure a great improvement to what had been there previously. (To say nothing of what could have been sited there, given the example of the industrial development immediately to the south.) A large sports complex has recently been established near the DART station, complete with fifty-metre lap pool; but most of the park's forty-plus acres remains undisturbed, with its neat rows of mature trees and well-tended flower beds, as well as the random scattering of crocuses and daffodils that supply passers-by with an early harbinger of spring. Not even the presence of a headless statue which, had it not been decapitated, might have been gazing (mournfully?) in the general direction of Croke Park can spoil the atmosphere. Fairview also has numerous playing fields for football or Gaelic sports at the south end where the River Tolka flows between its grim concrete banks, dappled with seagulls and enriched with the conventional selection of old tyres, supermarket trolleys and submerged bicycles, as well as a pair of swans who raise their cygnets there, urban birds well-enough adapted to see in humans a possible source of bread-crust meals and to ignore the occasional splash of a misdirected *sliotar*. The Dublin Port Tunnel – the largest single road building project yet attempted by the state – passes under Fairview Park and one wonders if the ghosts of some

Fairview Park

of the old fellows who used to liberate cargo there might not gaze down approvingly at the rich subterranean flow of commerce and ponder how best to gain access to it. Fairview Park is a green oasis at a corner of the bay that has not been much loved in the past, and it forms a lovely gateway to the north shore of Dublin Bay.

A Road by Any Other Name . . .

As one exits from under the Skew Bridge and travels east along the sea-front road, the industrialised zone of the port facilities falls away eventually; and the massed fuel storage tanks with their implicit promise of environmental catastrophe if not outright apocalypse give way to the inviting waters of the bay. From Fairview Park to the isthmus at Sutton is approximately eleven kilometres of sea views or, given the interregnum of the sand dunes of Bull Island, lagoon views. It is a popular drive, as weekend traffic will attest. This primary sea-front road is actually a multitude of roads, each emerging seamlessly out of the one before it, with Fairview Road begetting Clontarf

Road which in turn begets James Larkin Road at St Anne's, and James Larkin then takes unto itself Howth Road at Kilbarrack from which union issues Dublin Road. And Dublin Road passes through Sutton Cross as itself and then, always open to suggestion, decides that it is after all Howth Road (while approaching Howth, sensibly enough), only upon its arrival there to become Harbour Road (at the harbour, again not unreasonably, although one begins to weary of these incessant alterations). It is possible to argue that it is not the same road. Nevertheless, as it begins its merry loop around the Ben of Howth, what had once been Harbour Road bends hard right at the Martello and incarnates itself successively as: Abbey Street, Thormanby Road, Carrickbarrack Road, then, finally, as it returns to Sutton Cross – dizzy with accumulated appellations – Greenfield Road. Fortunately, there are very few road signs the length of it so visitors remain blissfully unaware of the adventure they are experiencing!

And so to the meadow and its bulls.

Clontarf: The Bull and its Meadow

The name Clontarf is ancient. Today it is inevitably associated with the famous battle which raged up and down the north side of the bay but for the most part happened closer to today's city centre. The area designated as Clontarf used to refer to a larger area, and the weir over the Tolka where so many Danes were slaughtered on Brian Boru's day of triumph was called the Clontarf Weir.

Bulls play an important role in the Irish psychic imagination (one recalls fondly Queen Medb's enthusiasm for them), and while the 'bull' used for the sand banks might be a variation on the word 'ball', Clontarf's bull is the animal itself, as is demonstrated by local rugby and GAA teams which, to intimidate their opponents, have adopted an appropriately dramatic red bull as their emblem. (But then as a logo, although historically more destructive, an expanse of sand would nevertheless carry less visual impact.)

Two splendid bay-facing amenities characterise Clontarf: the promenade green fronting Clontarf Road; and Bull Island. A third, St Anne's Park, although literally on the bay, nevertheless faces inward on itself and feels more landlocked, perhaps because its long, tree-lined entryway comes off Sybil Hill Road. St Anne's forms the northern boundary of Clontarf and will be discussed below.

Clontarf Castle before renovation

Clontarf also contains Clontarf Castle. History is what you make of it, and in this case the results are a peculiarly Disneyesque mock-Tudor castle characterised by the convenience of its surrounding asphalt car park with slots large enough to contain tour buses. Restored in the nineteenth century through the crude but effective methodology of total demolition of the original pile, the resulting faux Tudor-revival hotel boasts 'medieval' towers with ye olde machicolations from which besieged defenders might dump boiling oil (from the kitchen's deep-fat fryers, no doubt) upon unwary invaders who had drifted over from the surrounding housing estates intent on nothing more invasive than quaffing a pint of the black stuff. Perhaps the castle is best left to its own devices. Tourists and children seem to like it.

The promenade green at Clontarf is a relatively recent addition. About forty metres wide, it covers approximately sixty-five acres. The foreshore originally was a 'sloblands' of oozing mud, much as can still be seen beyond the seawall at low tide; and the construction of the promenade during the first half of the twentieth century established a clear demarcation between bay and shore. Seawalls were erected and sand pumped in from the bay, creating a level surface that reached Clontarf Road. Topsoil was spread to a sufficient depth to support grass and the clumps of bushes that were planted there, shelters were erected and a few benches placed in the intervals between them – and, with the exception of the now derelict Clontarf Baths and the slipway for the yacht club, that was about it. Much that could have been added to further 'improve' it wasn't. The green today has a settled, friendly, familiar feel to it; and it functions very much as the front garden/sports pitch for locals on summer evenings to develop their

The promenade in Clontarf

skills with football, rugby ball or hurley. The green invites participation. Joggers jog there, bladers blade, and strollers stroll. It is all very low-key and easy-going; dress is casual, people convivial, kids and dogs abundant. Ring buoys on long yellow nylon ropes are placed strategically along the seawall for use in retrieving errant footballs from the bay, an expertise common to the neighbourhood lads. (And despite dire warnings printed on them, the rings don't have much other application, since the bay there is so shallow that rescuing someone drowning within the reach of their yellow nylon ropes would require little more than advising the person in question to stand up.) The green is a neighbourhood park that has so far managed to evade further 'improvement', although one can imagine property developers salivating at the potential gains from all that unused shorefront land, ripe for yet more apartments if not an actual shopping mall or some other form of consumer-driven pseudo-entertainment.

The lifebuoy/football retriever on the promenade

The residences lining Clontarf Road present a melange of architectural propositions. Blocks of flats and apartments occur at the Fairview end, some very attractive, along with a few stand-alone houses. Moving east, single-family dwellings predominate, connected together in continuous terraces that come in sets of two, three or four matching units so that one wonders if the occupants of shared housing styles over time grow to resemble each other much the way roommates often begin to dress alike. There are a couple of formal Georgian terraces; slightly west of Vernon Avenue is a particularly attractive red brick one of elegant symmetry, with slightly larger units at each end; and down from it, set well back from the road, is an equally elegant classic terrace in grey brick. But these are the exceptions, and most of sea-front Clontarf comprises a series of sets of fused bungalows in short runs, as if an attempt were being made to display an entire range

Residences along Clontarf Road

of possibilities. One gets the sense that every type of domestic architecture from the past hundred years or so is probably represented somewhere along Clontarf Road. A good challenge would be to attempt to determine a meaningful pattern within these transmuting housing styles; yet the overall effect – although arbitrary – is hardly displeasing, and there is a sense of egalitarianism shared throughout the terraces facing the green, with no great mansions glowering down at their less worthy neighbours. The mood of the place feels eclectic rather than confused, cheerful and thoroughly liveable, no doubt in part because each individual unit participates equally in the spectacular amenity that is the bay.

Before it became a commuter suburb of Dublin, Clontarf's main village was organised around what is today Clontarf Castle. In the eighteenth century, growth of fishing on the bay led to the development on the shore of permanent fishing villages, one of which – the Clontarf Sheds, situated near a particularly rich oyster bed at about where Vernon Avenue intersects with Clontarf Road today – gives its name to one of the more authentic local pubs. The actual sheds themselves were small wooden buildings clustered along the coastline. They were used to gut, cure and preserve fish; and because they also served as the residences of those who did the gutting, curing and preserving, they were not praised for their exemplary sanitary conditions. The growth of this fishing industry shifted the centre of focus in Clontarf from the area around the castle to the sea front, and Vernon Avenue developed into Clontarf's main commercial street, a role it still plays today.

The oyster beds are long gone, of course, and the sheds with them – as is what had once been an equally prominent feature of this corner of Dublin Bay: Clontarf Island.

Clontarf Island

Clontarf Island was a comparatively large sand island situated near the mouth of the Tolka River at about where the East Point Business Park is today. It was never as large as Bull Island; but at the end of the eighteenth and beginning of the nineteenth centuries, it served a similar function as a popular recreation destination that was also used by fishermen, as well as by that particular breed of north-side entrepreneurs for whom the gallows at Ballybough Bridge stood as a grim reminder that not all misdeeds go unpunished.

The island had a single residence on it known as the 'Island House', but its main attraction was a long bathing pool enclosed on all sides by wooden stakes and tree stumps. A nearby shed served as a changing room, and on fine days the health-conscious could be found there paddling happily. This pool was much safer for swimming than the bay with its dangerous currents, and the tradition of purpose-built sea-water bathing pools continued in various guises, with full-blown developments at Clontarf, Sandymount and Blackrock, and the remnants of smaller ones occurring in tide pools from Howth to Bray – all, today, sadly derelict, although swimming in the bay is certainly still popular, with the celebrated Forty Foot at Sandycove a prime example.

References to Clontarf Island can be found in early writings about Dublin Bay, and it is assumed that it was a key staging site for the Danes as they arrived in preparation for the Battle of Clontarf. Much of the fighting at the end of the day happened around the mouth of the Tolka River, and the Danish forces that suffered the worst annihilation may have been

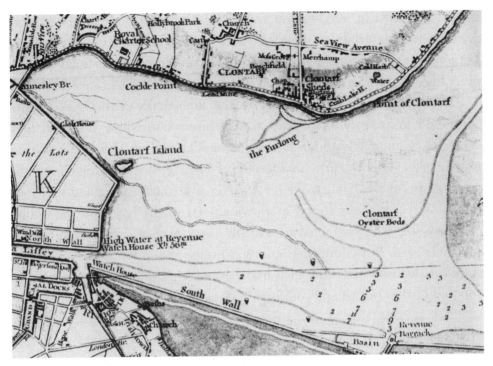

*Detail from John Taylor's Map of Dublin Environs, 1816, showing
Clontarf Island and Oyster Beds*

trying to regain their ships on that island which had become out of reach
due to the high tide.

Clontarf Island was used as a refuge for citizens in the Middle Ages
who were frightened of the plague or other pestilence; and it was also
employed, conversely, as a place of quarantine, with contagious victims
isolated there in 1650 during one of the worst outbreaks of plague in
the city. The plague bacillus wasn't the only source of death on Clontarf
Island. It also served as an excellent venue for settling affairs of honour,
with gentlemen facing each other's pistols there, well away from the
censorious eyes of the authorities who had declared duelling illegal, no
doubt reasoning that if someone needed killing, they would prefer to do it
themselves, in an orderly and organised manner.

Fishermen used Clontarf Island to mend their nets on the open beaches
or to winter their boats safely above the high-tide line, but the island's
main contribution to the city was as a source of gravel and sand. At low
tide, horse-drawn carts could cross safely, and load after load was hauled

away to be used in making concrete. Barges at high tide could carry off even more of the island so that even as citizens were flocking out there to observe birds in nature, swim safely in salt water, or shoot holes in each other, the island was steadily being diminished.

Throughout the first decades of the nineteenth century, as Dublin continued to grow, with construction projects flourishing much as they do today, Clontarf Island was getting smaller and smaller until, after a particularly violent storm in October 1844, residents living along the north shore of the bay awoke to discover that their island had vanished utterly. Wreckage was found in various parts of the bay, and the bodies of the people who had tried to weather the storm in their fishing cabins were retrieved. But Clontarf Island was no more and would never return, since the deposits of sand which had formed it originally were now being shunted farther out to add to North Bull Island.

Derelict Clontarf Baths today

The loss of the sea-bathing facilities was felt keenly enough for an attempt to be made at replacing them twenty years later at a spot opposite the GAA sports facilities where their derelict remains can be seen today, filled with bay flotsam, white Styrofoam packing inserts riding with a particular jauntiness. The entry to the Clontarf Baths is marked by a

Boats next to the Clontarf Yacht Club slipway

scruffy jumble of trees that are remarkable for their variety, as if a selection of species had been stuffed in there behind a wrought iron fence, then left to compete as a test of the theory of natural selection. Built in 1864, the Clontarf Baths were originally segregated with a wall running down the middle so that the genders would not have to commingle. (The wall was later removed, perhaps in recognition of the positive stimulation commingling provides.) Both cold 'plunge' and heated sea-water baths were available. A swimming club was formed to further develop what was already recognised as a healthful pastime – commingled or not – but the Clontarf Baths seem always to have been in a precarious financial state, and sufficient debts accumulated to sink the baths finally. Recent rumours have it that an attempt may be made to establish some sort of commercially viable venue on the site, although what that might be seems uncertain. There is a circular drive leading from Clontarf Road to the bath ruins that suggests the availability of parking – always sought – and one can imagine a restaurant there, although any attempt to begin developing the sea front will certainly meet fierce opposition. If something is built, it would certainly have an excellent view of the transformations wrought by the port facilities, for the gesture of the evergreen screen ends about there.

The only other landmark of note on the Clontarf sea front is the yacht club slipway from which dinghies and larger boats are launched during the summer. The Clontarf Yacht Club is one of the oldest on Dublin Bay and will be discussed in 'Sailing on the Bay'. The promenade green ensures that Clontarf will always be a particularly salubrious place to stroll and dream, kick a ball or whack a *sliotar*, greet flocks of brent geese as they glide in to feed, or watch the departing flight of a solitary grey heron, legs trailing, head tucked in tightly.

St Anne's Park

You come to watch the Clontarf eleven-and-unders challenge their rivals from Malahide on one of the fine football pitches, then stay after the match to admire the roses.

Dublin's second-largest park – in excess of 200 acres – forms the northern boundary of Clontarf, and its preservation in the face of the extensive development happening everywhere around it is a credit to the city authorities. On Saturdays and Sundays during season, it is alive with competition – football and rugby primarily but also with pitches configured for GAA sports – everything well organised and with teams representing all age groups participating, everybody in uniform and dreaming of bending it like Beckham.

St Anne's had a great house once – home to one branch of the Guinness family – established in the middle of the nineteenth century and burned down a hundred years later. All that's left of it now at the end of the long, tree-lined entry drive is a raised rectangular mound covered with grass as if forming an appropriate reminder of the transience of vain things.

The rose garden was a later addition, and on a fine day in mid-summer it can be lushly spectacular. A few outbuildings and walls from the great house era remain, and the entry drive lined with splendid old evergreens would have impressed visitors. St Anne's Park occupies land along the bay but makes no effort to engage it. The perimeter along the sea-front road is dense with maples and chestnuts, as are most of the other edges, forming natural barriers and adding to the sense of self-containment. There are no bay-facing hilltop follies here, no elevated arbours or faux-medieval towers from which one might be invited to gaze out on the bay. Perhaps the dominant presence of Bull Island just off-shore played a role in causing the landscape architects of St Anne's to focus so relentlessly inward. There can be few complaints; the parklands are splendid, with mature plantings everywhere – maples, pines and chestnuts. When walking on Bull Island, one is engaged constantly with distant vistas: Howth, the Poolbeg chimneys with the Wicklow Hills behind, the open waters of the bay stretching out to a limitless horizon. But walking in St Anne's is to be enclosed by parkland so that for all the open spaces that can be encountered, the genial ambience is that of the accessible, the nearby, and even the wide lawns with their soccer and GAA pitches still maintain something of the local to them. On the Clontarf promenade, the eye might be drawn to an immense container ship gliding into the port or

Playground in St Anne's Park

one of the ferries heading off to Holyhead; but here it is more likely to be a young family pushing a pram, or a couple of kids riding by on their bicycles, or the odd jogger suffering through his or her private fitness obsessions.

Raheny, Kilbarrack, Sutton

The sea-front road, its name segueing gracefully from James Larkin to Dublin, follows the curve of the bay with only the bike path separating it from the waters and/or mud flats of the lagoon and Sutton Creek. There is an interesting evolution of the styles of the houses here, with those at the Raheny end similar to the terraces of Clontarf while, once well into Kilbarrack, more and larger independently sited homes with surrounding gardens appear, albeit often seated at a much lower elevation in relation to the roadway and farther back from it. The road has been built up with the bike path on its sea wall even higher as a defence against flooding, and for all their spaciousness, these Kilbarrack houses maintain a more distant engagement with the bay. Not that much of the bay would be visible, strictly speaking, since the dunes of Bull Island would be in the way. Nevertheless, efforts have been made; and most of the sea front dwellings have incorporated large dormer windows on the second floors – some quite impressively designed – as if to secure what they can of their own glimpse of the bay even if the effect feels somewhat forced, like a man straining to peer over a tall fence.

The construction of the causeway has resulted in silting all along the lagoon, as was predicted, and at low tide the wide mud flats appeal mostly to wading birds seeking food. From the bike path, the view out over lagoon and dunes is spectacular, with one of the most wide-open vistas imaginable. It is all sky here, with Howth close enough now to pick

View across the lagoon from cycle path near St Anne's Park

out details, the twinned Poolbeg ESB stacks anchoring industrio-Dublin in the distance, and even farther south, the gentle backdrop of the Wicklow Hills.

This part of the north bay invites one to gaze out upon it in silence as one passes through it. But the temptation to linger seldom arises. It is another transition area, pleasant enough, but hardly sufficient to keep one from continuing on to Howth. There is a tiny bay-side cemetery on a rise in Kilbarrack with an antique church ruins, the ogival windows of which

View of the bay from the Marine Hotel

have been filled with iron prison bars to deny access to the undeserving and thereby adding to the general lack of welcome. One wonders if the authorities fear lawsuits from clumsy vandals who might trip over their own shoelaces while spray-painting their gaudy tags inside. The only other local landmark of note is a dinghy supply store which stimulates discussion as to the kinds of supplies dinghies might require, how frequently they would need to be replaced or upgraded, and could the servicing of dinghies actually be a viable business model? (Closer examination reveals that a full range of marine products are vended there.)

The bay is lost briefly to view as we approach Sutton Cross, although the Marine Hotel there has a lovely garden lawn that offers visible access to it, with outdoor seating along a covered porch and on the lawns themselves that in fine weather invites lingering over a pot of tea or a pint of the black stuff. The isthmus of Sutton Cross was once open water and Howth an island populated by Mesolithic settlers, as were Ireland's Eye and Lambay Island farther north. Today it is an intersection where one chooses between two routes into Howth. Both are recommended. Straight on leads to Howth Castle, the harbour and Howth Village. Turning right provides access to the inner curve of Sutton Strand, Shielmartin and the southern trailhead of the cliff walk. Either leads eventually to the other, happily enough, and both provide ample evidence of why preserving what is wonderful about Dublin Bay is so essential.

Chapter 10

North Bull Island

Although North Bull Island would seem to be a logical result of the construction of North Bull Wall, it was actually caused by the construction of both the two breakwater walls which bracket the mouth of the Liffey. (And it is worth recalling that the term 'bull' comes either from a corruption of the word 'ball', which means sand bank, or a reference to the sound of the tide flowing over sand banks, which to local ears sounded like the bellowing of bulls.)

Before the 'great walls' were built, the flow of the Liffey entering the bay would naturally veer off to the south – as would any river in the northern hemisphere. In addition to silt and other suspended particles carried by the river, the city's wastes were dumped into the Liffey and deposited in the bay by the southward flowing ebb tides. The rising tide would then reverse the process and shift the current flow north toward Howth, moving suspended material into the channel that is now known as Sutton Creek and so bringing it back down along the coastline where it became deposited. Silting in the river channel and the formation of the two immense sand banks was the result of this, as discussed 'The Great Walls of Dublin'.

The completion of South Bull Wall accelerated the formation of sand banks on the north shore since more suspended particles were sent deeper into mid-bay rather than following the original flow to the south, and so back around to the Sutton coastline, then on to Clontarf. This helps explain why even before the construction of the North Bull Wall, a permanent sand spit off the Dollymount coast had begun to emerge out of the underlying sand bank known as the North Bull. As more and more sand accumulated, the dunes remained dry even during the highest monthly spring tides. Grass seeds blown over from the mainland were able to colonise the dunes, and by binding them together with their root systems, added to dune stability. Thus the initial accumulation at what is today North Bull Island resulted from the first, south-side wall; and the 'other' suspended particles – courtesy of the willingness of the residents of the city to part with their effluvia – indicates one source of the extraordinary nutritiousness of the mud flats that formed in the lagoons between North Bull Island and the

The Bull Wall Bridge

Dollymount shore. The construction of North Bull Wall eliminated the possibility of any further south-westerly growth of the sand bank toward Clontarf, and the north-eastern boundary of the island was determined by the tidal action of the channel flowing along Sutton Creek.

Locals often drop the 'north' from the names here, resulting in Bull Island, Bull Bridge and even Bull Wall. It would seem sensible to recognise the relative spatial orientation of the two walls bracketing the Liffey mouth which have played such an important role in making Dublin Bay fit for shipping and so retain at least North Bull Wall; but references to north and north-less versions of all three can be found.

Bull Island today is a low-lying, dune-covered sand spit about five kilometres long. It is an extensive nature preserve – well-protected and well-appreciated – that can nevertheless be reached from Dublin's city centre in about an hour . . . by walking. It would be hard to find another major city with such a spectacular wilderness amenity that is so accessible (some think too accessible).

As it was being formed, the island remained separated from Dollymount because of the strong tidal flow that coursed along the Clontarf/Dollymount shoreline, maintaining an open channel between Bull Island and the mainland, with the flood tides driving the current toward the north-west corner of the bay, then the ebb tides reversing the flow. The construction of the causeway in 1964 ended the full extent of this process.

A series of elongated sand ridges comprise the central spine of the island, built-up by the action of offshore winds on the accumulated sand deposited there by wave action and anchored by dune grasses. These sand ridges can be dated approximately as to when they were formed and so provide a visual 'map' of the developmental history of Bull Island. The dunes themselves can be separated into sand dunes and grassland dunes. The pure sand dunes, mostly found on the bay-facing edge of the island, are colonised largely by marram grass and other hardy shore plants. The older grassland dunes have developed over time internally, and have evolved into an ecosystem with a wider range of flowering plants. Within these grassland dunes are marshy patches at elevations low enough to retain sufficient ground water and thus support vegetation not usually able to survive on the drier dune lands. (A fourth, artificially maintained dune-based ecosystem is formed by the fairways and greens of the two golf courses on the island.) Demarcations between the dunes, grasslands and fresh-water marshes are apparent enough although there are of course areas where habitats converge. The other major ecologically significant features of Bull Island are the lagoon with its bordering salt marshes on the inland side and the bay-facing beach.

Dollymount Strand is a broad flat sand beach that extends for the entire length of Bull Island. As with its south-side cousin, Sandymount Strand, the bay is very shallow here and the expanse of sand revealed at low tide is quite dramatic, with long-distance speed-wading conceivable as a new form of aerobic exercise.

On the landward side of Bull Island is a salt marsh and tidal lagoon. When the tide is low, extensive mud flats are exposed. The ecosystem that has developed around the lagoon supports large populations of migratory birds, making Bull Island one of Europe's main nature sanctuaries.

Bull Bridge, a few cottages, the splendid new sea-scouts facilities, the Interpretive Centre and two golf courses with clubhouses complete the list

Bathing shelter on Bull Island

of larger features on Bull Island, along with the old-fashioned, gender-specific bathing shelters on Bull Wall (that commingling issue again . . .) and a statue of the Virgin at the end of it, wearing a circlet of stars like an early adopter of the promise of the EU and balanced precariously atop her tall tripod, the better to monitor the goings-on of those below.

Bull Island Timeline

South Bull Wall was completed in 1786 (the date is variable since the wall was built in sections over a number of years, beginning with the Piles that were finished in 1730 and would have had some effect on sand accumulation at the north shore). Captain Bligh's map of Dublin Bay shows a recognisable expanse of dunes permanently above the high tide line. Twenty years later, the location for constructing the North Bull Wall was decided by the existing island, which had grown into a narrow spit of land tufted with a few scraggly patches of dune grass and reaching about three kilometres in length. (See 'The Great Walls of Dublin' for more on the construction of North Bull Wall.) Small, separate islands formed occasionally on the sand banks of the North Bull; the largest, Green Island, developed just under the bend of Sutton Creek and was gradually absorbed into the north-eastern tip of Bull Island during the nineteenth century.

Bull Island achieved its present length around 1900, with any further extension toward Howth made impossible by the tidal flow of Sutton Creek. The island has continued to thicken on the bay side with the accumulation of sand, and on the inland side with the continued silting in the lagoons. The plural is important. What was once a single lagoon, with the flushing action of tidal flow maintained by the decision to build a wooden bridge linking the island to the mainland at Clontarf, has been blocked by the construction of the causeway in 1964. This may or may not become a serious issue for the health of the island's overall ecosystem. There is still tidal flushing, of course, and fresh nutrients still arrive from the bay. It is possible that the salt marshes and mud flats will maintain themselves in a delicate but healthy equilibrium.

But it is also possible that they won't – that the silting will increase to the point that the mud flats dry out, destroying the habitats of the primary food sources that much of the island's huge population of migrating birds depends on. The causeway has drastically changed the lagoon, perhaps in ways not well understood at the time it was planned although there was certainly debate as to whether a second bridge should be built to ensure a continued tidal flow the full length of the island. In the end, the cheaper option of a landfill causeway was adopted. Despite renewed concerns recently, no attempt has been made to reinstate the continuous tidal flow down the Dollymount coastline, and serious questions remain as to the ultimate impact this alteration will have on the fragile ecosystems of the lagoons. Silting has increased near the causeway itself, particularly on the Sutton side, and permanent damage to the valuable wetlands of the north shore is a real worry.

Dollymount Strand

The causeway is in effect a continuation from Watermill Road, which forms the north-eastern boundary of St Anne's Park, and it extends about

Beach at Dollymount Strand

two and a half kilometres onto the island, ending at a roundabout and providing access to beach parking. The sole previous access point, Bull Bridge – a narrow, one-lane affair with traffic flow governed by a stoplight – was deemed unable to accommodate the cars of all those wishing to visit Bull Island so building the causeway road did solve a genuine problem. And for all the debate about it, there can be no question that vehicular traffic on Bull Island in summer has been successfully increased.

Two sections of Dollymount Strand have been set aside for the use of those who wish to share the warm sands and tangy sea air with their cars; and on a hot summer day, those parts of the beach take on the modern aura of a car park. Well-meaning people can disagree about whether this tilt in favour of automotive engagement has improved Bull Island or not. Many a young north-sider has had his first taste of the joys of the motoring life there on the hard-packed sands of Dollymount Strand, and even fully licensed and presumably experienced participants still find it stimulating to drive back and forth on the beach at low tide, occasionally executing daring turns or racing at high speeds, then power-sliding dramatically as a way of impressing fellow enthusiasts, as well as those attractive members of the opposite sex who are no doubt watching admiringly from the safety of the edge of the dunes.

That Bull Island benefits ecologically from the influx of cars in fine weather seems improbable. There are those who would argue that without easy access by car, many citizens would not choose to avail themselves of the amenities found there. Some might reply that they would not be missed. In any case, as we will see below, other even more dubious ideas on how to 'improve' Bull Island have been brought forward in the past although things seem stable enough for the moment, with the whole island – cars

Dollymount Strand

and all – designated as a UNESCO Biosphere Reserve in 1981 – Ireland's first. In 1994, Dublin Corporation made a Special Amenity Area Order to ensure that the island retains its Biosphere Reserve status. Bull Island is now a proposed Special Area of Conservation under the EEC Habitats Directive.

Bull Island is also Ireland's only example of an undisturbed sequence of shoreline habitats, including sand beach, fore dunes, mature dunes with grasslands and freshwater marshes, salt marshes and mud flats: in itself, reason for preserving it as a key part of our national heritage.

And Dollymount Strand truly is an excellent venue for sea bathing now that water quality has reached Blue Flag standards for safety; car-free zones do exist on the beach, sea shells are plentiful, God knows there's no shortage of sand for building sand castles; and although the bay there is too shallow for serious swimmers – one finds better water on the other side of Bull Wall – the novel sport of kite-surfing has established itself recently. So on any fine breezy summer's day, parents picnic, children frolic, dogs chase balls, sunbathers baste themselves with UV 15 while Grand Theft Auto fantasists test the filters and seals on their machines against the sand and salt of the bay, and over it all float gaudy parachute-kites like the immense cupped nylon wings of modern angels gliding, swooping, crashing into the water occasionally but for the most part just hovering benignly.

The Dunes and Freshwater Marshes

With the exception of summer, most visitors come to Bull Island for the complex of sand dunes and grassland dunes. It is an oasis of wild nature remarkably close to the city, and the island itself is easily long enough to provide plenty of space for a fairly demanding stroll.

The dunes are always above the level of the highest tides while the other ecosystems on the island – the lagoons and salt marshes – are regularly inundated. The elongated ridges of sand that form the body of the island run parallel along its main axis and are separated by valleys known as 'slacks', a few of which are low enough to allow the formation of freshwater marshes. The grassland dunes and slacks are criss-crossed by a network of walking paths that are much enjoyed by local strollers and dog-owners, and the older interior portions of them support a more varied habitat than would ever be found on beach dunes. The sand on the island is very fine; and although the dunes are held together by the vegetation

The dunes on Bull Island

growing on them, a hole resembling a small sand trap on a golf course will sometimes be encountered where the plants have died off and without their roots, the sand was blown out by the wind, leaving the empty declivity.

The fore dunes from a distance appear to be mostly sand and marram grass, a hardy plant which tolerates salt spray well and is always an early coloniser of dune systems. Gorse also occurs in the area of dry dunes and near the golf courses farther inland, as do a few other hardy plants that can anchor themselves in the sand, such as wild pansy and sea spurge. The fore dunes form a transition between the pure sand dunes just above the high-water line on the strand and the seemingly more complex ecology of the grassland dunes. Other valuable plants that can survive in these dunes include members of the pea family such as birds-foot trefoil, hare's foot clover and restharrow – all plants that add nitrogen to the soil and thus make it possible for other plants eventually to grow there.

The richest diversity on Bull Island is in the grassland dunes and slacks, and it is there that the greatest variety of wildflowers can be found.

From spring until autumn, a spectacular summer display adds colour to the scene there, particularly on the more mature inner slacks of the central grasslands. Familiar plants such as yellow rattle, lady's bedstraw, and various members of the stonecrop and vetch families abound, as do milkwort and forget-me-not and wild thyme. Orchids are also found throughout the grasslands, including the dense crimson spikes of pyramidal orchids and the similar lilac and mauve spikes of the common spotted-orchid. Rarest of all is a true exotic: the bee orchid, discovery of which can turn a casual stroll into a moment of transcendence.

Freshwater marshes are found at each end of Bull Island while the central portion remains drier. The only naturally occurring large plants, alders (natural in that the seeds were blown over from the mainland rather than planted as enhancements to the golf courses), are found in places along these marshes; and at the Sutton Creek end of the island is an area called the 'alder grove' where a particularly wide slack retains sufficient ground water to support several dozen of these trees. The two ridges that contain this slack are believed to have originally been the shoreline at 1906, then again the one that formed farther out thirty years later. The alder-grove slack is the lowest point on Bull Island, and it is close enough to the water table to support vegetation which is more commonly found in damp habitats on the mainland and could eventually become bog land.

In winter, the low marshes retain standing water continuously and resemble small ponds, while in spring and summer they become rich in wildflowers, with bluebells, marsh orchids with luscious wine-coloured flower spikes, marsh helleborine and autumn gentian among the more conspicuous.

Also at the Sutton Creek end of the island are the remnants of what had once been Green Island. Although it had been absorbed by the main island in the first decade of the twentieth century, the shape of it can still be made out as a circular configuration of dunes – in contrast to the more familiar elongated dune ridges found elsewhere.

The dunes are home to a wide variety of insects; and in late summer and early autumn, an astonishingly multitudinous population of large black slugs begins to appear, as is well-known to anyone who walks there at twilight, for to step on one of these monsters is to experience a memorable encounter with nature at its rawest.

More attractive residents are the Irish hares which thrive on Bull Island and are seen in groups, in contrast to their solitary habits on the mainland. A common house mouse is found there which has sand-coloured fur, somewhat lighter than is usual in the species. Although not enough time has elapsed on the island for a unique population to have evolved, the lighter-coloured fur may give individuals a better chance to avoid being taken by predators and so be an early step on the development of an evolutionarily unique variant. Field mice and brown rats are also found in the dunes, identical to their mainland cousins, and rabbits may be making a return there, which is not necessarily good news since their burrowing tends to damage the fragile dune systems. Reports of foxes and stoats have not been confirmed on Bull Island and it seems unlikely resident populations of those species have as yet established themselves.

The Irish Hare

The Lagoons and the Salt Marshes

Another noticeable feature of Bull Island are the lagoons and salt marshes that occupy the land-ward side along the shoreline at Dollymount. The lagoons are completely covered by the daily high tides and completely – or almost completely – exposed by the ebb tides. Fine mineral materials are constantly being deposited along the floor of the lagoon, along with organic detritus which is fed in from rivers emptying into the bay. Sewage, too, once played its part, although modern sewage treatment facilities today have eliminated this source of nutrients. (Thus the Blue Flags on our beaches.)

The salt marsh is the area between the dry dunes and the lagoon. Demarcation is determined by inundation. The dunes are always above the highest high-tide water line while the salt marsh is above the high-water line of the neap tides which flood the lagoon twice daily but it is within the reach of the highest monthly spring tides (which occur at the full and new moons) and so does profit from periodic submersion. The salt marsh is therefore sufficiently elevated to sustain higher plants which could never survive the twice daily flooding of the lagoon but that do benefit from the addition of nutrients that arrive twice monthly with the highest tides. It becomes a rich habitat for a wide variety of creatures, birds in particular.

The lagoon from Dollymount Sea Scouts Crow's Nest

The boundaries between the three zones are clearly distinguishable, with a 'cliff' forming at the high-water mark of the normal daily neap tides, and an absence of any salt-marsh vegetation in the dunes above the monthly spring-tide level. As silting continues along the edges of the lagoon, those areas become higher with accumulation and are eventually transformed into salt marshes which in turn also grow along their upper boundaries so that, once sufficiently elevated to deny the salt-marsh plants access to the periodic flooding they require, that area in turn becomes part of the dune system. Reduction in the size of the lagoon will probably result in a lessening in the numbers of creatures that live there and serve as the main food source for the vast flocks of birds which depend on Bull Island during their migrations or winter stay-overs.

The lagoon at Bull Island is actually composed of three distinctive intertidal areas: the mud flats, the glasswort flats and the sand flats. It is interesting to note that glasswort (*Salicornia*) – a small plant with fleshy leaves that slows the flow of incoming tide, trapping sand and silt particles and thereby adding elevation – is a key part of the mechanism that is raising the lagoons so that they will eventually become part of the neighbouring salt marshes. The sand flats occur in the southern lagoon and occupy the greater portion of the northern lagoon. Drainage channels from the salt marsh meander across the sand flats and merge with the incoming flows of Sutton Creek in the north and the Naniken Stream in the south.

In addition to glasswort, other plants are able to survive the spring tides, such as scurvy grass, sea lavender, thrift and sea milkwort. Sea aster

Entrance to Royal Dublin Golf Club

is also found, and, as with the other plants that inhabit the salt flats, it has comparatively succulent 'fleshy' leaves and stems that can store water.

The Royal Dublin and St Anne's Golf Clubs

The Royal Dublin Golf Course – Ireland's second oldest – was formed in 1885 and received its 'Royal' designation six years later. The original course was located near the Magazine Fort in Phoenix Park but soon moved to Sutton, then to its present home on Bull Island, where it has operated continuously, with the exception of the First World War when Bull Island was used as a training ground for British troops and the golf course was employed as a rifle and artillery range. After the end of hostilities, post-war compensation funded the redesign of the badly damaged links course which was finally completed in 1920. The clubhouse was destroyed in a fire in 1943, and not rebuilt for ten years due to uncertainty regarding the final development of the entire island. The new clubhouse opened in 1954 and has enjoyed periodic renovations and extensions.

The Royal Dublin Golf Club is an excellent links course. It has hosted the Irish Open Championship several times, attracting many of the world's finest professional golfers. Other important championship events held there include the Irish Amateur Open, the Irish Close, as well as the Carrolls Irish Open, the Toyota Challenge of Champions and the Forte PGA Seniors.

In 1959, legendary Irish golfer Christy O'Connor was appointed Club Professional, and he went on to win an impressive nine Irish Open Championships, including the 1966 Open which was played on his own Royal Dublin links.

Bull Island's other golf course, St Anne's Golf Club, rents its links form Dublin City Council. St Anne's was founded in 1921 as a nine-hole links course. In the early 1990s, it was allowed to expand into the full eighteen-hole links course which it is today. The original clubhouse – fondly remembered as little more than a tin shack (or maybe not so fondly remembered) – was replaced in 2003 with a splendid new club house which was designed to complement the unique ecology of Bull Island.

St Anne's Golf Club

Although the two golf courses seem an integral part of Bull Island today, some preservationists still see them as an intrusion on what should be wholly a natural park. They worry that the need to manage the fairways with mowing and fertilisation has resulted in an unacceptable modification of the natural habitat. That access to much of the island is also denied to the general public is a further irritation. Another view is that the two worlds suit each other fairly well, since the primary role Bull Island plays in the bay's ecology is as a bird sanctuary, something not directly harmed by golf courses, although roosting curlews in the salt marshes, their bellies stuffed with lug worms, might be annoyed occasionally by a badly sliced tee shot.

One need only remember some of the truly horrendous ideas put forward in the past to 'develop' Bull Island to feel that a pair of first-rate golf courses is not a bad compromise. It could have been a fun fair. (Or even an oil refinery?)

What Might Have Been

Ownership of the island has changed over the years. It was originally part of the Vernon estate, as was much of early Clontarf. The Vernons seemed benign-enough despots, and they did manage to thwart one of the more awful proposals made in which Bull Island would be 'improved' by transforming it into a sewage facility (and this at a time when a sewage facility meant the place where you dumped it) although the NIMBY implications are inescapable. Other bad ideas for the island are mentioned below.

Dublin Corporation developed a plan in 1868 to transform Bull Island into the city's main sewage dump. The idea was to transport the city's effluvia across the bay on barges where it would be deposited, presumably out of the visual – and olfactory – range of the residents who had produced it, and allowed to . . . well, one hesitates to speculate on what it was assumed the happy outcome would be. In every society, there are always those who see in empty land an opportunity to make use of it. The disposal of wastes hardly seems among the more sensible, particularly for sea-front land. Fortunately for Bull Island – and for all of Clontarf – powerful local forces, led by the Vernon family of Clontarf Castle and with the support of the Guinnesses of St Anne's and Lord Howth, were sufficiently formidable to defeat the noxious idea.

At the start of the First World War, the British army commandeered Bull Island and used it to practise trench warfare, complete with barbed wire and mock charges into the fire of enemy lines, something that would soon enough become all too real. The Easter Rising of 1916 ended much of this, although there was one incident in which British troops marching off the island on their way into the city during the fighting were ambushed by Volunteers at Skew Bridge. Nothing overt remains of Bull Island's brief martial past although old-timers remember finding bullets there as kids and seeing traces of rusted barbed wire that would emerged from the sand occasionally after storms.

Bull Island did have its share of smugglers' hiding places, and gentlemen occasionally used the open spaces of the strand to shoot holes in each other honourably, although not to the extent that took place earlier on Clontarf

Island. Bull Island is a sufficiently recent addition to the bay for its history to be driven mostly by the kind of large-scale, economically oriented 'developments' that require capital funding and planning permission and the approval of pliant politicians, rather than the more colourful events at Fairview and its now-lost island. Depredations in the eighteenth century took place under the shadow of the gibbet; today the best we seem to have is the possibility of 'naming and shaming' the despoilers. Not the most effective weapon to use against the more shameless types.

Another idea for 'improving' Bull Island was to convert it into a fun fair. Dunes would be paved, parking lots introduced, and where before had been found only the tedium of wind-swept dune grasses now would be an assortment of clanking rides, loudspeakers blaring jolly tunes at impressive decibel levels, and junk food emporiums, all of it sure to delight those who find stimulation in gaudy lights, mechanical noise and foods composed primarily of sugar and fat. Nothing came of it.

But in 1929, new energy brought new thinking, and a serious proposal to transform the entire Dollymount coastal area into a major seaside recreational centre based on Bull Island was introduced. Once again, major construction would be required. The lagoon would be sealed off with embankments fitted with sluice gates to eliminate tidal flushing so that a constant water depth might be maintained. No more messy mud flats. This newly improved lagoon could then be developed into a 'Coney Island' water park with various attractions while serving double duty as a national aquatic-sports stadium with complete facilities suitable for international competitions, all of it fully supported with grandstands for spectators and car parks for their cars. The entire development was to be surrounded by a wide motorway to encourage driving around it. (Why *do* some city planners look at Bull Island and think cars should be there?) Other areas nearby would be reconfigured to extend the concept of the aquatic pleasure grounds, with a large portion of Bull Island given over to the creation of a massive pleasure park complete with fun fair (again!), all of it designed to cater to city tourists who, it was assumed, found the existing natural amenities of Bull Island tedious. More grandiose concatenations would be added to capitalise upon the success of this plan. An aerodrome might be developed on Bull Island, with all attendant facilities for air travel (and more car parks too, no doubt), and the newly created lagoon could also become transformed into an important seaplane base.

Opponents to this development were not hard to assemble and included members of the two golf clubs as well as bird watchers, nature lovers and local residents worried about the destruction of what was after all perfectly fine as it was. Nevertheless, the project lumbered forward under the momentum of its own inevitability, and it stalled finally only because too many bureaucratic organisations were involved – the government, Dublin Corporation, Dublin Port, North Dublin Rural District Council, Howth Urban District Council – and they were unable to co-ordinate themselves sufficiently. Bureaucratic incompetence does have its benefits.

(Another similarly dubious idea was brought forward in 1930 when it was proposed that the entire section of the Liffey River between O'Connell Bridge and the Ha'penny Bridge be covered over and converted into a car park to service the increasing numbers of vehicles that were drawn into the city centre.)

It's hard to know what to think of such plans. Should we rejoice at the defeat of absurd ideas? Or fret that they had been broached at all?

One ponders the ugly dereliction of the baths at Dun Laoghaire or Clontarf and shudders to think that, had things worked out differently, much of Bull Island could look like that today, with the lagoon dead, the dunes paved, drifts of blowing rubbish collecting in the rusted old carnival-ride machinery that sits flaking mournfully in the wind, and nary a seaplane in sight.

Other Bull Island Facilities

Dublin Corporation took legal possession of Bull Island in 1954, allowing the Royal Dublin Golf Club to retain only the course itself and club house facilities. The Bull Wall and a narrow strip of land adjoining it are owned by the Dublin Port and Docks Board, as are Bull Bridge and the little cottages at the end of it. Dublin Corporation has transferred responsibility for the care of Bull Island to the Parks Department, making it the largest city park under their control.

The Interpretive Centre on Bull Island

The cottages clustered near Bull Bridge are the homes of the island's few full-time residents and were originally coast guard dwellings for those who were assigned the prevention of pirating or smuggling. The sea scouts have a club house there, newly redeveloped. Traditionally known as the 'Crow's Nest', it has been there in one form or another since 1912, when the Dublin Port Company granted the first charter for a sea scouts headquarters to Bull Island.

Opened by Dublin City Council in 1986, the Bull Island Interpretive Centre (also known as the Interpretative Centre) is mandated to assist in the understanding and preservation of the unique flora and fauna of the surrounding dune lands and salt marshes. With expertise in the specialised habitats of Bull Island, the centre is a valuable resource for schools and private individuals, and it also provides assistance to serious academics and researchers. As a large, natural environmental area that is easily accessible, the whole island functions as a living ecological laboratory.

Preserving Bull Island

Much of the bay feels fragile, and the hand of man has not always resulted in improvements.

Bull Island today seems safe enough; the bay perhaps slightly less so, although there are positive signs too (see 'The Future of the Bay'). One can only hope that local politicians will somehow manage to see it as within their legacy not to leave more blight, more industrialised waste on what should be our most precious amenity.

The temptation to do something to Bull Island seems short-sighted to us today. Yet many people in the 1970s fought unsuccessfully to preserve the remnants of the Viking settlement uncovered at Wood Quay. And what might strike some as a barren, wind-swept piece of land much too close to the city to be allowed to go unprofited-from, strikes others as a refuge from that very city and very much in need of protection. One man's rank weeds are another man's dune grasses, and what appears bleak and inhospitable to some others find uplifting and fascinating.

As of this writing, it seems unlikely that Bull Island will be seriously compromised any time soon, and the godwits and curlews and oystercatchers and dunlins and redshanks will continue to be found there, as will wintering brent geese all the way from Arctic Canada.

Probably we have reached sufficient economic development in Ireland to choose to preserve the beauty of our natural environment. Probably.

Chapter 11

Birds of the Bay

The bay's seasons can be defined by the calendars of its birds. The arrival of the brent geese in late autumn signals the advent of winter while the sight of resident grey herons stalking the mud flats and lagoons of the bay feels like an essential part of the long, lingering evenings of midsummer. Anyone fortunate enough to be living near swans will recognise the pleasure of spotting for the first time their new cygnets, brought out as if for display, awkward little brownish-grey feather bundles that are nevertheless somewhat swan-like already; you can see the promise there.

The shoreline of Dublin Bay is home to tens of thousands of birds and forms one of the most important bird habitats in Ireland. Dublin Bay is protected as a UNESCO Biosphere Reserve, the only one located within a capital city. It is also protected as a Wetland of International Importance and as a Natural Heritage Area. Thanks to these safeguards – and the efforts of countless Dublin residents who continue to work hard to protect the splendid natural environment of Dublin Bay – it is possible to see a diverse range of birds throughout the year, and to recognise in their continued presence an indication of the ecological health of the bay.

Brent geese

Appreciation of birds came somewhat late to Ireland; in earlier times they were viewed mostly as food, or as a source of blood sport, or as vermin to be driven off. The Irish Society for the Protection of Birds was formed in 1904, and by the middle of the twentieth century, ornithologists had emerged, arguing for study and preservation of wild birds, with an increased interest in migration patterns. In 1968, several groups converged to form the Irish Wildbird Conservancy (IWC) and this new organisation led the way in the preservation of bird habitats, the encouragement of scientific research, and the involvement of amateur birdwatchers in carrying out long-term studies. Today it is known as BirdWatch Ireland, and is the leading voluntary conservation organisation in Ireland, devoted to the protection of Ireland's wild birds and their habitats. There are several branches of BirdWatch Ireland within County Dublin; they hold monthly meetings and organise trips to local areas such as Bull Island or Dalkey Island. BirdWatch Ireland is a registered charity supported almost entirely from membership subscriptions, donations, grants and sponsorship. It has over 10,000 active members and supporters, and a network of twenty branches throughout the country actively promoting general conservation issues.

Birds typically are separated into resident and migratory species, and Ireland plays an important role for the latter category. In particular, seabird colonies of storm petrels and various terns, including the rare roseate tern, are found in protected parts of the Irish coastline and their preservation is actively encouraged.

Dublin Bay is the setting for seasonal migrations in numbers that are always impressive and sometimes astounding. In autumn, waders and waterfowl arrive from their northern breeding grounds while summer visitors are beginning their return journeys south. Birds which breed in the high Arctic regions depend on the relatively mild Irish winters to survive. These include the light-bellied brent geese, which are common on both sides of Dublin Bay from October to April, and can often be found at Sutton, on Clontarf Green and on the bay-side lawns at Fairview and on its football pitches, feeding on grass fields once they've gobbled up all the eelgrass (*Zostera marina*), their favourite shoreline food. Other birds common to Dublin Bay during winter months are the golden plover and the knot, medium-sized wading birds that can often be seen flying in dense flocks over Bull Island. In spring, the pattern is reversed, with birds from Africa flying in to spend their summers here; and Ireland's location at the far western edge of Europe makes it the first landfall for North American long-distant migrants.

The north side of the bay has the largest bird populations by far, thanks to the preservation of North Bull Island as an extensive natural habitat, with dune grasses and salt marshes for roosting, and mud flats and lagoons for feeding. (See 'North Bull Island' for more on the ecosystem there.)

The mud flats at the tidal lagoons at Bull Island can be hard to appreciate – unless you're a wading bird. The inter-tidal areas exposed at low tide appear lifeless; however, they support a diverse range of invertebrates which feed on the plankton washed inshore during successive tidal cycles. These in turn support the vast numbers of ducks and waders that live in Dublin Bay. Different bird species have adapted to feed on a certain range of invertebrates within the mud-flat ecosystem. The curlew, for example, has an extremely long beak and can reach the ever-desirable lug worms living deep within the mud flats. The dunlin, one of the smallest waders occurring in Dublin Bay, has a very short beak and can only catch small invertebrates found on the surface of the mud. Waders tend to feed only during daylight hours since they need to be able to spot traces of their prey; wildfowl are partly or wholly herbivorous and so can feed by touch. This difference in strategy no doubt helps to lessen over-crowding. Moreover, some species such as wigeon or redshanks feed almost continuously while curlews and godwits spend much more time roosting. Why they get away with an easier life is unclear. Perhaps it is because curlews and godwits are the only two species with lug worms comprising the bulk of their diet. If so, this may suggest yet another reason to salute the otherwise uninspiring mud-flats worm: its high nutritional value.

Curlew

Tufted duck

Bull Island is an important habitat for numerous species of wintering waterfowl, with large numbers of brent geese gathering on the grass of the promenade after they have finished off all the eelgrass in the area. Flocks of shelduck, wigeon and teal can be found on the lagoons; the north-east end of the causeway is good for pintails, while shovelers usually stay south of the causeway. The deeper water at either end of the island has goldeneye ducks and red-breasted merganser.

Waders are much in abundance on Bull Island. Knots and golden plovers sweep across the sky while the mud flats and salt marshes teem with dunlins, oystercatchers, redshanks, curlews, black-tailed godwits and snipe. Sanderlings can be seen on the seaward beaches, and lapwings seem to like the flats around Bull Bridge.

Unsurprisingly, masses of birds attract the attention of predators, and kestrels and peregrines can both be spotted sometimes in the area, as will the occasional merlin perched out on a pole. The salt marsh area east of the causeway also has short-eared owls which hunt in the salt marsh area east of the causeway.

Grey heron nest in the trees of St Anne's Park and are plentiful on the lagoons at Bull Island, as well as up at Sutton and down the length of Clontarf. The more exotic little egret is now often seen in late summer when they seem to take over duty from the grey herons in some areas, prowling the streams in the mud flats and along the edge of the low tide in the lingering twilight like their smaller and paler doppelgängers.

Golden plover

The south side of the bay is also an important site for wintering waterfowl, and although birds regularly commute between the south bay and the north bay, studies suggest that certain populations which occur in the south bay spend most of their time there. Several flocks of brent geese settle there regularly, feeding on the eelgrass beds at Merrion. Dublin

Bay is an important site for wintering gulls, especially black-headed gulls, common gulls and herring gulls, and it is considered the premier site in Ireland for Mediterranean gulls, which occur especially in late winter/ spring, then again in late summer into winter.

Grey heron

Over the summer months, attention shifts from the wintering geese, ducks and waders to the birds breeding in Dublin Bay. This includes three species of tern, small predominantly white birds that look like gulls. Terns hunt for fish by diving and can be seen in Dublin Bay between May and September. Common and Arctic terns are two of the species which regularly breed in Dublin Bay; small colonies are present in Dublin Port and on Dalkey Island. The latter colony is studied annually in the Dalkey Island Tern Project, which is run jointly by BirdWatch Ireland and Dun Laoghaire/Rathdown County Council. The main aim of the project is to manage the islands for terns, as well as to encourage a third tern species, the rare roseate tern, to breed on the island.

Sea Birds

Unlike the lug worm, whose world is pretty much limited to the hole it digs in the mud, the birds of Dublin Bay can fly, which expands their geographical reach considerably. Setting aside the migrants with their impressive travelling, there are pelagic birds such as fulmars or kittiwakes which almost never appear on land yet build shoreline nesting colonies in the safety of remote or inaccessible spots. Other birds such as cormorants, and sometimes shags, can be seen feeding offshore on both sides of the bay, or standing on offshore rocks with their wings held out as if inviting the admiration of featherless bipeds; yet they also are residents of the rugged cliffs on the coastline.

To get a true picture of the birds of Dublin Bay, one needs to take a short, summertime excursion. Islands are by definition a place apart, and Ireland's Eye seems particularly remote even though it is close to the largest urban population in Ireland. In early summer, the seabird colonies on the cliffs of Howth are crowded enough, but Ireland's Eye manages an even denser sea bird population. Nesting shelducks are in old rabbit burrows on the lower levels, with rafts of guillemots and razorbills off to the east side. Above, the cliffs teem with the nests of auks, kittiwakes and fulmars, while down near the water line are shags

Knot

on their nests. Other nearby residents include the great black-backed gulls and herring gulls, which can become aggressive in defending their nests. Gannets and kittiwakes have established a colony on the rocks offshore to the north-east, and along the cliffs running to the south, fulmars and kittiwakes nest in their hundreds, and at the off-shore rock to the south is a large cormorant colony. Also on the beach at Carrigeen Bay are the nests of oystercatchers, a stocky, noisy, black and white wader with red eyes, an impressively long orange bill and sturdy orange legs. You could not design a better bird.

The oystercatcher is a very common resident of the bay, a comically busy wader with much to say, some of it quite complicated and embellished with additional clicks and trills. It would be a dour soul indeed who did not smile inwardly at the sight of an oystercatcher on the job, busily probing

Oystercatcher

for worms or molluscs which when found it hammers open with alacrity. If another reason were needed why preservation of the bay was critical to our own human well-being, the oystercatcher would be a good candidate.

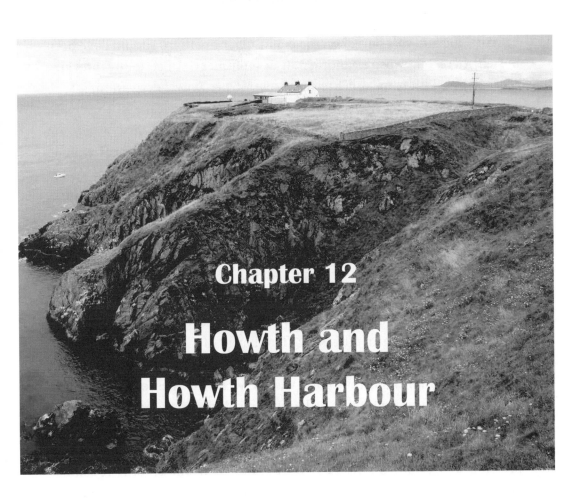

Chapter 12

Howth and Howth Harbour

Howth feels old. You would expect to find the odd tumulus. And for all the cheerful exuberance of the young Europeans who flock there like sprat on fine summer afternoons, as well as our own occasional contingent of plucky Irish lads out for a couple of scoops, the place never becomes overwhelmed. Temple Bar on a Saturday night it's not. The drunk shouting at two in the morning is pretty much doing it alone.

The name Howth comes from the Norse word *hoved*, meaning 'head'; while the Irish name, Ben Edair or Beann Eadair or Ben Edar or Ben Etar – 'Etar's Hill' (or Ben-na-Dir: 'Hill of Oaks'), seems less certain.

Who was this 'Etar' *aka* Edair et al.? Etar might have been the beloved wife of a Firbolg chieftain, or Etar could have been a chieftain of the Tuatha De Danann who replaced the easily impressed Firbolg. There was also apparently an 'Edar' who died fecklessly due to the unreturned love of his fair Aine and was buried on the peninsula, or perhaps should have been buried there but wasn't, another disappointment! Uncertainty prevails. One returns with some relief to the Howth-from-*hoved* derivation.

As we have seen, Norse invasions in the closing decade of the eighth century fell with severity on the Dublin coast; and the first attack on Howth is recorded in the year 819, with the raiders carrying off women to be sold into slavery. By the end of the ninth century, the name of the peninsula had changed from the Irish (Etar or Edair or . . .) to the Norse, and Howth had become an important Viking seaport.

The Battle of Clontarf did not extend as far as Howth, but some of the Danish invaders had left their boats there and the peninsula became a place of refuge for the losing side. Howth has always been easily defensible, thanks to the high seaward cliffs and narrow isthmus at Sutton. Some of the Danes regrouped there and fled while others stayed on apparently, and local names reflect their durability. The Battle of Clontarf weakened the Norse sufficiently that their sovereignty in Fingal was ended. This vacuum soon provided an opportunity for war between the men of Leinster and the men of Munster who met at Howth, resulting in a great slaughter on both sides, but with the Leinstermen finally getting the worst of it. There were to be other opportunities for butchery. During the Anglo-Norman invasion of Ireland, the resident Danes and Irish put up stiff resistance at Howth. The main battle took place on a bridge, and the hacking and slashing and chopping and stabbing was indulged with such brio that the stream flowing below soon filled with blood. A pleasant pub, The Bloody Stream, is now seated above the old stream itself, just at the DART station, and excavations in the area inevitably used to turn up old weapons and bones.

The winner of that famous battle, Sir Armoricus Tristram, was rewarded with ownership of Howth; and since his founding battle was fought on the Feast Day of St Laurence, his family assumed the name St Lawrence, in solemn commemoration of that sanguinary event. The St Lawrence family castle in the medieval period was one of the most important dwellings in all of Dublin, much favoured by the great and the good. Howth Castle today is a hodgepodge of styles and eras, interesting enough in its gloomy way, although attempting to detect any strategy behind the final design would lead to disappointment.

Howth was an early port, with evidence of trading voyages linking Howth to England found throughout the fourteenth century. Exports included hides and corn, and Dublin officials were stationed at Howth to prevent unauthorised shipments from departing. There were sufficient passengers landing at Howth for a mid-fourteenth century pestilence to have entered through the port there then spread to larger towns.

In the following centuries, Howth as a port played an important role in the growth of Dublin, with records asserting the right of the Corporation of Dublin to collect duty on goods landed at Howth, something the locals occasionally disputed although seldom with any success.

During the Elizabethan period, Howth grew into one of the largest towns in the area. Its port had a quay that was used mostly for passenger traffic, the main port of Dublin at the Liffey mouth having co-opted most mercantile traffic. Several of Elizabeth's chief governors are recorded to have embarked or disembarked at Howth, as did other notables during the mid-sixteenth century. Howth's position as a commercial port declined during the seventeenth century. Ships had grown larger and facilities for embarkation and disembarkation were better elsewhere. Fishing retained its importance, however – much as it does today – and packet-boat service to carry the mails between England and Ireland had the first incarnations of its long history, thanks to the skill and courage of Howth fishermen in open boats who would make the crossing over the Irish Sea when all other options failed. The fearlessness of Howth fishermen became legendary, and instances of daring occur periodically. During the English Civil War in the middle of the seventeenth century, Parliament blockaded Dublin Bay and the only way royalists in Ireland could communicate was by using the fishermen at Howth as secret couriers. They would set out in fair weather and foul, aware that detection by Cromwell's thugs would lead to unpleasant consequences.

Lord Howth's demesne came through the Commonwealth intact, with the sea reported as the boundary on all sides except for the west, which extended to Kilbarrack and Baldoyle. Lord Howth's property also included the harbour, and he had the right to take the choicest fish landed there. The management of local waters was Lord Howth's responsibility. Shortly after the Restoration, an attempt was made to lessen the danger posed by the peninsula to navigation by erecting what would evolve into the modern lighthouse, a raised platform with a great iron pan from which a coal fire blazed at night, and the Lord of Howth built a small wharf to service the ships bringing in the coal. (See 'Lights on the Bay' for more.)

Notwithstanding these early attempts at promoting maritime safety, the waters around Howth continued to be extremely perilous. A vessel was blown out all the way from Ringsend onto the rocks of Howth in 1674 and destroyed there. Three years later, another ship was wrecked on the rocks of Howth with great loss of life; and in 1696, the packet-boat coming from Holyhead was lost on the Sutton side of Howth Head, with all passengers drowned. With the beginning of the eighteenth century, the first serious attempts at resolving the problem of the port of Dublin were still decades away; and it is doubtful if anyone would have considered Howth as a viable part of that solution. It was too remote, too rugged, too wild. Howth had become an important fishery harbour, and it provided the city of Dublin with the bulk of its herring, an important food then;

Rocky shore near Howth

but in terms of traffic to England, the once-valued port of Howth had completely fallen into disuse.

Howth still participated in one aspect of international trade, however: smuggling. Caves dotted around the peninsula provided excellent hiding places for illicit cargoes; in the summer of 1764, revenue officers had seized sixteen casks of hidden tea only to be assaulted by brazen smugglers who then managed to recover most of their booty in a violent struggle during which two of their fellows were killed. Howth was unrepentant. Shortly after that battle with the king's agents, a fierce storm drove a lighter ashore at Howth. It was loaded with large casks of brandy; its crew was unable to defend it; predators lurked in the bracken and gorse; and Lord Howth himself felt obliged to take charge of the cargo, ringing it with his servants until its proper owner could be found. These same decades saw the first harbour pier at Dun Laoghaire built; and the Great South Wall was completed along the southern rim of the Liffey channel, with the hope that Ringsend might be made safer for shipping. There was some improvement, but the problem had clearly not been solved. Ships continued to be wrecked throughout Dublin Bay (see 'Famous Shipwrecks'); and shortly after the beginning of the nineteenth century, the Ballast Board opted for what today seems like a bizarre solution.

Two things were needed: a safe shelter for ships waiting to enter the port and a better station for the packet-boats. Immense sums had been spent in constructing the Great South Wall; yet despite the improvements, the ships of that era – dependent on sail – were unable to enter the Liffey channel in bad weather and were often forced to wait out storms exposed in the bay, with as many as twenty a year lost or seriously damaged as a result. The Pigeon House on the wall at Ringsend had become the packet-station; but like any other sea-going vessel, the packet-boats were dependent on winds and tides – and at the mercy of stormy weather – so arrivals in gales could be fraught and departure times were very uncertain, adding to the discomfort of passengers who were already facing sixteen, eighteen, twenty hours of rolling and tossing on the Irish Sea.

Two pamphleteers stepped forward: the superintendent of the Howth lighthouse and a local clergyman. Both enthusiasts plumped for Howth as the best site to meet the basic requirements of safety and convenience:

St Mary's with Howth Harbour in background

storm harbour and packet-station. In 1800, the first of a series of pamphlets proposed constructing a harbour on the northern side of Howth then digging a canal capable of carrying ships into the port at the Liffey. It was an audacious plan. The harbour itself would be remarkably long, extending from the town of Howth to the isthmus; and the canal would be cut through the isthmus, then follow down along the Clontarf shore, cross Fairview and empty finally into the Liffey. Needless to say, the scope of the project – to say nothing of the construction costs – would have been daunting. A similar plan was being mooted for a harbour at Dalkey with its own canal (and its own astronomical estimation of the funding required), but the Ballast Board was impressed by further arguments from the pamphleteers, asserting that Howth would be ideal as a station for the packet-boats since it was closer to Holyhead than Dalkey; that only a short pier would be needed at Howth; that the area could be guarded easily against attacks by foes; and that developing Howth Harbour would have the additional benefit of greatly increasing the fishing catch in the region, since with more places for more fishing boats to tie up, more boats would be available to brave the local waters and thus pull more fish out if it, thereby improving the diet of Dubliners.

The idea was attractive. Costs were assessed for the various projects and compared. And although it was already a worry that the harbour as situated might fill with sand (as it did), the Howth plan proved to be the cheapest option. A harbour sufficient for the packet-boats was agreed to – with no canal to Dublin nor any of the other embellishments the two pamphleteers had dreamed of – and funds were advanced.

Work began in 1807, and John Rennie, the famous Scottish engineer who would be so instrumental in the building of Dun Laoghaire Harbour, was consulted and would later take on some responsibility for finishing the project. Rennie had not been involved in the selection of the site chosen for the harbour and apparently expressed misgivings about it even after work was well begun. Second-guessing seemed the order of the day. Even the original pamphleteers had developed doubts and called on the government to rethink the choice of harbour site, or at least appoint a skilled resident engineer with sufficient expertise to oversee the project, the previous construction manager having resigned from his post. Most pundits seemed to have believed that if the harbour were built further east in Balscadden Bay, it would not fill with sand. Warnings went unheeded; the government persisted with its plans; Howth Harbour was built where it is today; sand poured in on the currents; and the result was such an immediate and unambiguous failure that it helped stimulate the construction of Dun Laoghaire Harbour soon after.

That being said, Howth Harbour is one of Dublin's great amenities. (That it is not on the bay itself might disqualify it from inclusion in this book; but it was the first attempt – and first failure – at solving the central dilemma of Dublin Bay and one which is still very much with us today: What should be done about a port that is located in a bay too shallow for it?)

Howth Harbour encloses fifty-two acres. The western pier is 823 metres long and is dedicated to the Howth commercial fishing fleet, far and away the largest in the Dublin area. The eastern pier measures 695 metres and ends in an excellent granite lighthouse with an attached lighthouse keeper's residence (see 'Lights on the Bay'). The harbour mouth, at 91.5 metres, seems too narrow and would not accommodate large ships easily but does thereby offer protection against high seas. The stone used to build the piers was quarried on the peninsula, although the foundation stone was imported from across the Irish Sea and the granite facings are from quarries on the south side.

West Pier in Howth

The harbour was finished in 1813, and the packet boat service was initiated there in 1818. Eight years later, it was shifted to Dun Laoghaire Harbour, which was nearing completion.

Howth Harbour has had its moment of imperial glory, albeit a somewhat muted moment. Prior to his visit to and departure from what would be renamed Kingstown Harbour in his honour, King George IV dropped in at Howth Harbour one sunny August afternoon in 1821. Crowds waved and cheered. The king apparently waved back. (A scurrilous rumour had it that the king was drunk; such irreverance will not be repeated here.) A carriage was waiting on the pier for the 'fatigued' king and off he went. And that's it. Nothing was renamed in his honour, no plaque commemorates the grand occasion, no ornate fountain, no obelisk, no street name changed; and the only 'king' of any note in the harbour is The King Sitric, one of Howth's better seafood restaurants and named after a different fellow entirely. It's as if George IV had never even been there. And while Dun Laoghaire is draped with Imperial flounces and furbelows, Howth has a rock near the West Pier with a plaque declaring

Fishing boats in Howth Harbour

in 1986 the official opening of Howth Fishery Harbour. The implications are clear. People are meant to work there. An obelisk would just get in the way. (There actually is one now, the 'Ready Boat Pillar', a complex artistic statement in mould-formed reconstituted granite, complete with matching litter bin.)

Prior to the mid-nineteenth century, when the branch railway to Howth was completed, the peninsula was primitive, a village of wretched thatched cabins inhabited by poor fishermen, and with St Mary's Abbey, its ruined old church, and Howth Castle about all that remained to indicate a richer past. Nevertheless, the citizens of Dublin liked Howth and came to picnic on the grass or on the rocks at Balscadden Bay, or to stroll on the head and admire the views of open sea, surrounded by heather and gorse, or even to creep off into the bracken. Joyce's *Ulysses* begins at the Martello at Sandycove, but it ends in Molly's remembrance of making love with Bloom in the bracken at Howth, a beautiful portion of her great monologue of lust and inclusion; and the wildness of Howth Head, the beauty of the cliff walk around it with various side trails leading up to higher points, is one of the most spectacular natural amenities on Dublin Bay. For all the development going on at Howth – and it is considerable – much of the original character of the place has been preserved. It comes as a surprise sometimes, when following a previously unexplored path, to round a bend and be confronted with a sprawling housing estate. That it can be a surprise stands as a testament to the success of the efforts at preservation that has kept so much of Howth intact.

Howth began growing in the latter half of the nineteenth century, the branch railway resulting in increased visitors and the establishment of hotels. The harbour itself filled with sand and was dredged and began filling again, as happens still. Commercial success seemed unlikely, and the folly of the construction of the harbour was summed up by the observation of a nineteenth-century pundit that not one boat-builder or rope-maker could be found there; no sail-maker or net mender or even carpenter or blacksmith was in operation near the port – and never would. He was wrong. Fishing boats had continued to operate out of Howth, and the fishing fleet grew in size and capability even as Howth as a port was still being denigrated. Today, Howth Harbour is home to a successful Irish commercial fishing fleet.

Business at the Harbour

At Howth Harbour, the West Pier and East Pier are very different from each other, with Howth's East Pier like a smaller version of the East Pier at Dun Laoghaire Harbour; although the lighthouse and keeper's residence at Howth are clearly superior to the south-side version and maintained in a much better state of repair. The East Pier is a long sweeping bend that faces out over Balscadden Bay with its marvellous cliff-side houses, one of which W.B. Yeats lived in for a couple of years; Puck's Rocks are farther on, and beyond them, the nostrils of the Nose of Howth.

Like the East Pier at Dun Laoghaire, Howth's East Pier is on two levels: the lower section is somewhat sheltered and directs the attention inward to the boats in the harbour while the upper one is more exposed to the weather but offers spectacular views out over open water that release

An aerial view of Howth Harbour

the soul and free the spirit. Most visitors seem to prefer strolling on the East Pier, the beauty of the cliffs and sky and sea being hard to resist; but the 'real' Howth Harbour is to be found on the West Pier and although there aren't any views until you get to the very end (unless the sight of a dead shark on display before a fishmonger's shop counts), the place is fascinating.

Five great fishmongers anchor the public business of the West Pier: Beshoffs, Wrights, Reids, Dorans, and Nicky's Plaice. All deserve praise and patronage. Across from them is the impressive structure of Howth's Dublin Wholesale Fishmarket, with its dedicated wharf and modern off-loading capabilities, as well as a few harbour seals lingering hopefully nearby even after the unloading has long since finished. Next to it is the lift-out facilities for the graving docks which lie farther to the west and are accessed along broad rail lines. Even large fishing boats can be manoeuvred onto a submerged lifting frame which is powered by two banks of four synchrolift hoists that raise the boat up to dock level from where it can then be rolled down to the working area.

The Howth Sea Angling Club has its clubhouse on the West Pier, and the Irish Coast Guard Station is just down from it. There is a wonderful Marine Supply here with sea kayaks displayed in a rack in front. Howth has no shortage of good restaurants, and two of the best are on the West Pier – Deep (and Deep 2 next door) and Aqua in the old yacht club building out at the end of the pier.

Boats in Howth Harbour

Centred on the shoreline between the piers is the clubhouse of the Howth Yacht Club, an impressive structure designed to take full advantage of its position on the harbour. (See 'Sailing on the Bay'.)

Old stone buildings line the west side of the pier, the stone a beautifully warm honey-coloured rock with massive granite quoins in places and window surrounds done in red brick or grey brick. What once must have been an old mariners' church now houses IC Trawl, specialists in net gear technology. What would be an old stone chateau were it in the south of France here is home to Thomas Mulloy Ltd, 'Fish Processors'. You even have a choice between two diesel oil and kerosene vendors on the West Pier.

Inside the harbour itself are the fishing trawlers tied up two and three deep; some are rusty old tubs and some fairly trim-looking boats. Most have large reels mounted on the stern for laying out then hauling in their nets, and in afternoons fishermen can be watched dragging out these nets along the pier roads to make repairs.

The elegant and the grimy are perfectly in balance here. It is a world of coiled ropes and rusted steel cables, of piled green nets and bright yellow bollards and the smell of diesel fumes, of fork lifts loaded with Styrofoam fish boxes and sea gulls picking at scraps in drying nets. At the far end of the pier is what remains of a defensive fortification, a stepped wall curved like an elegant stone staircase, perhaps four feet thick at the top and three times that at the bottom, certainly sufficient to repel cannon balls. The mirror image of it is found at the end of the East Pier, elegantly echoing the curves of the lighthouse itself, and the same constructions are also found on the two piers at Dun Laoghaire. At all of them, sea anglers can usually be found, filled with the hope and patience that their obsession requires.

The West Pier brings together in one place all the various aspects of fishing and fish. One would be tempted to argue that this is the proper business of the bay, the original use man found for it.

But then we read that fish stocks are not sustainable, that some species are in danger of extinction, and that local seas are warming, sending our beloved cod north and inviting into our waters as a replacement, tropical sea horses – hardly a fit pairing with chips.

Fishing nets in Howth Harbour

Chapter 13

Sea Angling

Dublin Bay offers a range of sports fishing opportunities. Some require hiking to reach – or even rock-climbing – but are often worth the effort, while others are no more demanding than taking a short stroll out a harbour pier. Most sites are accessible thanks to DART. You would almost think the city's urban train line had been designed specifically for the convenience of sea-anglers. The northern terminus at Howth is one of the most popular fishing venues, both for off-shore sportsmen and those with access to boats; while the DART station at Dun Laoghaire is sited practically on the busy West Pier. In between, and slightly harder to reach, is the Great South Wall at Poolbeg which extends out into the deeper waters of the bay. In the warm months, anglers will be found at all these locations while even when the weather is less than fine, the more resolute will be encountered on the piers, and the truly committed (or slightly demented) can sometimes still be seen on the exposed rocks at Howth, hope holding them fixed tight as limpets. There is some beach fishing in the Dublin Bay area, with the more popular venues slightly north of the bay, and the excellent off-shore boat fishing introduces almost too many options to record. But for the most part, it is piers and rocks that draw the serious sports angler and the casual bait-dropper alike.

Charter boat companies operate in Dublin Bay and beyond, leaving from Howth Harbour and Dun Laoghaire Harbour; and several areas on both the north side and the south side also have self-operated smaller boats for rent. Bullock Harbour is a good option. Anglers with their own boats will find public slipways for launching and landing although many of these are operable only during mid or high tides, so care must be taken in planning a fishing expedition.

Sport Fishing on the North Side

The two piers at Howth Harbour are both popular with anglers, with the East Pier apparently preferable although both are used, thanks to easy access to what is in essence deep-water fish stocks. Whiting, pollack, coalfish and codling are all caught during summer and autumn; and the piers themselves are very enjoyable to be on, with lovely views of Ireland's Eye nearby and Lambay Island just beyond it. Fishing conditions at the East Pier are said to resemble those found at the East Pier in Dun Laoghaire, with a rocky bottom on the seaward side yielding to sandy patches farther out for distance casters. The slightly less popular West Pier offers similar fishing, and the bottom at the harbour mouth between the two piers is sand and so a good spot for flatfish. Mackerel and garfish are also caught there during the summer, and mullet are drawn to the offal discharged by the commercial fleet. Dab and plaice can also be had occasionally.

And it should be acknowledged that if futility marks the day at Howth and disappointment prevails, the best fish-mongers in Dublin are arranged along the commercial West Pier so that one need not return home empty-handed; and if not even this option can completely assuage the sense of despair some anglers feel at the hopelessness of it all, several excellent village pubs are prepared to ease the pain, with the Abbey and the Cock in Howth village itself, and the Bloody Stream conveniently under the DART station.

In addition to the pier fishing available at the village, there are good fishing spots all around Howth Head and down the inside coast to Sutton. Accessing the various rock fishing spots is easy at Howth thanks to the cliff walk which goes all around the head although the cliffs are extremely steep and dangerous on the north-east side. Balscadden Bay, just off the East Pier at Howth, has a small but popular shingle beach that is fished for bass and flounder, particularly near the rocks on both sides. But it is the rocks and cliffs farther on that are even more popular.

In fact, 'popular' is the word for this entire area, and Balscadden Bay and the rocks that form the east edge of it can become too crowded in summer. It is easy to see why. The place is stunningly beautiful and easily reached. Mackerel in the summer is the big draw here, particularly at the 'split' rock near the Nose of Howth. As with other rock-fishing venues

Fishing boats in Howth Harbour

in Howth, footing can be treacherous and great care is required at times, particularly during wet weather when rocks become even more slippery.

Balscadden Bay itself can become so busy that serious anglers often avoid it in fine weather and move to other locations farther along. The cliffs are too high in most places on the back side of Howth Head but serious anglers do find ways of getting at places near the Nose. Underwater reefs often yield pollack and mackerel, sometimes dogfish or dab, and distance casters might reach wrasse under the rock pinnacles beneath the bird colony. It needs to be emphasised: these are high cliffs. Do not fall off. Bad results are certain.

Although the trail along the cliffs is much too high for fishing, the views from the Irish Sea side on Howth Head are spectacular and fishing spots can be reached after a twenty-minute hike. The best places are from the Baily lighthouse on around to Sutton Strand, with massive rocks jutting out into deep water. Here, too, footing can be dangerous in wet weather, but the opportunity to cast off the rocks into deep water is irresistible, and everywhere the scenery is breath-taking. Deep-water fish like mackerel, coalfish, plaice, dab, dogfish, wrasse and whiting are often caught here.

Just west of the Baily is a slight headland known as the Lion's Head. Like other rock-fishing sites along here, access is only for the very sure-footed as the down-hill trail can be slippery and falling would be, as they say, a very bad thing. Other than that, the spot is excellent, with a great view of the city in the distance. Best results tend to be associated with high tides, and pollack and wrasse are often taken. Fishing at dusk is an option, as long as the dangerous access trail can be safely managed.

The truly committed deep-water angler can launch small boats easily at Howth Harbour, providing access to good fishing grounds around Ireland's Eye and on the Kish Bank farther out in the Irish Sea. In addition to the species taken at Howth Harbour, mackerel in season and flatfish such as plaice and dab are also found out there. Finally, there is a dinghy club on the other side of the head at Red Rock at Sutton which has slips for launching small boats to go bottom fishing into the deep water of the main bay channels for bass and flatfish. At Red Rock, bottom fishing sometimes results in conger being taken, especially at night, and dab as well as dogfish, pollack, coalfish and wrasse are all possible.

The most common shore fishing on the north side is at Dollymount Strand, the very long beach on the bay side of North Bull Island. In summer, the place is impossibly crowded with beach-goers, often in their cars; but for the rest of the year, it is nearly deserted. The bay is very shallow here with a long tidal draw so that while some beach fishing takes place in summer, the best time to try it is during the evening tides in autumn. It would be hard to call the techniques used at Dollymount Strand 'surf casting' since there isn't much surf; but the results can be surprisingly good, particularly with an incoming tide at night, when the occasional nice bass can be taken although dogfish, flounder and plaice are more common. Autumn is also the season to try fishing off the Bull Wall Bridge and embankment, where pollack, codling, whiting and even bass can be found. At very low tides, bait diggers can be seen in the exposed sand flats, searching for the ever-desirable lug worm.

Moored fishing boats in Colimore Harbour

Sport Fishing on the South Side

Fishing from the Great South Wall and the Poolbeg Lighthouse can yield mackerel in season, as well as conger eels and small pollack. In addition to the usual deep-water species found in the bay, large shoals of big mullet are occasionally spotted in the Liffey itself, usually on an incoming tide. Some anglers swear by the hot water outflow from Poolbeg Power Station as a smart option. Bottom fishing at Poolbeg also produces the odd flounder and the occasional nice bass. As an angling venue, the Great South Wall is conveniently close to the city centre although getting out to it requires a hike thought the wastelands of industrio-Dublin and, depending on wind direction, the presence of the Ringsend Wastewater Treatment Plant may or may not make itself felt. Once out on the wall, the views of open water and various Dublin Bay landmarks are unsurpassed, and at the Poolbeg Light, you are as close to the centre of the bay as you can get without a boat.

Like Dollymount Strand on the north side, there is some shore fishing on Sandymount Strand but the extreme shallowness of the bay at this point limits it to periods of high tide. At low tide, lug worms can be dug as bait but for the most part, anglers tend to seek out other, more promising venues.

Dun Laoghaire Harbour is the south-side equivalent to Howth Harbour, albeit much larger. Access is easy, thanks to the DART, and all fishing spots are only a short walk from the station. The West and East Piers in Dun Laoghaire Harbour are both excellent for sea-angling, with pollack and mackerel in season, and with whiting, codling and bass also taken. People also fish inside the harbour for dab, plaice and conger in summer and try float fishing from inner coal quays for mullet. There are public slipways to launch boats for deep-water fishing around Scotsmans Bay to the south and farther down to Dalkey Island.

Some local anglers will argue in favour of limiting efforts to the West Pier since the East Pier is the usual strolling route for visitors, residents and their children. It seems probable that the fish don't know how crowded with humanity the East Pier becomes in fine weather, and so the rebel who stays with it might be well rewarded. The fact is, both piers seem equally popular and neither seems over-crowded, with plenty of open water for everyone.

Two fully equipped charter boats operate from Dun Laoghaire Harbour and offer general ground, wreck and reef fishing off the Kish Banks and the Burford Banks. If disappointments rule the day and the take-home catch amounts to nil, it is but a short stroll from the West Pier to the Purty Kitchen – Dublin's second-oldest pub – and a fine place for the solace of a good pint. (Yes. They have an excellent seafood menu.)

Scotsman's Bay also has public slips from which small boats can be launched, typically limited to mid and high tides. Bullock and Coliemore both have launch spots for general ground fishing around Dalkey Island. Species available include mackerel in season, plus dogfish, plaice, dab, codling and whiting. Coliemore Harbour is also a good place for pier fishing for codling, pollack and conger. Bullock Harbour is a tiny enclosed harbour filled with boats fitted with outboard motors. It has a pleasant, old-fashioned feel to it, and is very much there for the angler. Bullock Castle stands just above the harbour – looms over it even – and behind the harbour on the seaward side are diving rocks from which boys dare each other to jump off, like a smaller, localised version of the more famous Forty Foot at Sandycove. Bullock Harbour has a nice, out-of-the-way feel to it. A big marine supply store – Western Marine – is there, as is the Dublin City Sea Angling Club. Boats for hire is a good business at Bullock Harbour, as at Coliemore, and easy access to south side off-shore fishing sites makes it an area worth exploring for anglers.

On Lug Worms

At low tides on the mud flats around Clontarf or Sutton, or on Sandymount Strand in the south, solitary individuals shod with wellies and equipped with buckets and spades can be seen far out on the broad expanses of exposed sand and mud obsessively digging. Or at least they look obsessed. Visitors often think they are searching for cockles – and in some places they might be, although cockles are no longer much fancied here – but what they more probably want is bait.

Or, more precisely, lug worms.

It would be hard to over-praise the lug worm as one of nature's better ideas. The lug worm lives in a permanent burrow and feeds by passing sediment through its system, extracting nutrients and depositing the remains on the surface as a little piled coil, something very familiar to anyone who has strolled the strands and mud flats at low tide. Curlews love lug worms, and can be spotted at low tide probing for them. But many popular species of ocean fish are also enthusiastic about lug worms which is why there is today an occupation which, for want of a better job

Lug worm casts

description title, might be categorised as 'lug-worm digger'. In fact, this way of earning a living has grown so rapidly in recent years that there is a real worry the over-digging of lug worm nurseries may diminish the ability of the species to sustain itself. (Yes, lug worms like to live near each other and that is the term used for areas where baby lug worms are found snuggled together.)

People who have seen a lug worm do not argue in favour of their preservation on grounds of cuteness or wild beauty. Pandas or cheetahs they are not. But every species is worth preserving. And besides, good bait deserves effective management for the benefit of future generations.

The best way to identify a lug worm burrow is by finding the 'cast' (that piled coil) and the 'blow hole' beside it. Below the hole lies the worm, perhaps a few inches deep, perhaps as much as two feet deep. Some seasoned lug-worm extractors have abandoned the crude tool of the spade in favour of the more-efficient lug-worm pump. This is not a wholly welcomed development, apparently. In untutored hands, worm-pumping can be a hazardous process since if the mechanism is dialled up for maximum suction, one risks bursting the worm. Knowledgeable lug-worm-pump aficionados operate with their suction washers set initially to 'light' then increase the setting gradually, always aware of the need for moderation since few things in this world are more useless than a burst lug worm.

Chapter 14

Poolbeg to Seapoint

The Poolbeg Peninsula

The Poolbeg Peninsula is about ninety acres of reclaimed land, much of it occupied by the ESB power generating facilities. 'Poolbeg' means something like 'little hole' and refers to the section of deep-water which stood off the mouth of the Liffey. Before the construction of the Great Walls, Poolbeg provided safe anchorage for ships and the name was therefore attached to the lighthouse, a familiar landmark at the far end of the Great South Wall.

The first structure of any note on Poolbeg Peninsula was the Pigeon House – originally 'Pidgeon's House' – a blockhouse built at the end of the Great South Wall, also known as the 'double wall', which extended from Ringsend, replacing the original piles. The Pigeon House was finished in 1761 and used by the Ballast Office to store tools and materials, with a man named John Pidgeon appointed resident caretaker. By 1765, the Pidgeon family were supplementing their income by providing refreshments for cross-channel passengers and day-trippers out to view the construction of what would eventually become the Great South Wall. In 1790, the Pigeon House (without its 'd') became the official cross-channel landing site for packet ships carrying mail and passengers between Britain and Ireland; and in 1793, the Pigeon House Hotel was constructed. This impressive building of cut stone still exists, a melancholy relic in a weed-choked yard awaiting whatever the world has in store for it. Renovation? Demolition? More benign neglect?

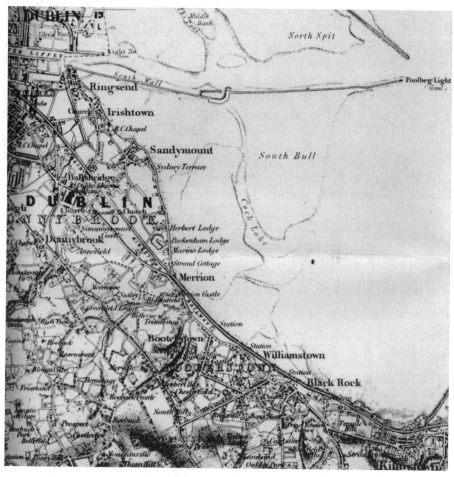

Detail from One-inch Ordnance Survey Map of Ireland, 1860
extract from Sheet 112

The British military occupied much of Poolbeg at the end of the eighteenth century and used it as a defensive installation, a transaction which supplied the funds necessary to begin the construction of North Bull Wall. A portion of the fort's walls can still be seen near the Pigeon House, and part of the entryway gate has been preserved on Pigeon House Road. After the departure of the military, Dublin Corporation bought back the property for use as a power station, choosing the site because it was close to the growing demands of the city and had the necessary supply of water from the Liffey for cooling. The Pigeon House Station opened in 1902 and generated electricity under the authority of the Dublin Corporation Lighting Committee until 1929 when the newly formed Electricity Supply Board took over responsibility. The Pigeon House Station was a reliable supplier and continued to operate during times of uncertainty, including the 1913 Lockout, the First World War, the 1916 Rebellion and the Civil War in 1922–3. The city eventually outgrew the capacity of that plant, and the first incarnation of the present power station was approved. The old Pigeon House facilities remained on standby status and wasn't fully decommissioned and closed until 1976. Like the abandoned Pigeon House Hotel, the old power station remains as a deteriorating wreck today, the cooling tower partially demolished, the structural ironwork rusted to a shade approaching that of the red brick of the walls. It stands as a reminder of how poorly industrial-age derelicts decay if they aren't somehow refurbished. Yet one wonders why nothing has been done to manage them better; they are a part of urban history that we may someday regret not having had the foresight to restore and repurpose.

The modern ESB Poolbeg Generating Station began producing electricity in 1971. It operates on both oil and gas, using either fuel with equal efficiency, and is the only facility in the ESB system capable of this flexibility. Oil tankers unload their cargo directly at the open-piled jetty, and the oil is then stored in five tanks with a capacity of 140,000 tons. The Poolbeg Station currently provides about thirty-five per cent of the country's electricity and is rated the most efficient power generating plant in Ireland.

The Poolbeg Chimneys

At 207 metres, the chimneys are far and away the tallest things on the bay; and while visible from virtually anywhere in Dublin, they are not universally admired for the industrial note they add to the city's foreshore. Perhaps it's for the best that there are two of them; one might feel unloved

Chimneys at Poolbeg

and lonely. (Although they appear to be identical, close examination reveals that they are different in shape and girth – the forward one bold and resolute, the other slightly more svelte, delicate even.) The chimneys seem too prominent for our relatively low-profile city; yet without that height, noxious particles might get in our Guinness.

To those returning after an extended period abroad, the chimneys are a sure sign of home. They may seem a somewhat coarse emblem – lacking the grandeur of the Arc de Triomphe or Brandenburg Gate, perhaps – but they are what you see first when arriving by water and clearly signify Dublin Bay, much the way the Opera House does Sydney Harbour and the Golden Gate Bridge does San Francisco Bay: magnificent feats of imaginative architecture and practical engineering that have become so integral to the landscape, their removal would be keenly felt. (And the next time you curl up in front of the warm hum of your electric fire ready to enjoy yet another rerun of *Friends* on the telly, you can thank the Poolbeg Station for making it possible.)

Yet for all that, not everyone finds the chimneys visually appealing. Perhaps they could be enhanced. One recent proposal was to decorate them with twinkling lights, much in the way the Eiffel Tower was covered with strobe lights for the millennium, an enhancement that so charmed the French, a new allotment of high-tech fairy lights has been plugged in for special celebrations, such as when *Les Bleus* win the World Cup. Whether our chimneys get a similar treatment or not is pending although breath should not be held.

(One remembers the Countdown Millennium Timer that was inserted into the Liffey, perhaps in the hope of attracting eager celebrants who would join together in a mass counting down of the days until the advent of the magical 2000. Alas, the 'Chime in the Slime' disappointed. It seems the Liffey's water was too nutritious (which does not however imply that beneficial results might accrue from drinking it); the device became so obscured by algae it could no longer be seen in the murk and Y2K had to find its excitement elsewhere.)

Whether or not our chimneys get a tarting-up, and whether or not such an effort and expenditure improves matters, they will be our signature structure for the foreseeable future. That the symbol of industrio-Dublin is a pair of chimneys is not entirely inappropriate. Better them than 'The Spike' which, for all its warmth and charm, somehow fails to capture the soul of the city, at least not as well as did the much-lamented 'Floozie in the Jacuzzi'. And seen from sufficient distance, the chimneys do have a certain poignant appeal. On a clear autumn evening, with the first touch of chill in the air, hike around to the Baily Light on Howth Head and gaze west. There they are in the distance, emerging from a glittering scatter of city lights with their emitted vapour traces forming into elongated golden lozenges against the aquamarine sky perhaps, catching the last of the sunset rays even as the face of the bay itself broods darkly on . . . whatever bays brood on. Worse things could be there. An oil refinery would be worse, for example. Or an industrial incinerator.

Irishtown and Ringsend

Irishtown and Ringsend enjoy very little exposure to the bay. They are close to it historically – and geographically – but have been shoved into the background due to the physical alterations that have taken place over the years as land is 'reclaimed' for various uses, not all of which delight the senses.

Ringsend was originally a long narrow peninsula that was separated from the rest of Dublin by the estuary of the Dodder river. The Irish for peninsula is *rinn*, pronounced 'ring', so it seems likely the name came to mean 'the end of the peninsula'.

Locals call the place 'Raytown', reflecting its history as a fishing village; and two major Irish football clubs, Shelbourne FC and Shamrock Rovers FC, were founded in the area. There is also a long tradition of rowing with two clubs, St Patrick's and Stella Maris, and the traditional Ringsend Regatta still takes place annually. Ringsend took over from Dalkey in the seventeenth century to become Dublin's chief seaport. One dubious claim to fame is that in 1649, Ringsend was where Oliver Cromwell landed with over ten thousand soldiers and set off on his campaign of righteous slaughter. The name 'Irishtown' derives from an order issued in the middle of the fifteenth century that required all native Irish to depart from Anglo-Norman Dublin. The area now known as Irishtown was just outside the city walls then.

As with Fairview Park, attempts have been made to improve matters for those living near the desolation of industrio-Dublin at Poolbeg, and it seems churlish to be less than delighted by them. (And, as with the north-west corner of the bay, in the eighteenth century a gallows was erected at Ringsend for the edification of the locals.) Sean Moore Park is a wide, green expanse that links the eastern edge of Irishtown to the bay. There are benches, paths for strolling, and football pitches that provide a local venue for future incarnations of Keano to begin honing their skills. Ringsend Park and the new Irishtown Stadium with its eight-lane running track, glass-fronted gym and aerobics studio plus all-weather five-on-a-side pitches are further attempts at neighbourhood palliation.

Another entry on the 'things-aren't-so-bad-here' side of the ledger would seem to be Irishtown Nature Park. On fine days joggers follow the curved path around the inner slope of the bay and head out the length of Poolbeg Peninsula, their eyes lifted, gazing out over open water where dolphins frolic in the waves, or down Sandymount Strand filled with happy families bonding. Alas, the nature park isn't convincing. There are bay-facing benches spaced along the main path but rather more litter than is usually found in parks, and rather fewer visitors. It seems a little ragged and unkempt. A large, somewhat faded sign at the entryway testifies to the benefits to be gained from appreciating nature and displays the wide selection of plant species that grow there, ready to be appreciated. Many favourites are included: blackthorn, holly, alder, ash, you name it. The sign acknowledges that the whole area was once a former landfill dump which became colonised by plucky little plants eager to make the world a better place. Fair enough.

Yet there is a point at which one recalls why bank holidays tend to be spent elsewhere; and upon rounding a bend in the rising path, one is confronted abruptly by the hulking presence of the Ringsend Wastewater Treatment Plant, confirming the olfactory alarm bells that had already long since been sounding. This is not an area most people visit. No chapter in *Ulysses* was set here. It is not even on my Dublin Streetfinder

Irishtown Nature Park sign with Ringsend Wastewater Treatment Facilities

Colour Atlas & Guide; although in that the sewage facilities are not alone: much of the reclaimed land at Poolbeg has been left disquietingly blank, not unlike the empty areas on the edges of early seafarer's maps where, confronted by the unknown, mapmakers drew fanciful pictures of mythical monsters to indicate a certain unease at encountering what might be lurking out there. Squeamish locals may complain, but the sewage treatment facilities aren't going away. We will explore other, similar choices in 'The Future of the Bay'.

And there are positive things to report. The Irishtown Nature Park *has* become a viable habitat for many common passerines such as skylarks, linnets and reed buntings, as well as for kestrels, which one assumes hunts them there. The southern edge of Poolbeg down around to Sandymount is a protected area for wildlife, and perhaps hoping for the best is the best we can do, given some of the proposals currently under consideration for the development of what is today derelict land. Cormorants, gulls, waders and other wildfowl are drawn to the bay there, and a grassy field between the park and the sewage works was set aside as a feeding zone for brent geese although one wonders what they make of the noisome colossus beside them.

The bay itself has certainly profited from the new sewage treatment plant. It was not so long ago that raw sewage was sent spewing directly into the bay, with predictable results. The first sewage treatment plant established at Poolbeg removed the solid portion of polluted wastes from the city and settled it as sludge while the rest was released directly into the bay. The sludge was loaded onto a ship and dumped out where the bay meets the Irish Sea. In 1999, Dublin Corporation (now Dublin City Council) built the new waste water treatment works, which is also linked via a submarine pipeline to a pumping station at Sutton. As a result, there is now a single treatment facility that handles all the sewage of the entire Dublin area. Waste water is filtered, aerated and exposed to UV light before being allowed into the bay. Solid wastes are converted into a kind of fertiliser. As a result, Dublin Bay is cleaner than it has been for centuries, and our reward is the Blue Flag status at major sea-bathing venues at Dollymount Strand and Seapoint. It's all good . . . unless you happen to live downwind.

Of course, sewage treatment has to take place somewhere. (And the advent of a sewage treatment plant must stimulate the most fraught of all possible NIMBY reactions, understandably enough.) Nevertheless, the Irishtown Nature Park seems almost like a cynical attempt to mask the awfulness of what has been done – is being done; is planned for doing – to this part of the bay, and we should not feel like we have to accept a dump site overgrown with plants and pretend it's a garden, even if the plants are identifiable. Bull Island on the north side of the bay is a genuine nature preserve. The Irishtown Nature Park is a fraud that seems to exist mostly for its inclusion in an annual report.

Yet for all that, Sean Moore Park does give access to the bay; and when the tide is out, it's possible to walk on hard sand down the length of the south shore all the way to Seapoint, with only the need to circumvent the occasional stream emptying into the bay requiring ingenuity if not actual agility.

It is an open, invigorating world of sand, sea and sky that would be hard to overpraise, and one heads down into Sandymount Strand with a sense of relief. Gazing back at Poolbeg is not reassuring. Unlike on the north side, no attempt has been made to screen with trees the industrialisation that disfigures the shore. Perhaps that is more honest, with the stacks of shipping containers, and the ESB power station with its fuel tanks openly displayed. Or perhaps it is merely arrogant, the gesture of those who believe that the city and its economy are dependent upon them so they can do whatever they want.

Sandymount Strand

The strand at Sandymount is the functional opposite of that at Clontarf where the promenade is inviting but few care to venture into the muck at low tide (other than those seeking their beloved lug worms of course). At Sandymount, it is the strand at low tide that beckons; and although a similar walk south can be managed during high tides by following Strand Road and the sections of promenade and bike path which run along the shoreline, this is nowhere nearly as satisfying as on the north side. (Although it may be eventually; see 'The Future of the Bay'.) At Sandymount Strand – at least as we have it today – the tides are determinant.

Dollymount Strand on the north side of the bay is equally dramatic in the long pull-back of its tidal draw, although you have to journey out to see it, and casual passers-by on the north side are familiar with the mud flats of Clontarf or the lagoons at Dollymount. Yet Sandymount Strand at low tide is distinctively spectacular. Driving past it along Strand Road (aka Beach Road when closer to Irishtown) is always to experience the astonishing fact of just how far out on the strand you can walk. From the shore at low tide, there seem to be no limitations as the hard sand beckons. Posted warnings point out that what ebbs later flows so the unwary might find themselves in difficulties if too far from shore. For all that, little human figures – some equipped with dogs, others with small children, a few on their own – disperse themselves around the fantastic expanse of sand in random configurations, as if there were a subtle force directing their wandering patterns. There are other options on the hard sands of the low-tide strand – jogging and horse-riding both occur there, as does bait-digging for the endlessly desirable lug worm. Yet what that flat expanse of hard sand really calls for is casual, aimless wandering. And this at a place that is fairly uniform all over so that wherever you end up will not be remarkably different from where you started out. There is something seductive about all that openness that drags the stroller into it, as if we too are somehow urged outward by the draw of the moon.

When the tide is in, there is little to observe along the coast at Sandymount. A promenade/bike path runs the length of it until interrupted by shorefront houses just before Strand Road crosses the DART tracks and intersects with Merrion Road to produce Rock Road. The promenade and green are much narrower than the one at Clontarf and somewhat more oppressed by the busy traffic that flows endlessly on what has become a

Promenade along Sandymount Strand

major thoroughfare running down the south side. There are comparatively more car parks situated along the green than at Clontarf, too, suggesting use by visitors as much as by residents, and even the local Martello Tower seems marred by renovations that are ageing badly.

The houses along the Strand Road present a more varied selection than the similar neighbourhood facing the Clontarf promenade, with the road itself playing a more detrimental role due to the comparatively shallower front gardens. Bay views would be uniformly dramatic, of course; and there are some lovely old Georgians and Victorians mixed in with more modern designs as well as what would be considered fairly standard mid-level family housing, were it not for the desirable location. Not found are the kind of unified, elegantly classic terraces that make the sea front at Blackrock and Seapoint and Monkstown so impressive; although the strand is but a short walk inland to Sandymount Green and other equally splendid old neighbourhoods with the peaceful calm that makes this part of Dublin delightful.

Still, at high tide things feel cramped here, hemmed in. No doubt the road itself is at fault. Traffic on what is the main artery into the city is certainly continuous and at rush hours intense. But is there any solution, other than the very expensive proposition of an underground transit system such as are employed in other major cities? Adding more, wider roads will bring in more, faster-moving cars, leading to more congestion, more demands for parking and ultimately still more even wider roads. The San Francisco earthquake of 1989 levelled the elevated Embarcadero Freeway which had dominated – and disfigured – the eastern shoreline of San Francisco Bay. Its destruction was seized on as an opportunity to rescue the foreshore from vehicular traffic and return it to the city's citizens. This simple decision (not so simple at the time) today stands as one of the great demonstrations of the benefits of city renewal, and the eastern shore of SF Bay is now vibrantly alive. Dublin could do worse than learn from San Francisco's experiences with managing the scale of development. One hopes it will not require an earthquake to bring this point home.

The Sandymount Baths

The Sandymount Baths are a relic of what had once been one of the popular sea-bathing facilities that were constructed around the rim of the bay, with other notable derelicts still found at Blackrock, Dun Laoghaire and Clontarf. The baths now are a configuration of concrete walls with the back section missing. For a ruin, it is remarkably well maintained, painted a pleasant sand-coloured beige; and inside the main walls of the baths can be found what is arguably some of the most beautiful graffiti anywhere in the city – more characteristic of art school expertise than the puerile tagging indulged in by insufficiently occupied adolescents. The baths were once linked to the shoreline by a bridge, now gone, and pools of sea water were maintained at a constant depth to facilitate swimming in safety. This idea of contained fresh sea-water bathing seems quaint today, with our modern lap pools like the fifty-metre extravaganza near the Clontarf Road DART Station. Yet swimming in the sea is a fundamentally different proposition from the kind of mindless (if healthful) back-and-forthing in lap pools where the only distraction is the counting down of how many are left until you can quit. The continuing appeal of the Forty Foot in Sandycove, the Martello at Seapoint or the bathing facilities on Bull Wall in Clontarf demonstrate that some hardy folks, at least, still see the good in the bracing dip in the bay.

The derelict Sandymount Baths

The Booterstown Marsh

Currently, there is no bay-side transit through Merrion other than along Merrion Road, which borders the somewhat confined Booterstown Marsh before again becoming a promenade/bike path at Blackrock Park, albeit one totally blocked off from the bay by a stone wall on the far side of the DART tracks. The Booterstown Marsh is the only remaining salt marsh lagoon on the south shore of Dublin Bay, and as such it provides a glimpse of a natural habitat tucked within what is a distinctly urban setting. The marsh was acquired by An Taisce from the Pembroke Estate in 1971 and is managed as a protected environment with heritage significance. The area itself is a brackish lagoon marsh fed with both salt-water and fresh-water intakes, and it serves as a resting spot for migrating waterfowl. Dublin Bay is an internationally important feeding and roosting area for ducks, geese and waders, and it probably holds the highest concentration of wintering waterfowl of any Irish estuary, albeit with the majority of them on the north shore of the bay. Nevertheless, the Booterstown Marsh does represent the last fresh-water and salt-water natural habitat on the south side, and it deserves preservation for the benefit of species such as moorhens, reed buntings, sedge warblers, teal, snipe, lapwings, as well as various waders and seabirds.

Marshlands used to be a much more prominent feature along the south coast of Dublin Bay. Booterstown Marsh was part of Merrion Strand until early in the nineteenth century when reclamation and development began to destroy the fringe of lagoons, tidal pools and marshes that extended from Dublin City to Blackrock. In 1834, the new Dublin to Kingstown railway was built on a raised stone-faced embankment that cut across this part of the bay, and separated the marshlands and tidal lagoons from the

The DART at Booterstown

sea between Merrion and Blackrock. Eventually, the original lagoons along the coastline were filled in, leaving only the Booterstown Marsh and, in a somewhat more genteel form, the pond at Blackrock Park. From the mid-nineteenth century, the marsh area was grazed or cultivated, and cultivation ridges can still be detected on the eastern side of the marsh. Much of the lagoon was drained for growing crops during both World Wars, and this resulted in a restriction of in-flowing streams. After the land fell into disuse, marsh vegetation gradually reclaimed the arable land and the lagoon reformed itself, returning much of the salt marsh to its original state.

An Taisce has declared Booterstown Marsh to be an important bird sanctuary; although this gives it no legal protection, it does indicate its value to the community and should lead to its inclusion in the proposed National Heritage Area which will protect the shore and bay from Dun Laoghaire to Merrion Gates. It is also hoped that the Booterstown Marsh will become part of a proposed Special Area of Conservation for south Dublin Bay, further underscoring the ornithological significance of the marsh.

The marsh today seems to exist in a kind of awkward limbo, with no current access to it for visitors and its borders rigorously defined by Rock Road and the DART tracks. Booterstown DART Station dominates the south-eastern edge of the marsh, its curiously futuristic configuration of glass and steel suggesting the relative strength of the competing forces in operation here. (The DART station at Blackrock has a similar design.) Still, the marsh has managed to regenerate itself and better days may be coming. One certainly wishes the marsh well, for this part of the bay could use the encouragement of some natural venues. Nearby on Rock Road, the immense new Elmpark development seems to be a more typical example of what the future holds in store here, with the addition of more density to an already highly developed area.

Blackrock

The name comes from a black rock offshore that once marked the boundary of Dublin's city limits. Another marker, a slightly asymmetrical ancient stone cross, can still be found in the village and may indicate the site of what had once been an ecclesiastical edifice here of which no trace remains. Strollers chatting on their mobiles pass this old stone cross without a glance. Blackrock today is the site of the Blackrock Shopping Centre; yet the place still manages to maintain something of the feel of an old-fashion seaside village, with art galleries, boutiques, pubs, restaurants and cafes. (As well as a healthy selection of mobile phone supply outlets to ensure things don't become too twee.)

Blackrock Park extends from the Martello at Williamstown to the town of Blackrock itself; and although it is on the bay, it is totally cut off by the DART tracks which have a high stone seawall as a protection against the robust surges of high tides on the winter bay. The park itself is a lovely expanse of trees and green lawns, with a pond much favoured by seagulls that is a remnant of what had once been a tidal lagoon. Mothers with toddlers occupy themselves on the lawn, pensioners occupy benches, and preoccupied teenagers skulk at the perimeter of station-side facilities, fizzing with hormones.

Like the larger St Anne's on the north side, Blackrock Park is a precious urban amenity that happens to be beside the bay without involving itself particularly with it. Given the configuration of the DART tracks here, it could hardly be any different. (If we were doing it all over again now, would we return Blackrock's foreshore to it and site what is one of our most successful forms of public transportation elsewhere? And if so, where? Underground?)

For all the loss of its sea front, Blackrock is a charming seaside town that made the wise decision to route through traffic away from its narrow main streets. Not every urban area can have this option, of course, but those that do would be well advised to emulate Blackrock's success at re-establishing the more human scale of a pedestrian-dominated high street. Blackrock residents use their town well and visitors come for the pleasure of being there – and this without the draw of bay access! Perhaps some of it is simply habit. Blackrock was known as an important pilgrimage site in the middle ages, and it had evolved into a popular bathing resort in the eighteenth century. Grand houses were erected here and there, a few of which are still standing, Blackrock House and Newton House being visible from the street. The place was the domain of elite families at first; but day-trippers soon found it and venues for public entertainment were

Salthill DART Station

established to meet the needs of visitors journeying out from the city. Blackrock gained something of a reputation for the ready availability of its wines and spirits, sufficient to restore those chilled by a brisk dip in the sea or those in need of restoration simply at the thought of doing it.

Another derelict sea-bathing establishment stands just off-shore from the DART station here, almost as if connected to it, with the rusting blue diving platforms of the Blackrock Baths like bizarre extensions of the overpass stairs used to gain access to the opposite platform.

Perhaps the most impressive bay-related structure at Blackrock is Idrone Terrace, a large, sea-facing terrace south of the station, built in the nineteenth century and well maintained, as it deserves to be. The DART tracks are low here and unnoticeable, and the symmetrical terrace, with its uniform front staircases leading up to entryways and façades painted in various shades of cream, pale yellow and white, provides a pleasing and unified whole that speaks of the elegant values of an older Dublin. Modern Dublin is well represented in Blackrock by the UCD Michael Smurfit School of Business nearby, and the community here so pleasantly exemplifies one positive aspect of the quality of life to be found on the south side of Dublin that its lack of direct participation with the bay seems excusable.

Seapoint

Fluttering proudly from the top of the Martello Tower at Seapoint is a cheery sky-blue flag that guarantees nearby waters safe for bathing. The Blue Flag Programme indicates that things also get done right in a sometimes fraught world, and it is certainly fitting to see what was once a fortified gun emplacement meant to defend us from the depredations of Napoleonic warships now decorated with a new form of defence against an even more insidious waterborne foe: human sewage. (See 'Water Quality'.)

Extending north from the Seapoint Martello Tower is Brighton Vale, a sea-facing terrace with a few separate dwellings on the end that is as much a part of the bay as it is the shore. Brighton Vale was constructed in the nineteenth century and remains the only residential street located on the seaward side of the DART tracks between Merrion Gates and Scotsman's Bay. The consistency of design of this Victorian row of single-storey structures is wonderful, with each unit participating as a variation on a common theme of raised entryway doors bracketed by bay windows that here seem to take on a second meaning, the individual dwellings painted various pastels, shades of beige or whites and greys, all of it perfectly in harmony with the shoreline and the bay. Farther inland, on the slope above Seapoint Avenue, is Trafalgar Terrace, another example of the combination of the efficient use of space with

Martello tower at Seapoint

classical architectural elegance that derives from an earlier, slower time. (And may God strike with pustules and boils any developer who tries to replace these lovely old terraces with tower blocks of apartments!)

Seapoint seems the ideal place for the lazy days of summer. In fine weather, sun bathers and ocean swimmers gather at the stone platforms around the Martello Tower in a community of loyal users similar to those at the Forty Foot at Sandycove. It is social, pleasant, relaxed, healthful. It also feels rigourously local although one assumes interlopers would be tolerated, if not embraced. A sand beach extends down towards Monkstown and the first jetties of Dun Laoghaire Harbour, and on a hot afternoon will have a good assembly of families with kids, the odd dog or two. Yet the differences between Seapoint and Dollymount Strand would be hard to miss. Here at Seapoint things are small, low-key, residential; while at the wide-open spaces of the north-side's long strand, a vast summer multitude descends upon the middle sections of the strand where parking is allowed, utterly transforming the beach and nearby dunes.

Seapoint also marks the end of the sand banks of the South Bull, and so forms the southern boundary of the low tide walk from Sandymount. If the main activity at Sandymount Strand is aimless wandering at low tide, here it involves getting wet.

The beach itself at Seapoint opens to the south, facing Dun Laoghaire Harbour and consisting of sections of sand with large rocks interspersed as if by the hand of a designer. Swimming would be best here at high tide since the inlet is shallow. A slipway leading off the stone seawall provides direct access into deeper water and is much employed by serious sea-bathers whose heads can be seen south towards the jetties off Monkstown following a course well established by repetition. Surfing is said to be possible although it would be a fairly tame form of the sport, given the low bay waves (perhaps it is winter storm surfing); kayaking and canoeing would be a more probable choice. Seapoint has a manned life guard station throughout the bathing season. And although the bay between Blackrock and Monkstown appears benign enough on a warm summer day, one of the worst sea disasters to occur on Dublin Bay took place here in November 1807 when two ships were wrecked with the loss of hundreds of lives (see 'Famous Shipwrecks'.)

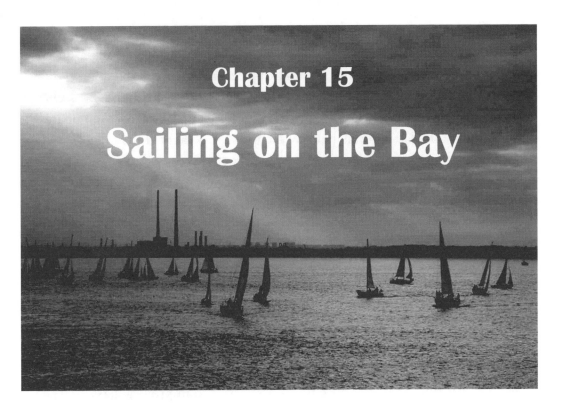

Chapter 15

Sailing on the Bay

Dublin Bay Sailing Club

Dublin Bay Sailing Club is the largest yacht-racing organisation on the Irish east coast; it provides regular weekly racing for everything from small dinghies to ocean-going forty-foot yachts.

Operating from Dun Laoghaire, the club's members are mostly drawn from the four local yacht clubs although visiting yachts are invited to participate. The club maintains a starter's hut on Dun Laoghaire West Pier but has no other premises. Racing runs from the end of April to the end of September, with slightly different schedules depending on the day of the week. Keelboats and dinghies race on Tuesday evenings and on Saturday afternoons while Thursday evenings host races for keelboats only.

Keelboat races start either on fixed lines on the seaward side of Dun Laoghaire West Pier or from a committee boat stationed not far from the harbour mouth and follow a fixed course extending from Salthill on the western side of the bay to the Burford Bank on the east and finishing at the line off the West Pier.

On Saturday afternoons, Dragons and J24s race on Olympic-style courses, joined occasionally by the Ruffian and Glen classes.

Dinghy racing on Saturdays takes place on Olympic-type courses in Seapoint Bay, while that on Tuesday evenings is in Scotsman's Bay. On certain Saturdays in June and July, racing is suspended to accommodate the annual one-day regattas held by the four local yacht clubs.

One-design Boats

One-design boats are so termed because the sailboat's hull conforms to the rules of whichever class it is in. One-designs are racing boats that compete with each other in regattas. In order to keep a level playing field, all boats in a class must be as alike as is enforceable.

This of course can make for some great sailing. One-design does not always mean absolutely identical. Some one-design classes allow for modifications in rigging or perhaps deck layout; others allow no variation whatsoever. It's all dependent on the specific rules – and these too can evolve over time or in response to sailors' desire to improve a class.

The Water Wag Class of sailing dinghy is the oldest one-design class in the world. Their origins began in Killiney, County Dublin, and they have raced regularly in Dun Laoghaire Harbour for about a century. Water Wags are fourteen-feet long and clinker-built, which means having overlapping external planks secured with clinched nails. Water Wags are usually sailed by two people. Water Wags adopted a modified design in 1900 by changing to a transom stern, but all boats still had to be of the same design and specifications so the concept of one-design racing was preserved. Today, Water Wags still maintain the traditions of their class, and proud owners sail these lovely old boats in Dun Laoghaire Harbour every Wednesday evening in summer. The oldest boats in this class are about ninety-seven years old; the newest boats were launched this season. Water Wags are easily recognised. They have distinctive silver-spruce planking, straight stem, and raked transom. Sails consist of a low centre of effort gaff rig, with the main boom extending aft of the hull. Sails carry a number between 1 and 40. The spinnaker is a colourful flat triangular sail which is only to be flown on its long pole when the wind is astern.

Howth Seventeen-Footer

Another legendary one-class boat is the Howth Seventeen-Footer. The first five craft appeared competitively in 1898, and the fleet was expanded by another dozen boats over the following sixteen years. Dun Laoghaire was home to about half of the fleet but eventually all the vessels ended up in Howth. The fleet size is traditionally regarded as comprising seventeen boats so the loss of two boats, the second sinking in 1984, resulted in the decision to build two further vessels. Accordingly, faithful attention to original specifications and skilful hands of apprentice shipwrights saw the construction and launching in 1988 of the *Isobel* and the *Erica*.

The Howth Seventeen is a sailor's boat. It requires an experienced hand to manage the 335 square foot of sail and the peculiar rig. The challenge makes mastery all the more rewarding.

South-side Yacht Clubs

The National Yacht Club has graced the waters of the Irish Sea and far beyond for more than a century. The present clubhouse was erected in Dun Laoghaire in 1870 to a design by William Sterling. The club had

Sailboat in Dun Laoghaire Harbour

been known by various names, including the Kingstown Royal Harbour Boat Club; the 'Absolute Club' although this change of name was never registered; the Edward Yacht Club; and finally the National Yacht Club. Sterling's design for the exterior of the club was a hybrid French chateau and eighteenth-century garden pavilion, and today it continues to provide elegant dining and bar facilities. The club provides a wide range of sailing facilities, from junior training to family cruising, dinghy sailing to offshore racing and caters for most major classes of dinghies, one-design keelboats, sports boats and cruiser racers. It provides training facilities within the ISA Youth Sailing Scheme and National Power Boat Schemes. The club is particularly active in dinghy and keelboat one-design racing and has hosted two World Championships in recent years.

The Royal Irish Yacht Club is situated in a central location in Dun Laoghaire Harbour. The Club was founded in 1831 and features the first purpose-built yacht clubhouse in the world. The building is now a listed structure and retains to this day all its original architectural features.

There are many racing, sailing and cruising classes active in the Club. The Dragon Class has a long association with the RIYC which has hosted many regional, national and international Dragon regattas over the years and is a favourite venue for Dragon events. Water Wags are another popular class at the club, as is the 1720 Club Sportsboat racing keelboat. Shipmans, Sigma 33s, J24s – the largest one-design class in the world, and considered ideal for family day sailing as well as fast competitive sailing. The RIYC hosted the J24 World Championships in 1990. Finally, Cruiser class ships are well represented at RIYC.

The Royal St George Yacht Club began as the Kingstown Boat Club, whose members' main interest was in rowing. Membership grew rapidly and well-known yachtsmen joined. The clubhouse was designed as a miniature Palladian villa in the neo-classical style. (The builder also constructed Sorrento Terrace in Dalkey.) Work was completed in 1843, but growth in membership soon required an extension of the original façade, which involved clever duplication of the existing Ionic portico with the erection of a linking colonnade between. The George has a long tradition of racing and cruising, with a wide range of classes represented, including Water Wags, IDRA 14s, and other dinghies, with about fifteen Enterprises, a very large dinghy that is excellent for both crusing and two-man racing. One-designs include 1720s, Dragons, Glen, J24s, DB24s, Ruffians, and others as well as cruisers and juniors such as 420s, Lasers and Mirrors.

North-side Yacht Clubs

The Sutton Dinghy Club was founded in 1940. Located on the south side of the Howth Peninsula with easy access to the whole of Dublin Bay, as well as to the sheltered waters of Sutton Creek, it is the leading dinghy sailing club on Dublin Bay. The club offers adult and juniors courses to provide the best introduction to sailing, using the thoroughly modern Laser Pico along with the more traditional Vaurien. The club also has a fleet of dayboats, consisting of a Jaguar 22, a Figaro 19 and a Caravelle, for those who prefer more stability.

The Sutton Dinghy Club racing season runs from April to October, with Club Racing on most Sunday mornings and on Wednesday evenings when daylight permits. Club Racing is based on class of boat, with classes currently raced including GP 14, Mirror, Laser, Optimist, IDRA 14, 420, and Laser Pico dinghies. Sailing also takes place through the winter months. A handicapping system gives everybody an equal chance of winning so that weak sailors are encouraged to improve and the Club champion does not walk away with every trophy at the end of the season.

The Clontarf Yacht and Boat Club is one of the oldest yacht clubs in Dublin Bay, having been founded in 1875. The club provides sailing and boating facilities for the greater Dublin area, and members participate in cruising, racing, fishing and general recreation on the water. Club members have attained National Champion status in E-Boats, Mermaids, Fireballs, GP14s, IDRA14s and Lasers. Club members are active in cruising, and CY&BC has earned a reputation as a club with a strong vibrant sailing fleet, with a potential to return a welcome invitation to ports visited.

Boats next to slip at Clontarf Yacht Club

The club is located on the coast road at Clontarf, and has achieved a reputation for its ability to host national and international events, including E Boat Irish National Championships, Fireball Leinster Championships,

IDRA14 Open, Mermaid National Championships and International Match Racing.

The cruising section of the club has built up a good relationship with a number of clubs on the West Coast of England and Wales, and cruisers from these clubs visit Clontarf. Also the club fleet visits Northern Ireland on a regular basis and are always well received and entertained by the host club. The club is active in advancing the sport of sailing by providing well-qualified instruction. Juniors sail in Optimists, Mirrors, 420s and Lasers; and during the summer, instructors are employed to provide a structured learning environment. Instruction is also offered to adults who wish to gain experience sailing a range of boats from dinghies to large cruisers. Adults with experience can also take advantage of courses based on internationally recognised ISA (Irish Sailing Association) standards.

Howth Yacht Club

Sailing has been associated with Howth since 1895 when the Howth Sailing Club was formed. In 1968, that club joined with the Howth Motor Yacht Club to create the present Howth Yacht Club, Ireland's largest sailing club and regarded as one of the premier racing clubs on the Irish sailing scene. An adult training course offers new members access to the sport of sailing while every summer, the Howth Yacht Club runs a junior sailing course, with instructors qualified to Irish Sailing Association standards.

The Howth Yacht Club operates with a 300-berth marina, additional moorings in the harbour and a large dinghy fleet. Howth sailors have won countless national and international championships, representing Ireland even up to Olympic level. The Club has also earned a reputation for its abilities in race management and has hosted numerous Regional, National, European and World Championships over the years. Howth has long been associated with the oldest surviving one-design keelboat class still actively racing in the world, the Howth Seventeen-Footer.

Chapter 16

Water Sports on the Bay

Coastal Rowing

The sport of coastal rowing can be traced to the mid-nineteenth century when boats and crews raced out to meet incoming schooners for the piloting contract. Fishermen also would race at dawn to be first at the best fishing grounds. What began as a means of earning a living evolved into a sport. Four-oar races and six-oar races were held, with only the six-oar competitions allowing boats that were built specifically for racing. Although the sport lost much of its popularity with the advent of modern, engine-powered boats; competitive coastal rowing has seen a resurgence in popularity, beginning in 1988 when two neighbouring rowing associations – one in Cork and one in Kerry – held a regatta pitting coastal rowers in these two very competitive counties against each other. The Irish Coastal

Rowing Federation today represents about fifty clubs around Ireland, four of which row on Dublin Bay: the Dalkey Rowing Club, St Michael's Rowing Club in Dun Laoghaire, and the St Patrick's Rowing Club and Stella Maris Rowing Club, both at Ringsend. A new 'one-design' boat was introduced in 2002 to standardise competition.

There are also more than a dozen non-seagoing rowing clubs in the Dublin area, including university clubs for men and women, affiliated to the Irish Amateur Rowing Union. Dublin Bay would be inappropriate for the sleek shells used in the sport of crew, but the Liffey hosts crew competitions and other events as well as pleasure rowing, so they are close to the bay if not actually on it.

Wind Surfing, Surfing and Kite Surfing

Wind surfing, at least, has become easier to enjoy thanks to improved equipment and better training courses. Just about anyone can enjoy the rush of taking off across the water, balancing against the power of the rig, enjoying the sun and the wind and the water. All forms of surfing sports are now more accessible, thanks to changes in design and advances in materials technology. Boards are lighter and more stable, and the rigs used for wind surfing and kite surfing are easier to control.

Which is not to say they aren't active sports that require a good deal of skill to master. Lessons are available, and various clubs and associations are there to help the novice get started. True wave surfing on the bay is improbable, to say the least; and although there are attempts to take advantage of winter storm tides, using the wind for propulsion is much more feasible.

The Irish Kitesurfing Association was set up to help those interested in getting started with this fascinating new sport, also sometimes known as 'kite boarding'. Managing the gear requires some expertise, particularly on blustery days, but practitioners can be watched off Dollymount Strand on any breezy summer day, with their occasional long floating leaps sailing high off the surface of the water particularly thrilling to watch. There is a Kitesurfing Training Centre based in Clontarf; training courses are scheduled for every weekend from March to October, with all equipment provided.

There is also a windsurfing centre based in Salthill, Dun Laoghaire that provides facilities for windsurfing and canoeing lessons; changing rooms are available and equipment can be hired.

Surfing tends to be better outside the bay, with a couple of schools in Malahide. One local option is the Surfdock Centre, located on the Grand Canal Dockyard in Ringsend, with surfing, windsurfing and sailing courses. Surfdock also runs junior courses and corporate nights, and stocks popular brands of water sports equipment and surf wear.

Canoes and Kayaks

Canoes originated on the lakes of Canada and aren't ideal for the rougher waters of the bay although they are seen there occasionally. The Irish Canoe Union was formed in 1960 and is recognised by the Irish Sports Council and the Olympic Council of Ireland (OCI) as the governing body

Kayaking in Sandycove

of the sport and recreation of canoeing in Ireland. Its mandate includes the promotion of canoeing in all its forms, the organising of competitive and recreational canoeing events, and the selection and training of competitors to represent Ireland at international events. They also arrange the holding of instruction in canoeing skills and techniques, and provide general services for anyone interested in or associated with the sport and recreation of canoeing.

There are over twenty clubs in Dublin, including sea scouts and university clubs, that actively support canoeing, kayaking and sea kayaking. The Irish Sea Kayaking Association is a voluntary group with the aim of developing and promoting the sport of sea kayaking in Irish waters. Sea kayaking is very popular on Dublin Bay, with many excellent sites for exploration around off-shore rocks and islands. The ISKA encourages the responsible enjoyment of our marine heritage and low-impact recreation. This includes sea paddling, exploration of and camping on deserted islands, education and safety. A strong emphasis is placed on training and education, in order that the sport can be enjoyed with minimal risk to the participants.

Dublin Bay Diving

Scuba diving and snorkelling are popular around the Irish coastline, with dive sites on the west coast considered world-class. The waters from Donegal to West Cork are filled with marine life, dramatic underwater scenery, and usually with excellent visibility. But Dublin Bay is also a rewarding location for underwater exploration, with dive sites appropriate for those still discovering the support as well as more challenging venues for the more experienced divers.

Scotsman's Bay is a good starting point for novice divers since it is a sheltered beach that provides relatively shallow water to practice. There isn't much to see, however, and visibility is poor unless divers access deeper water farther out from boats.

The Muglins and Dalkey Island are more exciting dive sites although they are only appropriate for experienced ocean divers. The Muglins is an oval rock north-east of Dalkey Island, and it is a very scenic dive, with nooks and crannies filled with marine life. The current can be strong here, and if it is too strong, divers often move around to Dalkey Sound on the inside of Dalkey Island. There's not as much to see as at The Muglins since the dive is in an open channel with a sandy bottom.

Wrecks are popular dive sites in Dublin Bay. The *MV Bolivar* struck the Kish Bank in 1947 and today lies in fairly shallow water so experienced ocean divers can explore the remains of the ship with fairly good visibility. The *RMS Leinster* is a large late-Victorian mail and passenger ship that was torpedoed by a German U-boat in 1918, with the loss of over 500 lives. The wreck is beyond the Kish Bank about twelve miles from shore, and although heavily damaged it is still largely intact. Permission to dive the wreck must be obtained from the owner. Moreover, tidal currents are strong in the area and the Stena Line HSS ferry to Dun Laoghaire passes nearby.

The *HMS Vanguard* is an intact mid-Victorian iron battleship that sank in 1875 and was only rediscovered in 1985. She is lying within the depth range for experienced divers, about fourteen nautical miles out to sea off Bray Head. The wreck lies on a sandy seabed, tilted over towards her starboard side. She is not often dived but provides a challenging and unique experience

Scuba Diving

for those divers who do explore her. As with all ships over a hundred years old, the vanguard is protected under the National Monument Act so permission to dive is required.

The Irish Underwater Council was founded forty years ago to organise and promote sport scuba diving and snorkelling in Ireland. When it began, there were only six Irish clubs, but the sport has grown and today almost eighty clubs are distributed all over Ireland with about half that number found at Dublin Bay. In addition to the usual activities associated with diving, members of the Irish Underwater Council also promote activities as various as underwater orienteering, snorkel races, underwater hockey and rugby, as well as underwater photography.

It is not all fun and games, however. The Scientific Commission promotes underwater biology and archaeology by organising courses on marine identification and co-operating with the Nautical Archaeology Society and the Irish Maritime Archaeology Society.

Dublin universities actively support diving in Dublin Bay. The University College Dublin SubAqua Club started in 1993 and has grown into a large group with almost 100 members, with a strong focus on training. UCD SubAqua can now instruct on all Irish Underwater Council training courses. At Trinity College, Dublin University Sub-Aqua Club (DUSAC) was founded in 1968 and is one of the most active diving clubs in Ireland, with a very good safety record. The club dives throughout the year in Dublin Bay, as well as around the country and abroad. DCU Sub-Aqua Club was founded in 2001 and is fast-becoming one of the most popular sports clubs on the campus. Finally, Aquatec is the diving club at the Dublin Institute of Technology.

Chapter 17

Water Quality

The Blue Flag

It seems a simple solution: if you have something you don't want, something unpleasant, something smelly, just toss it in the river and let the river flow flush it away. Out of sight, out of mind.

Civilisations are built on their waste-management capabilities. Imperial Rome was very good at it, medieval Europe less so. Middens and cesspits were ubiquitous in early Dublin, and today they provide fertile pickings for anthropologists and archaeologists. In seventeenth- and eighteenth-century Dublin, even wealthy homes still relied on cesspools for all kinds of domestic sewage, with the bay the ultimate destination. As the city grew, the problem did too. By the middle of the nineteenth century, the construction of a sewage system with water closets resulted in an increase of raw sewage flowing into the Liffey, transforming it into an immense open-air sewer that at low tide was almost unbearable for passers-by on the quays or bridges.

In 1896, an improved system of trunk sewers that ran along the north and south quays channelled wastes to a treatment facility at Ringsend from where it was released – slightly altered – into the Liffey estuary. Some poorer quarters continued to discharge their effluvia directly into local streams and rivers which fed the Liffey – the poor Poddle was a noisome stream at one time – and not until the 1980s was the entire system brought under a degree of control. Before the building of the new Wastewater Treatment Facility, there was a sewage treatment works in Ringsend, which removed about forty per cent of matter from the sewage then let the rest straight through into Dublin Bay. The 'sludge' as the solid matter was termed got loaded onto a ship and dumped out beyond the tidal currents of the bay. Once again, out of sight, out of mind. The effect this had on the sea floor seems to be debatable, but it could hardly have been positive.

Finally, in 1999, Dublin decided to build a single treatment plant to handle all the sewage wastes for the entire Dublin area. A pumping station was built at Sutton with a pipe under the bay that connects it to the new Wastewater Treatment Facilities on Poolbeg. The new system filters and aerates all wastes and exposes it to UV light before releasing the liquid into the bay. The sludge that is now produced is converted into a granular fertiliser, which is a big improvement to dumping it out on the Kish Banks. Although the new treatment plant has left locals unhappy with the smells, it has helped ensure that pollution from human wastes has been eliminated from the bay, resulting in water clean enough to bathe in and earning Dublin Bay its current Blue Flag status at popular bathing sites.

Visitors at Seapoint or Dollymount Strand – the bay's two Blue Flag bathing venues – are invited to examine the results of regular water quality tests. Rules of behaviour are also posted. (Interestingly, those hardy souls who choose the Forty Foot at Sandycove are not burdened with such information.) Measures of *E. coli* bacteria indicate relative water cleanliness, not because *E. coli* is such awful stuff but because it is an indicator of the pollution level of water in terms of how much human faecal matter it contains. The Blue Flag is awarded on a yearly basis, so continuing to qualify every year demonstrates how successful this aspect of the rehabilitation of Dublin Bay has been. Other nearby Blue Flag beaches farther north are at Donabate and Malahide; while to the south, Killiney and Greystones in County Wicklow also currently have Blue Flag status.

For a bathing site to earn a Blue Flag, it must display information relating to coastal zone ecosystems, update the information regularly, and also post descriptions of the Blue Flag Programme and regulations governing the qualifying area's use. The bathing site also must comply with all local regulations, it must be clean, with waste disposal bins available and regularly maintained, and there must be clean sanitary facilities with controlled sewage disposal. Lifeguards, lifesaving equipment and first aid supplies must all also be available. The list of requirements goes into more detail for various specific conditions but the overall promise of the Blue Flag Programme is that the bathing facility can be trusted as healthful and safe.

Chapter 18
Dun Laoghaire

The 'Disappointed Bridge'

The history of Dublin Bay returns again and again to the story of the struggle against silting and sand. In some ways, Dublin Bay is poorly suited for use as a port, particularly at the Liffey mouth where Dublin Port has its facilities today. The port itself evolved as it did over the centuries, and as ships grew larger and drew more water, what had once been solutions – building quays to narrow the Liffey and thereby deepen it – were found to be no longer adequate. If one had to create a new deep-water port to serve Greater Dublin today, the area at the Liffey mouth would probably not even make the shortlist. Nor, for that matter, would most other parts of the bay, with one possible exception: Dun Laoghaire.

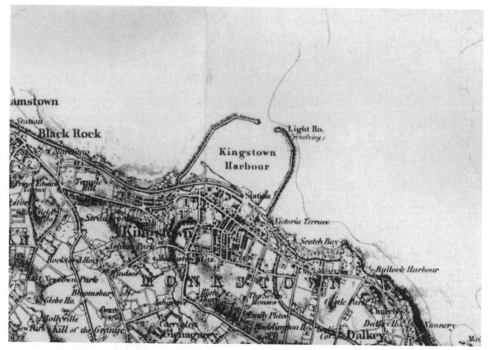

Detail from One-inch Ordnance Survey Map of Ireland, 1860
extract from Sheet 112

Dun Laoghaire Harbour, *aka* Kingstown Harbour and characterised by Stephen in *Ulysses* as a 'disappointed bridge', anchors the southern end of Dublin Bay much the way Howth peninsula and its harbour does the north side. The two are otherwise dissimilar. Dun Laoghaire is cosmopolitan, suburban, city-facing, civilised, engaged; Howth is remote, romantic, wild, and withdrawn, facing out into the Irish Sea (or at least that's part of the image of the place). At one time, the two areas competed to provide what Ringsend could not: a place of asylum in storms. Dun Laoghaire ultimately won out and has played a more important historical role in the growth of the city than has Howth; and while Howth retains the quiet charm of a sleepy little fishing village (albeit one with gourmet restaurants and stylish boutiques), Dun Laoghaire today functions as a vibrant component of Dublin City, and one must travel on down to Dalkey to find the south-side equivalent of Howth.

And why are fishing villages 'sleepy' (particularly little ones)? Is it because fishing is hard work and fishermen exhaust themselves? Or because the tangy sea air is itself somehow somnolent? Maybe it's caused by diet. Whatever the reason, people often claim they sleep well beside the sea so perhaps there is something inherently slumberous about it.

Dun Laoghaire takes its name from a circular fort – a *dún* – built on the coast by High King Laoghaire in the fifth century, perhaps sited at about where the bridge over the DART tracks to the Coal Harbour is today. No trace of it remains. From the Middle Ages to the sixteenth century, the protected waters between Dalkey Island and the mainland functioned as the best place to seek shelter from storms in the south bay; and the village of Dunleary, as it was called then, was little more than a dreary cluster of fishermen's houses arrayed along a creek, probably at around where the Purty Kitchen pub is today.

Although Ringsend was the usual point of embarkation and disembarkation during this period, records show that the Monkstown/ Dun Laoghaire coast was also used by travellers to reach ships riding at anchor there, and a small quay was built for this purpose. (Dun Laoghaire was, of course, still Dunleary then; we'll stay with the modern name for consistency.) During the Restoration, the Earl of Essex landed there on his arrival as Lord Lieutenant; and the appointment of an excise officer indicates the increasing importance of this part of the bay at the end of the seventeenth century, as does the stationing of a man-of-war offshore. Having warships on the bay was hardly pleasing to the locals, since they were vulnerable to being forced unwillingly into naval service, and reports of skirmishes against press gangs record injuries, sometimes severe.

By the eighteenth century, the Liffey channel into Dublin Bay had become too dangerous for large ships to enter, particularly during low tides; and vessels often had to await more favourable conditions. They found some safety in the deep pools at Poolbeg and Clontarf; but they also avoided the South Bull entirely or at least delayed facing it until the weather improved by mooring off the Monkstown/Dun Laoghaire coast as well as in the Dalkey Sound further south still. Passengers used small boats to come ashore, then made their way into Dublin by land. A coffee house was built in the village for their entertainment, and the area was already seeing the first signs of things to come. (The Purty Kitchen pub dates itself from 1728, making it the second oldest pub in Dublin, predated only by The Brazen Head on Bridge Street, and pretty much the oldest anything in Dun Laoghaire.) The south coast in the early eighteenth century was already becoming more than just a place of refuge from sandbars. Visitors were also beginning to come out from Dublin for the salubrious sea breezes, and like Blackrock, the village became popular as a sea-bathing location. Remarks published in the eighteenth century promised that honest residents and good ale could be found there, although visitors were cautioned to bring their own meat and wine with them.

Water-borne travel and trade continued to expand during this period, and with no good solution to the continued danger to shipping at the Liffey mouth yet determined, the popularity of Dun Laoghaire as a landing place led to the construction of a pier there built from locally quarried granite and completed in 1767. It extended 149 metres out into the sea and provided some shelter to the small local fishing fleet, as well as a landing site. Remarkably, it still exists today, tucked away down in the north-west corner of the modern harbour and enclosing what is called the 'Old Harbour'. Shipments of coal began arriving there in 1768, a year well-remembered because it also marked the completion of the South Wall at Poolbeg, leading to the eventual establishment of the Pigeon

A view of Kingstown Harbour and Dublin Bay

House Harbour at the Liffey mouth as the destination for mail packets in 1790. The Old Harbour at Dun Laoghaire was a handsome, semi-circular construction, enclosed by high banks of gravel along one side and by the pier itself, which together sheltered the small harbour from all winds except from the north-east. Nevertheless, like Howth Harbour and many other small harbours on the east coast of Ireland, it soon began filling with sand at a rate which the dredging capabilities of the time were unable to manage.

The story of the development of Dublin Bay as the main port for Ireland shifts from place to place. Within the span of fifty years, the completion of three major maritime civil engineering projects – the first pier at Dun Laoghaire (1767), the South Wall and lighthouse at Poolbeg (1768), and the harbour at Howth (1813) – stipulate the three Dublin Bay regions which were to compete for preeminence throughout the first half of the nineteenth century. Succeeding projects – the construction of the asylum harbour at Dun Laoghaire and the building of the two Bull Walls – shifted the balance of power clearly to the centre and the south coast of the bay. One wonders how different Dublin Bay might appear today had the Sutton side of Howth been chosen for a harbour, naturally shielded as it is from the fierce north-eastern gales which caused such havoc with mariners.

Throughout the latter half of the eighteenth century, the Viceroys and their families continued to use Dun Laoghaire for their arrivals and departures, as did various British notables and other VIPs. Even after the Pigeon House at Ringsend had been established as the primary destination of the mail packets from England, passengers were still sometimes put ashore at Dun Laoghaire when the weather was bad. Nobody wanted to tempt the bulls that still made the approach to the Liffey mouth so treacherous.

The Asylum Harbour

Dublin Bay needed both a reliable port and a place of refuge. The port at the Liffey mouth had long since become firmly established as the commercial port, the place for loading and off-loading cargo, and a wide range of

Carlisle Pier

ancillary interests – customs, carting, warehousing – insisted that it remain so. Ringsend was also linked to the Shannon River and the midlands via the Royal Canal and the Grand Canal and so formed a key entrepôt for the central portion of Ireland. Nevertheless, for all that, Dublin Port was so insecure when the tide was out or when storms were churning up the waves on the bay that other options were deemed necessary. Ships were being wrecked, cargo destroyed, lives lost. Even if the port was to remain at Ringsend, a place of real asylum must be created nearby.

One early idea was to establish a deep sea harbour at the relatively secure section of deep water between Dalkey Island and the shore. Laying up on the lee side of Dalkey Island provided some shelter from storms blowing out of the north-east. Another idea was to build a new, larger harbour at Dun Laoghaire that could be used as a place of asylum. But an interesting addition to the argument in favour of building the asylum harbour at Dun Laoghaire was the suggestion that a canal could be extended from Dun Laoghaire to the Grand Canal Docks at Ringsend, eliminating the need to enter the Liffey directly. The north side also managed to include itself in the debate, bringing forward the suggestion that the asylum harbour should be built at Sutton or on the north side of Howth; and for many of these plans too, the structural designs and estimated costs often included a ships' canal to link to the capital.

Improbably, Howth turned out to be the winner; yet even as Howth Harbour was being completed (and before it had begun silting up), plans for a new harbour at Dun Laoghaire were still under consideration.

Early in this debate, the famous Scottish civil engineer John Rennie was brought in. Rennie was responsible for numerous canals, docks, harbours and bridges in the British Isles, and he is still considered one of the most distinguished civil engineers of the age. His opinion mattered, and he had declared his preference for Dun Laoghaire as the best site for a new harbour in Dublin Bay and held to it firmly despite the nod going to Howth. Moreover, John Rennie was a fervid canal man. Perhaps an inland coastal waterway would become the ultimate solution.

The Ships' Canal

Rennie's plans for Dun Laoghaire included a double-armed harbour with a system of locks that would neutralise the effects of tidal flow, maintaining a constant water level on the inland waterways and permitting continuous traffic. The canal would gain access to Dublin Port at the Grand Canal Docks, which also would have to be managed against the tidal flow of the Liffey estuary. Thus, this proposed new harbour at Dun Laoghaire would be both a safe asylum harbour and one of the most innovative commercial docks anywhere in Ireland, using Dublin Port and the two existing canals to route cargo inland.

Rennie died in 1821 without seeing his dream realised. There was always another option being mooted, the one that in the end proved successful. The scouring effect created by the Great South Wall proved that the concept was valid. The construction of the North Bull Wall in 1824 appeared to be deepening the Liffey channel sufficiently to indicate that direct access to what was already well established as Dublin's primary port would become feasible, even for larger vessels. There was no reason for the expense of funding a new canal, opponents argued. Ships would simply

Dublin and Kingstown Railway, from the footbridge at Sea Point Hotel looking towards Salt Hill

sail straight into the now-deepened river channel and off-load at the port docks right in the centre of the city. Nothing could be more convenient.

These decisions were not reached lightly. Dun Laoghaire and Ringsend were still in competition for predominance (Howth Harbour had silted itself out of contention); but in the end, the idea for a coastal canal was rejected as impractical, given the topography in question and the Liffey's tidal variations at the bay-side quays. The new Dublin-to-Dun Laoghaire railway (Ireland's first and the world's second) which was completed in 1834 was sufficient to end forever the consideration of a new canal. Dun Laoghaire would be used as an asylum harbour, as it had originally been intended, and Dublin Port at Ringsend would be the region's main commercial port. Interestingly, the railway that had seemed like a possible fallback should it become necessary to transport cargo from Dun Laoghaire into the city never functioned that way: it was for passengers only.

Building the Harbour

The original plan approved a harbour with a single pier – what would eventually become today's East Pier – but at an early stage of construction, John Rennie, who had been appointed as a directing supervisor, sought a second pier as well as an extension of the original pier, arguing that this new design would force sand and other drifting deposits across the mouth of the harbour rather than into it. Rennie's expanded plan was finally agreed to by Parliament in 1820.

King George IV leaving Kingstown Harbour

King George IV visited Ireland in 1821 and departed from Dun Laoghaire on the royal yacht. To mark this occasion, the town renamed itself Kingstown and the harbour became the Royal Harbour of George IV. A nice monument marks the occasion. The royal departure itself was fraught. HRH embarked and set sail, putting out along the coast of Wicklow only to be driven back by high winds and rough seas. Until the storm abated, the king was obliged to take shelter at the very pier he had left from, his royal self much inconvenienced by the storm. One wonders if the local dignitaries and well-wishers all reassembled, with the help of a military band, perhaps, and stood on the pier in sodden uniforms in the rain waiting gamely once again for the kingly departure. Whether or not that happened, the utility of an asylum harbour had certainly been demonstrated, and construction proceeded apace. The whole region was soon bustling with activity. By 1823, at the peak of the quarrying and construction phase, there were between 600 and 800 workers on the Dun Laoghaire Harbour project.

Stone for the harbour was extracted from a quarry at Dalkey Hill. It was transported down to the building site on a funicular railway composed of paired sets of three trucks, each of which could carry about six tons of rock. The truck-sets were linked together with a continuous chain and ran on a track of iron rails. The tracks descended steeply from the quarry to about where the present railway bridge is at Barnhill Road. Part of it can still be seen near Dalkey Avenue, and the path along the railway from Dun Laoghaire to Dalkey is still known as the 'metals'. The tracks then continued towards the harbour in a series of further funicular inclines. Although most of the stone used to build the harbour came from the Dalkey Quarry, some was also sourced at Glasthule where a Martello Tower had once stood, at about where People's Park is today. Stone also came from an area known as the Churl Rocks, today's Moran's Park.

The funicular railway was ingeniously engineered. At the top of the hill at the quarry, a huge friction wheel was mounted vertically between two massive frames with a second, smaller wheel at the bottom of the hill. The weight of the full trucks going down pulled the empty ones back up, and a brake mounted on the friction wheel regulated their speed. On flat ground, horses were used to pull the trucks along the rails and around to the construction site. The system was certainly efficient; and it was said that the granite was 'poured into the sea' at a rate of about thirty metres a month.

By 1840, sufficient stone had been transported to the harbour and the funicular railway was closed down, with the section of track between Glasthule and Dalkey sold to developers and repurposed as part of the mysteriously named 'Atmospheric Railway', which ran for about ten years then dissolved into the swirling mists and was seen no more. (See 'Sandycove to Dalkey'.)

John Rennie's original scheme had proposed a harbour mouth that was 450 feet (137 metres) wide, ending at pier heads with short jetties. An opposing view held that given the prevailing winds, such an entrance was too narrow for safe entry, and a much wider entrance was proposed, with a breakwater some 1,200 feet (366 metres) outside the harbour mouth, shielding it against wave surge. A third proposal was brought forward that advocated extending the East and West piers, resulting in an entrance that would be 650 feet (198 metres) wide, which was thought required in order to prevent the formation of a sand bar. Decisions by Parliament to proceed, and the arrival of money to do so, came in fits and starts. Both piers had reached a penultimate state of construction around 1831, with the final decision regarding the harbour mouth still fiercely contested. Delays became an embarrassment, and it was decided finally in the early 1840s that the piers would be terminated as they are today with rounded-pier heads, resulting in a harbour mouth 750 feet (229 metres) wide.

Samuel Lewis's *Topographical Dictionary of Ireland*, published in 1832, gives a good description of the make-up of the two piers:

'The foundation is laid at a depth of 20 feet at low water, and for 14 feet from the bottom the piers are formed of fine Runcorn sandstone, in blocks of fifty cubic feet perfectly square; and from 6 feet below water mark to the coping, of granite of excellent quality found in the neighbourhood. They are 310 feet broad at the base, and 53 feet on the summit; towards the harbour they are faced with a perpendicular wall of heavy rubble-stone, and towards the sea with huge blocks of granite sloping towards the top in an angle of ten or twelve degrees. A quay, 40 feet wide, is continued along the piers, protected on the sea side by a strong parapet nine feet high.' (Caroline Pegum, 'The Background History of Dun Laoghaire Harbour', November 1996; Dun Laoghaire Harbour Company website)

Little is known of the workers who laboured under extremely difficult conditions. Many lived with their families in shabby huts and stone cabins they had built themselves on Dalkey Commons or at other common lands near the work site. Most were locals from Dublin and Wicklow, but there were also skilled stone-cutters brought in from Scotland. Life on Dalkey Commons would not have been particularly pleasant for any of them. The huts and cabins seldom had sanitary facilities. Drinking water came from local springs that became polluted by the discharge of raw sewage, resulting in outbreaks of typhus and cholera. It was a hard life. The work was arduous and dangerous, with the use of blasting at the hillside quarry particularly hazardous; injuries were frequent, and the lack of available medical treatment led to maiming, disfigurement and death. Records of the Harbour Commissioners and the Commissioners of Public Works who took over the project in 1831 are filled with petitions and pleas and complaints from the families of workers who were injured or killed.

Complaints about the behaviour of these impecunious new residents in the Dalkey area were also common. Local landowners complained that workers were squatting illegally in Dalkey and tried to get them evicted although no other options were made available to them. Theft from the harbour was a problem, hardly a surprise given that pay was poor and the cost of living exorbitant in what was at the time a legitimate 'boom town'. Workers petitioned the Commissioners following a reduction in their weekly wages, pleading that they were required to live in 'the dearest market in Ireland' where food was too expensive, and any form of

Dun Laoghaire Harbour mouth

lodging was double what could be demanded anywhere else in the country. Whether they received any relief or not is unknown.

There were riots and insurrections, inevitably related to working conditions; but even during the grimmest times the labourers would have found some consolation in the fact that they retained their freedom. Not so the unfortunates who were languishing in the prison hulk *Essex* which was permanently moored in the harbour from 1824 to 1837. Prison hulks were ships with their masts removed that were used to warehouse convicts awaiting transportation to Australia. The *Essex* hulk – an American frigate that had fought against the British in the Pacific and was captured in 1814 – was moored about fifty yards off the East Pier, roughly opposite what is now the National Yacht Club. The prisoners were never allowed off the hulk and were not used in the construction of the harbour. (The last transport ship carrying convicted prisoners from Ireland to Australia set sail from Dun Laoghaire Harbour in 1853, bound for Fremantle, Western Australia, where it arrived just in time to celebrate the construction of Fremantle Prison, the last establishment built by convict labour in Australia and today one of Western Australia's premier cultural heritage sites.)

A moveable floating lighthouse had been maintained at the end of the East Pier during construction; it was replaced by the current lighthouse with its battery emplacement in 1842, bringing the great asylum harbour of Dun Laoghaire to completion. Considered one of the most magnificent harbours in what was then the British Empire, the East Pier reached a final length of 1,290 metres and the West Pier was 1,547 metres. Together, they enclose 251 acres of water.

As the main work on the piers was wound down in the 1830s and 1840s, more and more workers were being laid off with little hope for finding alternative employment. The lucky ones were kept on to finish the pier heads and the East Pier lighthouse. The Victoria Wharf and the new coast guard station would also have provided some employment, as would the building the anemometer on the East Pier. But most of the labourers were out of luck. They petitioned the local authorities for relief, only to be denied – a sorry end to an otherwise admirable project.

Dun Laoghaire Harbour joins the Great South Wall and North Bull Wall to comprise the three most impressive feats of marine engineering on

Dublin Bay. The sleepy little fishing village of Dunleary – once dismissed as the 'inconsiderable and dirty abode of a few fishermen' – was well on its way to becoming Kingstown, a fashionable seaside resort, although the labourers whose efforts made it possible probably had little reason to celebrate.

Perhaps they celebrated anyway. In 1832 an anonymous letter writer complained that there were thirty-seven public houses operating in the town, to the detriment of the morals of the locals, no doubt. For all that, the work got done and the resulting harbour is a credit to the perseverance of those who planned it and the tenacity of those who built it.

The Growth of Dun Laoghaire

In addition to the name he left behind, King George IV's departure from Dun Laoghaire in 1821 conferred a new status on the region as well as on the harbour piers then under construction. The growing town expanded up the hill facing the harbour, with George's Street, originally the connecting track between the pair of now demolished Martello Towers that once kept locals safe from Napoleon, forming the main thoroughfare. In 1826 the mail service from Britain was transferred from Howth to Dun Laoghaire. It was first accommodated by a wharf near the present bandstand on the East Pier then moved to the Traders Wharf immediately to the east of the Old Pier. In 1859, the Carlisle Pier – designed to accommodate the largest steamboats then in use – was opened and the mail service continued at that location until the mid-1970s. Even during World War I, the mail boats sailed, although the loss of RMS *Leinster* to a torpedo twenty-six kilometres from Dun Laoghaire Harbour resulted in over 500 deaths. The Carlisle Pier, now a sad derelict, was also the site of the slip for the first lifeboat service, and the splendid new Life Boat House is next to it. The future of the Carlisle Pier is under consideration, with common agreement that it should not simply be left to deteriorate further.

The opening of Ireland's first railway in 1834 linked Westland Row and the new harbour, ensuring the continued development of Dun Laoghaire as a commercial success and driving the rapid expansion of the town as a fashionable place to live. The railway – and the improvement to Dublin

Port resulting from the building of North Bull Wall in 1824 – also ended forever the plan to create a canal linking the harbour to the Liffey.

In 1860, Dublin Steam Packet Company ships crossed to Holyhead in about five hours and forty minutes. Fifteen years later, this had been reduced by two hours, and in 1896, the crossing could be made in just under three hours. The railway met the packet ships on the Carlisle Pier, making Dun Laoghaire an integral part of the national rail network and conveniently linking Ireland to Britain. The railway was not intended for cargo, however, and facilities for managing heavy freight were never developed at the new harbour.

Coal had been part of the story of the Old Harbour, and the coal-importing business continued to be exceedingly active at the new one. In 1835, there were already twenty registered yawls importing coal. The Outer Coal Harbour was constructed in 1855, and within a few years, coal was easily the biggest business in town, although today not a trace of it remains.

The East Pier Battery

It would be a poor facility indeed that didn't create within the soul of the imperial Britisher the desire to mount a gun somewhere on it. Conquerers must defenders be (which perhaps helps explain why Beckham doesn't start for England anymore).

A defensive battery had long been established at Glasthule but was rendered strategically useless by the construction of Dun Laoghaire Harbour. It was demolished in 1843 to make way for the Dublin–Kingstown railway line which was being extended as far as Dalkey. In 1857, construction began on the current defences, a circular battery on the eastern pier-head once armed with massive cannons. (One benefit of building it, proponents argued at the time, would be to provide employment for the working classes during the winter months. Fair enough.)

The battery was entered through a barrel-vaulted passage that led from the pier to the ground level magazines where the ammunition was stored. There was an upper battery with three gun platforms and a lower battery, also with three more platforms. In the fort were quarters for officers and soldiers designed to accommodate twenty-four men.

The 1860 edition of the *Official Railway Handbook to Bray, Kingstown and the Coast* contains the following description:

> Round the lighthouse has been lately built Kingstown Fort, a small but powerful defence should an enemy show himself within range. From its prominent position it commands the whole bay; it is completely manned, has many guns of large calibre, a powerful magazine, and a means of heating balls to a white heat. The walls round it are curved at the tops so that any balls striking them would glance away harmlessly.

Gun shot was heated in a furnace, and it must have taken a good deal of time to reach the desirable 'white heat' stage, which suggests a more leisurely form of warfare than we enjoy today. One can imagine the defenders spotting a dubious sail on the horizon and scrambling to get the buns in the oven then breaking for tea while they baked.

East Pier light with battery

The armament installed in the fort consisted of three 68-pound guns mounted over casements on the upper battery, four 32-pounders on the lower level and one or two 24-pound guns which could be used to fire directly into the harbour itself. Firing from a steady platform gave shore batteries an advantage over attacking ships, and the three 68-pound guns facing out at open sea were formidable weapons that commanded a considerable range with great accuracy. For all that, no attack has ever been launched against Dun Laoghaire Harbour. The battery's history is happily uneventful and it was – and is – used mostly for the firing of gun salutes, being one of two such installations in the country, with Spike Island in County Cork hosting the other. Stripped of its armaments at the beginning of the twentieth century, bedecked in fairy lights as was the whole harbour, the battery fired its blanks in 1907 to welcome of King Edward VII and Queen Alexandra on their royal visit to Ireland.

Dun Laoghaire Today

The current harbour stands pre-eminent among Dublin Bay's most impressive marine engineering feats, and examples of fine workmanship are everywhere, with the massive granite bollards along the East Pier particularly impressive. The coal industry is long since gone from the harbour, and the fishing industry has declined to the point of irrelevance. Some of the old facilities are still in operation, with the new Life Boat Station Visitor Centre a prominent addition.

The Dun Laoghaire Harbour Company was established under the Harbours Act of 1996 and charged with developing Dun Laoghaire Harbour as a marine tourism gateway to Ireland, maintaining and enhancing the recreational

Dun Laoghaire Lifeboat Service

and amenity value of the harbour and promoting investment and commercial development to support the historic harbour's long-term maintenance. All available evidence seems to point to its successful realisation of this mission.

Onshore, the Victoria Fountain has recently been restored to the ornate – if somewhat excessive – style beloved in that extravagant age, with its predilection for elaborate details and decoration. The Victoria Fountain was manufactured in Glasgow and erected on the foreshore to commemorate Queen Victoria's visit to Dun Laoghaire in 1900, a year before her death. The Germanic queen's monument was badly vandalised in 1981 but is now restored and reinstated to its original glory, not far from another reminder of the vagaries of the past: the anchor of the *Leinster*, cruelly sunk by a German torpedo in 1918.

Walking the Piers

The East Pier (1817–23) seems the more inviting of the two for strolling while fishermen tend to cluster on the West Pier, perhaps due to the proximity of the Trader's Wharf with its ice plant that was established in 1972, leading to the addition of a fish market there.

Near the entry of the East Pier is the inshore lifeboat station, a lovely old granite building constructed in 1800; and an all-weather lifeboat is moored in the harbour (see 'Lifeboats'). Out on the pier itself is the somewhat shabby bandstand and glass-sheathed audience shelter, both erected in 1890 and awaiting the council to get around to refurbishing them. Farther out still is the Boyd Memorial, erected in the memory of Captain Boyd and his crew who drowned in a rescue attempt in 1861. Just down from the Boyd Memorial is the old anemometer, established in 1852 and upgraded into an automatic weather station in 2000; and at the end of the pier is the East Pier Lighthouse and battery, beautifully constructed works of civil engineering art that were built of granite blocks in 1850s.

The shore between the piers houses several notable structures. Just inside the East Pier is the National Yacht Club, an elegant old building designed by William Stirling in 1870. The Royal St George Yacht Club is on the foreshore between the Carlisle Pier and the Car Ferry Pier, and the Royal Irish Yacht Club – the first purpose-built yacht club in Ireland and opened in 1848 – is just to the west, with the yacht marina behind it, sheltered by a curved breakwater. Farther west still is the Dun Laoghaire Motor Yacht Club, established in 1958 (see 'Sailing on the Bay').

The north-western corner of Dun Laoghaire Harbour is the oldest part of it. The original 'Old Harbour' extends up to about where the still-existing Old Pier from 1767 is, and out from this is the Traders Wharf, constructed in 1855, which in turn shelters the original Coal Harbour. On shore near the Traders Wharf is the King Laoghaire Stone, marking the site of the ancient ring fort (*dún*) from which the town gets its name.

The West Pier (1820–27) is the longer of the two, with a breakwater extending well out into the harbour. The Dublin Bay Sailing Club's Starters Hut is just above the breakwater junction and serves as the nerve

Dun Laoghaire's East Pier

centre for many of the races held in the south bay. Farther out on the West Pier is the original Lighthouse Keepers House, a lovely granite structure built in 1863. Like the East Pier, the West Pier terminates with a lighthouse erected in the mid-1850s.

The Commissioners of Irish Lights first established workshops in the harbour in 1875. Today their depot includes mechanical, electrical and electronic workshops for the overhaul of navigation aids, the fabrication of marine equipment and the re-fitting of boats. Their state-of-the-art ship

Stena Line boat in Dun Laoghaire Harbour

the *Granuaile* is used to manage the system of buoys and lights that make Irish waters safe, and it can often be seen loading and unloading stores and navigation aids in the harbour. (See 'Lights on the Bay' for more.)

The Marine Activity Centre is located at the base of the West Pier, behind the Dun Laoghaire Motor Yacht Club. It was opened by Roinn na Mara in June 1989 to provide a facility for training in sailing and other water sports, safety training courses and lectures on marine matters. Three organisations operate in the centre: the Dun Laoghaire Vocational Educational Committee, the Irish National Sailing School and the Irish Youth Sailing Club.

The Dun Laoghaire Harbour Sea Scouts, an Irish-speaking troop, are based in this corner of the West Pier, next door to the Irish Youth Sailing Club. The St Michael's Rowing Club maintains the tradition of skiff rowing in Dun Laoghaire that originated in the nineteenth century when 'hobblers' used to race against each other to reach arriving ships and offer their unlicensed services as pilots. (Hobblers were supposed to restrict themselves to tying up ships at docks, but the temptation to pilot them was hard to resist.) The St Michael's Rowing Club was formed in the 1920s by redundant hobblers and members of the famous Workman's Club who instructed the young men from the area in the skill of rowing. This tradition has continued down to the present day, and club members can often be seen rowing out from their base in the Coal Harbour.

SID, as 'The Sailing in Dublin Club' is known, is based in Dun Laoghaire and offers people who love sailing the opportunity to sail regularly without having to buy a boat. The club provides a fleet of dinghies for one or two-person use, and a yacht which can carry up to six people.

Dun Laoghaire today

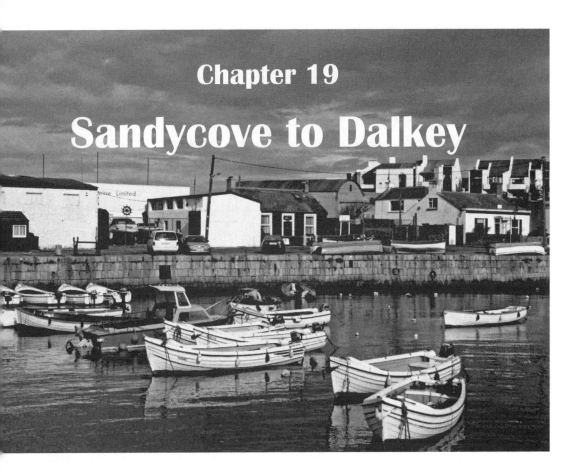

Chapter 19
Sandycove to Dalkey

Scotsman's Bay

Dun Laoghaire Harbour and its town fit together as a self-contained unit that appears neatly bifurcated: half land, half water. No other portion of Dublin Bay feels quite so equally balanced. Howth, for all its quaint harbour and popular sea-angling spots, is a lump of land mostly: gorse, heather, bracken, limestone, then rhododendrons and the bright emerald green of golf fairways; bay and sea surround it as a backdrop, always there but at a distance. So too with other regions. Clontarf is suburban, residential, as is posh Dalkey. The nature preserve at Bull Island seems closest, perhaps: an ecosystem balancing dunes and lagoons, beaches and bay water; a place where the hand of man has been lightly employed; while the diametric opposite would be the Liffey mouth, bracketed by Poolbeg and the port facilities that together form the heart of industrio-Dublin where the hand of man is being employed very heavily indeed. (Which is not to say that we don't need a port, or that we might try and get by without electricity.)

The bay at Dun Laoghaire feels like an amenity that is being used but not abused. The great civil engineering efforts of the nineteenth century have been preserved and advanced through the twentieth and into the twenty-first. Although Dun Laoghaire is growing, with huge new developments facing out over the harbour, it doesn't feel out of balance – at least not yet (see 'The Future of the Bay'). Perhaps it's a matter of scale, with the very large harbour – it encloses 250 acres of water – sufficient to hold the onshore developments in equilibrium. The two lovely church spires have not been overwhelmed by modern buildings looming above them, unlike the way churches in Manhattan sit forlornly in the shadows of neighbouring skyscrapers. Or at least, it hasn't happened yet. Perhaps Dun Laoghaire's greatest piece of good fortune was not to have been converted into a primary commercial port for the bay, despite the efforts of the brilliant Scottish engineer John Rennie, who hoped to link his asylum harbour to the city's port at Ringsend with a canal.

Scotsman's Bay curves gently between the East Pier of Dun Laoghaire Harbour and the dramatic outcropping of rock that thrusts itself out into the bay, enclosing Sandycove beach and forming the celebrated Forty Foot. Just south of the East Pier are the derelict Dun Laoghaire Baths, like those at Clontarf and Blackrock, an old-fashioned form of entertainment that no longer seems viable on the bay. The baths were constructed between 1905 and 1911, replacing the Royal Victorian Baths dating from 1843; they consisted of an entrance building, an open-air pool and a toddler's pool fed by tidal seawater, with heated indoor pools added in the 1970s. Many locals will have childhood memories of happy days spent at the baths, and the pools and other facilities retain their shapes – the elongated rectangle for serious swimmers here, the shallow pool for toddlers there – which makes the sight of them decaying in the summer sun even more dispiriting. Something needs to be done with these forlorn relics on the foreshore. (The Sandymount baths could be retained as a curiosity, requiring only the occasional fresh coat of paint.) Moreover, the location of the Dun Laoghaire baths between the East Pier and Scotsman's Bay makes them

The Dun Laoghaire Baths in better days

a tempting site for potential real estate development, which has not gone unnoticed, unsurprisingly (see 'The Future of the Bay'.)

A promenade walkway follows the shoreline around Scotsman's Bay, with a wide green separating most of it from the road and residencies of Glasthule and Sandycove. It is actually two walkways, one at street level and another right on the breakwater so that during storm tides it would no doubt become impassable. Various configurations of staircases connect the two levels in places, and the design of it seems almost a visual extension of the complex southern embankment of the East Pier with its various staircases, medial platforms, benches and cannons erected here and there. At the mid-point of the Sandycove Promenade is the large bronze sculpture of a sea urchin, a perfectly suitable act of enhancement that characterises the pleasant atmosphere of the shoreline here. One of the area's better seafood restaurants, Cavistons, is nearby although it serves only at lunchtime.

The 'sandy cove' would be hard to miss on a warm summer afternoon. A couple of patches of sand interspersed with rocks form the southern edge of the inlet. Beyond the cove is the outcropping of rock crowned with the Sandycove Martello of James Joyce fame, and the Forty Foot is just up the

Aerial view of Sandycove

hill or around the rocky point. Another foreshore derelict, the Sandycove Baths, with a small, overgrown and littered park nearby, is totally out of keeping with the general ambience of the cove and almost spoils what is otherwise a lovely neighbourhood amenity – almost, but not quite; for the cove itself is a childhood haven, with shallow safe water, and a boat slip that serves equally well as an easy way into the water and a place for sunbathing. It feels small, manageable, local. Some lovely houses along the road might instil envy in those who suspect that such domiciles are beyond their means – and the estate agents' estimation of sea views adding twenty-five per cent to a house price would, with these dwellings, probably have to be revised even further upward. But the area is so pleasant, so cheerful, that not even suppressed covetousness could long mar it.

The Forty Foot

Yes, 'togs must be worn'. Moreover, the most famous place to get wet in Dublin Bay is 'considered to be an unsafe area. Due to the presence of submerged rocks, diving is especially dangerous.' Now, the exit from the gene pool of any person non-cognisant of the risks involved in flinging oneself headlong into water that is a conspicuous jumble of massed rocks – some submerged, some not – would probably not constitute a loss to the evolutionary forward progress of the species. Nevertheless, one feels warned.

The name 'Forty Foot' comes not from the depth of the water but from a regiment of soldiers which used to be stationed nearby – the 42nd Highland Regiment of Foot, now known as the Black Watch. There are hooded cement benches that can be considered bathing shelters although privacy is very much what you make of it. The actual main access point to the waters of the Forty Foot is quite small, and for all its history and myth, seems somewhat unprepossessing. Locals and regulars – and visitors, too – gather here on Christmas Day for the annual Christmas swim. Some assert that the water is 'not that cold'; others don't. There's an informal competition for the silliest bathing costume; and bystanders share flasks of hot whisky, both to restore chilled bathers after the dip and bolster them before it. The Forty Foot was immortalised in the opening chapter

The Forty Foot Baths

of James Joyce's *Ulysses*, and it hasn't changed much since then, with the obvious alteration resulting from the addition of women and togs. Any improvement would only serve to lessen it. For all the warnings, kids still jump off the rocks backing the main entry point, as they always have and always will.

The Sandycove Martello houses the James Joyce Museum, appropriately enough; and it is a thrill for any lover of Joyce's work to be able to go up to the roof and look out on the vista he saw and wrote about. The tower itself has been fully restored and the small grounds around it paved and finished so that the overall effect is a bit hard and cold – too much granite will do that – making it an odd repository for the rich sinuosities of Joyce's prose. One wonders what Bloom would have made of it.

South of Sandycove the main road leaves the shore and passes through neighbourhoods of lovely old terraces – the red-brick Breffni Terrace on Breffni Road particularly notable – until it regains the sea front, briefly, at Bullock Harbour with its old castle.

Bullock

Bullock Castle dominates the small harbour and adds a note of historical drama to what is otherwise a pleasant, old-fashioned kind of place with new developments and other improvements visible nearby. Bullock itself is an ancient town that once rivalled Dun Laoghaire and Dalkey. The town was given to Cistercian monks who also gained local fishing rights, and it was to protect these lucrative fisheries that Bullock Castle was built in the twelfth century. Long ignored and settling into decrepitude, it has been recently restored.

Bullock has seen its moments of drama. Bullock supported the rebels in 1641, and was the site of a horrific reprisal when a party of soldiers descended on the village, intent on vengeance. The inhabitants had heard of their approach and put out to sea, but the soldiers followed in boats and captured them well off shore. Fifty-six men, women and children were forced out of their boats and drowned in the sea.

Bullock Harbour was also one of the sites of the first stationary lifeboat service in Dublin Bay, along with Sandycove and old Dunleary

Boats in Bullock Harbour

(Dun Laoghaire). The Sandycove station opened first and all were in operation by the early decades of the nineteenth century. Lifeboats today are stationed primarily at Dun Laoghaire and Howth but the long tradition of providing help to mariners in trouble had its inception on the south shoreline of Dublin Bay (see 'Lifeboats').

Behind Bullock Harbour on the seaward side are diving rocks, a smaller, localised version of the more famous Forty Foot at Sandycove, a little harder to reach. Bullock Harbour has a nice, out-of-the-way feel to it although like much of the south coast of Dublin Bay, nearby modern developments have changed the area remarkably.

Dalkey and Dalkey Island

Dalkey and Dalkey Island form the southern-most border of Dublin Bay, much as does Howth in the north. Dalkey Island lies about 300 metres offshore and comprises about twenty-two acres. Some of the finest Mesolithic remains found in the Dublin area come from Dalkey Island, including spear points and arrow heads that are today in the National Museum. Students of the island have dated these earliest remains to around the fourth millennium BC. Evidence has also been uncovered that suggests continued human occupation of the island during the Iron Age and the Early Christian period, and Dalkey Island was also used as a Viking base. It is today inhabited only by wild goats and rabbits.

The name 'Dalkey' comes from the Irish, *Deilig Inis*, Island of Thorns. The Vikings took the first syllable of the Irish name and added their suffix for 'island', and this evolved into 'Dalkey'.

The Martello Tower on Dalkey Island is one of eight built by the British Admiralty to defend the Dun Laoghaire coastline from Napoleon.

Martello Tower on Dalkey Island

The ruins of an old stone church there, named after St Begnet, is thought to have been abandoned when the Vikings took over the island and began using it as part of the trading port they had established on the bay. Apparently the church was renovated sufficiently to serve as living quarters for the builders who constructed the nearby Martello tower and gun battery. An older wooden church may have been there originally, and the outline of a promontory fort can be seen at the northern end of the island.

Sightseers and fishermen visit the island during warm weather. The surrounding waters are considered an excellent dive site (see 'Water Sports on the Bay') and the fishing is said to be good there. Boats at Coliemore or Bullock Harbour can be hired for the short trip out there.

The very deep channel between Dalkey Island and the mainland was known as the 'Dalkey Roads'. Before the construction of the asylum harbour at Dun Laoghaire, ships used to take refuge against storms on the lee side of the island. Dalkey Island was apparently once a candidate for an oil terminal. The idea was abandoned, fortunately, preserving the shoreline area of Dalkey.

To the north-west of the island are the Carraig Rock, Clare Rock and Lamb Island, parts of them visible only visible at low tide; while to the east of Dalkey Island are the rocks known as 'The Muglins'. They pose a danger to shipping and have been fitted with a lighthouse. (See 'Lights on the Bay'.)

Dalkey Village

History permeates Dalkey. For all the celebrity residents who have established their homes here, the village manages to restrain itself.

Dalkey became an important port after the Anglo-Norman invasion and was used by vessels trading from the continent and England. Seven castles were built as defensive installations that could also serve as warehouses to store goods, and two are still standing today: Goat Castle and Archbold's Castle. Unfortunately, as a seaport Dalkey was also vulnerable to other imports, and it is believed that it was through Dalkey port that plague entered Ireland in the mid-fourteenth century, leading eventually to the death of a quarter of the Irish population.

Goat Castle dates from around 1429; it is well-preserved and today forms part of the Dalkey Castle and Heritage Centre. For those who wish to moderate their pursuit of culture, it is conveniently located next to The Queen's, Dalkey's oldest pub.

The freemen of Dalkey have the right to elect a king. It is a rare honour, as the king's full title of 'King of Dalkey, Emperor of the Muglins, Prince of the Holy Island of Magee, Baron of Bulloch, Seigneur of Sandycove, Defender of the Faith and Respector of All Others, Elector of Lambay and Ireland's Eye, and Sovereign of the Most Illustrious Order of the Lobster and Periwinkle' indicates. The current ruler, King Larry the Second, was elected in 1983. His duties are not thought onerous. The Coliemore Road is Dalkey's main coast road, with the smallness of Coliemore Harbour making it hard to see it as the important port it once was. Boats to Dalkey Island can be hired here.

Dalkey Quarry is a now disused granite quarry that provided the stone used to build Dun Laoghaire Harbour. It is now a popular rock-climbing location within Killiney Hill Park. During the construction of the harbour, the quarry was connected to Dun Laoghaire via a tramway known as 'The Metals', parts of which are still visible in some parts of Dalkey. (See 'Dun Laoghaire'.)

Dalkey Quarry

Dalkey was also the terminus for the Atmospheric Railways which originated in Dun Laoghaire and remained in operation for ten years.

The Atmospheric Railway

An atmospheric railway is one which uses air pressure to power the train. It functioned somewhat like the pneumatic message-forwarding systems in which air is pumped out of one end of a closed tube, creating a vacuum which in turn causes a cylinder to be propelled forward. The Dun Laoghaire to Dalkey line was the first attempt at a commercial application of this attempt at moving passengers.

The debate at the time was how to use steam power to move loads on land. Should the steam engine that powered the train be mounted on it, resulting in what we know as the steam locomotive; or could the power source be situated more safely at the end of the line and used to create a vacuum which would then pull the train – the 'atmospheric' system? To some pundits, having the power source as part of the rolling stock seemed an unnecessary additional risk. Steam engines at the time were cumbersome and dirty and dangerous; billowing coal smoke was unpleasant, sparks flew and burned holes in garments or even caused track-side fires. There had to be a better way.

The atmospheric system required a continuous pipe that was seated in a trench between the tracks. The pipe housed a large, tightly fitting piston connected to the rolling stock riding just above and behind it by an armature which passed through a slot on the top of the pipe. A pumping station at the Dalkey end of the system created a powerful vacuum in the pipe ahead of the piston, thereby pulling the train forward. The trip up from Dun Laoghaire rose on a slight uphill gradient so for the return journey, the piston was lifted out from its pipe and the train carriages rolled decorously back to Dun Laoghaire.

That's right, a slot ran the entire length of the pressurised pipe. Yet as improbable as it sounds, the system worked and the train served passengers more or less reliably (often 'less', alas) for ten years.

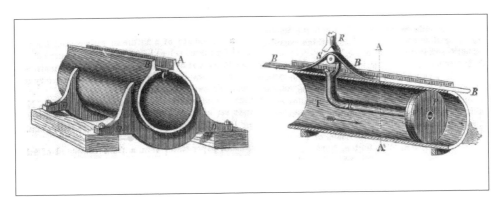

To keep the system air-tight, leather seals covered the slot along the length of the pipe. A mechanism riding just ahead of the linking armature forced them open for the connector to pass through, and a second mechanism just behind the connector forced them closed again.

Unfortunately, the leather used for the seals along the pipe dried out, became brittle and cracked. In order to maintain adequate flexibility, the leather was smeared with tallow. A man was hired to handle this chore and he trotted along behind the advancing train, smearing on the tallow where needed. Unfortunately, rats liked the tallow and gnawed the leather as well, ruining the seals so that leakage occurred, pressure fell, and the train ground to a halt. Leather seal repair and replacement became a burden on the system. Yet for all that, the Dun Laoghaire to Dalkey Atmospheric Railway was considered a success, and it persevered for ten years, yielding finally in 1854 to the steam locomotive service that was being extended from Dublin to Bray.

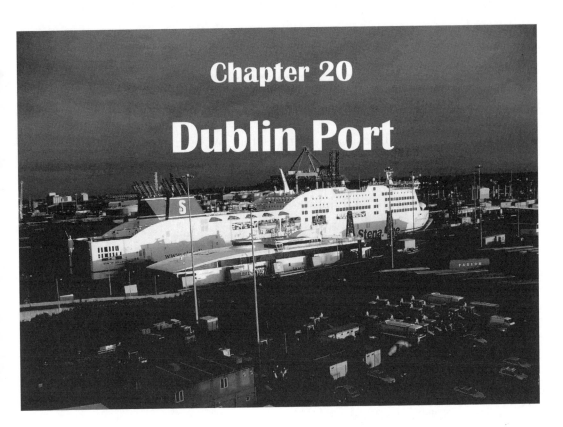

Chapter 20
Dublin Port

The Problematic Port

Even before the Vikings, boats travelled along the coastline and up the Liffey, connecting the bay with the inland plains. Early hide-covered boats drew almost no water, and even the primitive wooden boats of the time had flat bottoms and fairly shallow draughts. They could be beached on the sand bars at the river mouth and navigated upriver, given tide and weather. The Vikings made their primary settlement at the Liffey mouth for the same reason: conditions suited their vessels perfectly.

As boats grew larger, things soon seemed less favourable. The silting of the river, the bay's tendency to fill with sand, the tidal draw and fierce seasonal storms all combined to create hazards for medieval mariners whose boats required deeper water than the early Irish or Viking vessels had needed. They took the risk because a port existed, which at the time meant the jetties and wharfs used to off-load or on-load cargoes, and the various land-based extensions necessary to facilitate water-borne trade – stevedores, carters with dray animals, storage facilities, markets, a network of roads, as well as local merchants with the commercial skills and access to capital sufficient to sustain the system. Wood Quay and Fishamble Street are arguably the first embodiment of a Dublin Port that we would recognise as precursor to the major facilities now bracketing the Liffey mouth.

By around 1300, sections of stone quay walls had been constructed on the south side of the river at about where they are today. Building out into the river provided reliable access to deeper water. Yet in the middle of the fourteenth century, Dublin merchants complained that anchorage for large ships was impossible at the harbour port and they were required to drop anchor in the Dalkey Sound and off-load their cargo onto lighters that could make the journey into Dublin Port – an inconvenience, a costly inefficiency and, in times of bad weather, a sometimes fatal hazard.

Siting Dublin Port at the mouth of the Liffey and in the heart of the country's growing capital was problematical from early days. The existing infrastructure – and inertia – kept it there. Moving it seems always to have been judged too costly, and local vested interests whose livelihoods depended on the port and its facilities would have fought against any changes – and they did fight at times and do still.

The development of a commercial port in the sense that we use the term today involved the assignment of rights and responsibilities for managing its physical infrastructure. In the sixteenth century, with the continued growth of trade, maintenance of the quays and slips along the Liffey was allocated to specific individuals who in return for their efforts were allowed to levy charges on vessels using these facilities. Quays became property. An overseer was appointed, for example, to ensure that refuse or unneeded ballast was not dumped into the already too-shallow river; and this position evolved into one that also preserved the integrity of the banks on the south side of the river, indicating that mariners at that time were already damaging the shoreline by scooping out ballast there. Another growing problem was the abandonment of old hulks which, once judged unseaworthy, were left derelict where they foundered, adding to the hazards at an already difficult harbour.

The history of the port's steady move eastward is discussed in 'The Riverside Quays and the Custom House' but the need to improve the port was of constant concern throughout the seventeenth, eighteenth and nineteenth centuries – and, indeed, is still a matter of debate today. New vessels always seemed too large for the berths available to them, and petitions to construct larger quays and to create deeper channels occur and reoccur throughout the centuries. Dublin Corporation 'owned' the river and was therefore responsible for the deteriorating quality of the port and subsequent damage to the city's fortunes. Civic forces acted, and at the end of the seventeenth century, the Ballast Office Committee was established as the first step in renewing the port. Ballast was essential to ships departing empty or only partially loaded, and sand was the most convenient form available. Scooping it out of the sides of the riverbanks tended to reduce their integrity, sending more sand settling into the river channel. Restricting the taking-on of ballast to certain areas mid-channel would in effect serve the additional purpose of dredging out the too-shallow river. The Ballast Office itself employed lighters to deliver sand-ballast to ships; it had other duties as well, among them measuring the tonnage of arriving vessels in order to determine how much dues they owed the port. Controlling where ballast could be taken meant establishing a channel that would be maintained at a level deep enough for navigation. This idea – that an official body should be responsible for determining and maintaining an adequate shipping channel – was an important step forward in the development of a modern port facility. The authority of the Ballast Office also led to the construction of the Great South Wall (see 'The Great Walls of Dublin') which eventually prevented the South Bull from encroaching on the Liffey channel – for the most part.

The Imperial Port

The Ballast Office Committee was replaced in 1786 by a port management organisation that came to be known as the Ballast Board. In addition to the previously established rights and responsibilities of the Ballast Committee – dredging the channel, repairing the quays, etc. – the newly empowered Ballast Board put in place more comprehensive financial and regulatory controls in the hopes of securing sufficient funds to make needed repairs – another theme that runs throughout the history of Dublin

Port. The harbour at Dunleary (later Kingstown then Dun Laoghaire) was declared a part of the port of Dublin; the board was empowered to carry out improvements there, and also take responsibility for managing buoys in the Dalkey Sound.

Dublin Port on the Liffey in 1890, looking west

Responsibility for lights and lighthouses was assigned to the Ballast Board in 1810; in 1811 the first floating light on the Kish Bank was established, and the present Baily Light on Howth was completed in 1813 (see 'Lights on the Bay'). The board established the first lifeboat service in its efforts to improve maritime safety, and the number of Irish lighthouses grew from only fourteen when the port assumed responsibility to seventy-two by 1867, the year in which the Dublin Port Act formally separated the Ballast Board into two components: the Port Authority which was limited to Dublin Bay, and the Commissioners of Irish Lights, who were awarded the responsibility for managing the lighthouses and other marine safety facilities around Ireland.

The harbours at Howth and Dun Laoghaire lie outside the port of Dublin geographically but were both under the control of the Dublin Port Authority. (The history of the construction of both harbours is discussed elsewhere.) The packet station for the Royal Mail was shifted from Howth to Kingstown (Dun Laoghaire) in 1834 on the strength of the new asylum harbour under construction there plus the establishment of the railway line between Dublin and Dun Laoghaire. By 1836, Kingstown Harbour had become independent of Dublin Port, and the City of Dublin Steam Packet company won the mails contract for Kingstown/Dun Laoghaire.

The first half of the nineteenth century saw the development of increasingly larger, faster steam-powered ships (see 'Ferries on the Bay'). This meant that water depth at the port was even more critical. Sailing ships at lows tides could become incapacitated, but when the tide returned they floated with no harm done. Not so with new ships coming on the scene. The first steamships were powered by paddle wheels which could be easily damaged by running aground or even trying to operate in water that was too shallow. The advent of the steamship era was a huge boost to trade. But it meant that deep water had to be maintained alongside the quays at constant level if the larger ships were going to be able to berth there.

Shipping companies put pressure on the Port Authority, and eventually a timber wharf was built at the east end of the North Wall, perpendicular to it and running along a north–south axis. A deep pool was dredged so that water deep enough for even the largest paddle-steamers to berth safely at low tide was maintained. This area was later expanded into today's Alexandra Basin. The berthing facility on this new wall was still exposed to bad weather, particularly easterly gales, so a breakwater was constructed another 300 metres to the east of the new wharf and running parallel to it. Another pair of new deep-water wharves were constructed on either side of the entrance of the Royal Canal Dock but shipping was increasing at such a rate that the port facilities were scarcely able to meet the needs of merchants even with these and other new wharves that were erected along the north quays.

Other additions to what was becoming a full-fledged port facilities included quay-side shelters in which cargo could be stored temporarily after off-loading, graving slips that enabled hull repairs to be carried out

Dublin Port on the Liffey in 1890, looking east

on dry land, and customs facilities with bonded warehouses. The building of a new graving slip large enough to handle the new City of Dublin packet steamers required adding land, part of which was acquired from Dublin Corporation and part of which came from the Vernon Estate, which claimed ownership of all the foreshore lying between the river channel and Clontarf. A retaining wall was built running east–west along the edge of this area, all of which was reclaimed land created by dumping material dredged from the river channel. The history of dredging and dumping the material on the foreshore to create new land runs through the centuries in a kind of Sisyphean response to the natural propensity of the bay to fill with sand.

For all the expansion and development of the mid-nineteenth century, demand was outpacing available berthing facilities. A report filed in the early 1860s complained that every berth was filled and approximately forty ships were moored in tiers or anchored in the river, all waiting for an opportunity to tie up and discharge their cargo. Further extensions were required and the port again began building farther out into the bay, extending the North Wall and adding new deep-water berths.

Building of the North Wall Extension continued, with the first block laid in 1870 and the project completed in 1882. The Prince and Princess of Wales visited the new extension in 1885, and the basin it contained was named 'Alexandra' in honour of the Princess. Filling in a portion of the bay on the Clontarf side of the port facilities was approved in 1868 for the construction of a chemical manure works with jetty. Ten years later, the Vernon Estate rebuffed attempts by the board to secure all of the Clontarf foreshore, bounded on the western side by the railway embankment and East Wall, and on the east by Bull Wall. Had the port been successful, all of the north west corner of Dublin Bay would no doubt have soon ceased to exist.

In 1879, the port tried to circumvent the Vernon Estate's attempt to preserve the bay by getting a bill passed through Parliament. They were partially successful. Permission to purchase much of what it wanted of the north west bay was granted; but the water extending out 1,000 feet from the Clontarf sea wall was denied it. The bay here is extremely shallow, as anyone who has walked along the promenade at low tide can attest, so using it for berths would always have been unlikely. Filling in the bay would have created new land for industrial or commercial developments, such as today's successful East Point Business Park, but at the expense of the natural amenity of the bay. Still, undaunted, in 1897, the port managed to reclaim more land from the bay as the port continued to expand north towards Clontarf. In this case, the land was leased to the Anglo-American Oil Company which wanted to store petroleum in tanks on the foreshore; and in 1899, the first oil tanker arrived and discharged its cargo there.

By the end of the nineteenth century, the filling-in of the bay to create land that could then be leased to enterprises such as the chemical manure plant and the oil storage facilities had begun to give the port the shape it has today, with industrial facilities joining the more conventional 'port-like' activities of managing cargo and passengers. The revenues that the port accrued from creating then leasing land helped to offset a decline in earnings at the end of the century, and securing adequate funds was often a problem. The port bore the responsibility of maintaining its facilities and dredging the river channel which, despite the building of the Great Walls, still needed to be done regularly. Despite the heavy increase in port traffic, the income derived from port dues was insufficient; and powerful shipping interests prevented the port from charging more. Insufficient revenues led to the partial curtailment of dredging in the last decades of the nineteenth century, and this resulted in increased numbers of ships going aground along the south side of the channel. The Ballast Board had been put in place at the end of the eighteenth century to ensure that Dublin Bay would be a safe and secure harbour and port. One hundred years later, despite innovative marine engineering and heroic efforts, the sand once again seemed to be gaining the upper hand.

In 1899, a new port authority board responded to a survey by the British Admiralty which demonstrated the unacceptable shallowness of the sand bar and the river channel. Despite its precarious finances, the port contracted with a new dredging company that used modern suction dredgers; and by 1903, sufficient sand had been pumped ashore to fill more reclaimed lands near the graving dock. The success of this operation led to the purchase of a large suction dredger that was able to maintain adequate water depths into the second half of the twentieth century. Jetties continued to be extended and land filled in, allowing the construction of facilities for a second petroleum company which leased two acres of reclaimed land. The port had begun generating its own

Unloading crates of tobacco on George's Dock, late 1940s

electricity as well, and this led to the construction of electric cranes which would improve the port's capacity for managing bulk cargoes. A one-hundred ton crane came into operation in 1905, and a number of smaller cranes were added to the berth along the North Wall Extension.

Reconstruction of the South Quays was begun in 1870 and completed in 1913. Water on this side of the river channel also was now deep enough for ships to enter and depart no matter what the tide. The Great War interrupted development of the port as a commercial facility since the North Wall Extension and Alexandra Quay were used for military purposes. After the end of hostilities, the timber jetties had deteriorated and the port needed sufficient funds to replace them with more durable masonry and concrete quay walls. The port successfully managed to increase the amounts it could charge for usage of its facilities although doing so required a prolonged struggle.

Ireland Owns Its Port

The Irish Free State took up a variety of issues regarding ports and harbours in 1926, and a report published in 1930 revealed inconsistencies in management and functions of ports throughout the country, much of it due to the prevalence of local statutes and governing bodies. The importance of water-borne trade was clearly recognised by the government, and the involvement of local officials was viewed as something of an impediment to developing a comprehensive, efficient and profitable maritime trading network. Not much was done, however, and the 'Emergency' of 1939–45 resulted in further delays. The Harbours Act of 1946 established the basics of the system of port management that is still in place today, laying out the management responsibilities for port facilities.

The 1930 report also noted that ships were continuing to increase in size so that many Irish ports were – or soon would be – incapable of receiving them. Dublin Port, it was concluded, would be best equipped to handle future shipping needs of the country, the shallowness of Dublin Bay notwithstanding. The late 1930s saw the first large cruise liners arriving in Dublin Bay, and a passenger terminal was constructed at Alexandra Quay

Unloading coal with a four-tonne bucket, 1956

to handle this new service, with four or five ships a year berthing there up until the beginning of World War II.

World War II also halted another plan to increase revenue for the port: an oil refinery. The idea had been brought up and approved in 1936. Fifty-three acres of reclaimed land was to be made available, and another seventeen acres was filled in to create a site large enough to meet all the oil-refining needs for the country. Two jetties were built with pipelines connecting to oil tanks where the crude could be stored before it was refined. Dredging would be required in order to create deep-water berths for the oil tankers, and this was duly authorised. By the end of 1938, the landfill had been completed, the jetties built, and construction begun on parts of the refinery itself. Oil tankers had also been constructed to carry the crude to Dublin Bay; and although most of the project was completed by 1939, financial and other difficulties halted further construction and the project was suspended until after the war.

The war had created shortages since insufficient shipping was available, and this had further underscored Ireland's total dependency on water-borne trade and the inadequacy of the country's own shipping capacity. In 1941, Irish Shipping Limited was founded as a national flag-carrier, with the Minister for Finance as majority shareholder. Three shipping companies, also shareholders, managed a fleet of ships that by the end of the war totalled fifteen vessels.

The commercial expansion that followed the end of the war also brought increased shipping traffic to Dublin Bay; and despite financial constraints, the port was able to respond by completing Ocean Pier at Alexandra Quay. New electric cranes were ordered to replace those worn out from use, and the first fork-lift trucks in Ireland appeared at the port, an indication of the port's determination to modernise its facilities. ESB bought the site that had been set aside for the oil refinery and repurposed it into a power-generating plant, which came on-stream in 1949 as the

Managing loose timber before containerisation, 1960s

'North Wall Generating Station'. Congestion on the quays caused by oil tankers off-loading resulted in the creation of a single zone dedicated to petroleum tanks and pipes, with new jetties constructed for the exclusive use of oil tankers.

Bigger new ships required berths with deeper water, and a new dredging company was employed to continue and extend the never-ending struggle against silting. Need for sand as ballast had long since ended since modern ships use seawater, so the material dredged from the bay and channel was dumped, along with city rubbish, on the foreshore to continue building out the south side of the river at Ringsend to create sufficient land for the planned ESB generating station which would replace the old Pigeon House facilities.

The port facilities continued to expand in the 1950s, with new lifting cranes, a new dry dock, and new facilities to handle LPG as well as coal and oil. The first ships fitted with large ramps on the bow for roll-on/roll-off services had begun to appear at European ports, an innovation that greatly improved the efficiency of ferries. The on-shore installation of ramps to handle this traffic was finished in 1956 but the actual service itself was long delayed due to the opposition of Dublin dockers. (See 'Ferries on the Bay'.)

The foreshore south of the port facilities was part of the Pembroke Estate, and dumping on the land south of Pigeon House Road exceeded what had been authorised by the owners, resulting in reclaimed land which the port feared might be developed by the Pembroke Estate. In 1963, the port in conjunction with Dublin Corporation and ESB bought 650 acres of foreshore to secure future development possibilities from Poolbeg to Ringsend.

By the mid-1960s, all the improvements and extensions initiated by the port at the end of World War II had been completed; but the continued evolution of sea-borne trade meant that further developments would be required. Land reclamation continued in batches of twenty or thirty acres on the south side of the river and another hundred-acre parcel opposite Clontarf. The old story of dredging the channel and reclaiming land seemed to be plodding along on its familiar weary way. Yet the world of shipping was undergoing a profound transformation – probably the single biggest change since the advent of steam-powered vessels – and the effect on Dublin Port would be monumental.

The concept itself was not new. Goods had been shipped in purpose-built containers for decades. But the application that was being developed was very definitely new, and the promise it held for improved efficiency would become transformative. The innovation was in the standardisation of the container itself, the introduction of cargo ships that carried nothing

Samskip Pioneer *in Dublin Port, 2006*

but containers, and the development of port facilities specifically designed for managing containers – mainly the immense mobile derrick cranes that are today ubiquitous at commercial ports. Standardising containers made it possible to quickly transfer a unit of stored cargo from the ship it arrived on to the lorry that would carry it on to its destination. The improvements in cost and efficiency realised by this new form of cargo management would be hard to overstate – as would the decimation of an entire workforce of stevedores and dock workers. The late 1960s saw the addition of derrick cranes with varying lifting capacities placed at several quays at the port, and more would be added as the port extensions continued to advance into the bay, with new deep-water berths configured for the immense container ships which were already appearing.

Innovations continued to occur at a rapid pace. By 1968, with opposition by dockers weakened, roll-on/roll-off passenger ferry service was at last inaugurated, and the port's continued growth and success seemed assured. Lift-on/lift-off container shipping and roll-on/roll-off management of cars and lorries had together transformed the business of the port and tremendously improved the efficiency and success of its operations.

There were some disappointments, however. In 1972, another attempt was made to gain permission to construct an oil refinery on the bay, this time on foreshore to be reclaimed from south of the Pigeon House at Sandymount Strand. Public opposition from local residents was fierce, not surprisingly. And although the plan was defended as being in the national interest and therefore too important to be influenced by residents of Sandymount and Ringsend who for reasons of their own did not want to live next door to an oil refinery, the application for planning permission was eventually denied. A general recession in trade throughout the latter half of the 1970s and into the 1980s limited the port's abilities to expand its facilities. Dredging was sustained so that the deep channels into the port were sufficient to meet the needs of container shippers who were also able to use a new container terminal on the South Quay.

The Harbours Act of 1996 defined the limits of Dublin Port. It essentially covers everything in this book. Dublin Port includes the River Liffey from Rory O'Moore Bridge. Its eastern boundaries are configured as a straight line connecting the Baily Light to the North Burford Buoy, across to the South Burford Buoy and ending at Sorrento Point. In other words, Dublin Port occupies Dublin Bay.

Dublin Port Company

Dublin Port Company is a self-financing, semi-state organisation whose business is to facilitate the flow of goods and passengers and attendant tracking information through the port. Two-thirds of all containerised traffic in Ireland is funnelled through Dublin Port, as anyone whose morning commute includes the roads along the coasts or quays can attest.

Dublin Port's growth reflects the astonishing success of the Irish economy. In 1995, the port handled slightly less than twelve million tonnes of cargo. Ten years later, the total has reached almost twenty-seven million tonnes. Over that same period, imports have grown from seven and a half million to seventeen and a half million tonnes while exports more than doubled. Similarly, 4,795 trading vessels used the port in 1995 while the number in 2005 was 7,917. Clearly, the 'Celtic tiger' can be seen within these figures. Moreover, the greater increase in tonnage relative to vessel numbers indicates an improved cargo capacity per ship over this ten-year period, supporting anecdotal evidence that ships are getting larger and more economical to operate. This trend also means that ever larger ships will draw even more water and thus require new, deeper berths.

The port operates a number of cargo-handling services. The port is Ireland's primary centre for lift-on/lift-off services (*aka* 'Lo Lo', which sounds like a name for a panda), and operates two dedicated terminals as well as the common work area in Alexandra Quay. Trade is handled at these three terminals by Dublin Ferryport Terminals, Marine Terminals and Portroe Stevedores, with daily service from Dublin to the UK and mainland Europe as well as weekly services to Iberia and the Mediterranean. Containers are handled by two 64-tonne and one 105-tonne mobile derrick cranes. Lo Lo accounts for less than a quarter of the port's total throughput, with average annual growth of about seven per cent.

The Granuaile *leaving Dublin Port, 2005*

Roll-on/roll-off services (that would be 'Ro Ro', also fond of munching on tender bamboo leaves) is the single largest segment of the port's business, with five ferry companies that cater to both the freight and tourism markets. In the last six years, over €85 millon has been invested in port facilities with the major share going to develop Ro Ro facilities (discussed in 'Ferries on the Bay').

The port has discharging facilities for liquid bulk such as oil, bitumen, chemicals, LPG and molasses. A dedicated petroleum zone has storage capacity for 330,000 tonnes and is linked to four oil berths by a common user pipeline system so that oil tankers can discharge their cargoes directly into the storage installations of any of the oil companies. A new comprehensive fire-fighting system has been installed on the Eastern and Western Oil Jetties.

Dry bulk is handled at sites on both the north side and south side of the river, with loading and discharging facilities for peat, coal, grain, animal

Crystal Serenity, *Dublin Port, 2005*

feed-stuffs, fertiliser, sand, etc., as well as lead and zinc concentrate from Tara Mines. Five mobile cranes, four rated at 64 tonnes and one capable of lifting 104 tonnes operate at Alexandra Quay, as well as various grabbing cranes, conveyers and hoppers. Finally, break bulk is still managed on

Dublin Port Tug

the north side of the port although the company is planning to exit this business.

Tourism is an important and growing source of revenue for Dublin Port. Around seventy cruise liners are scheduled to visit Dublin Port in 2006, with smaller vessels entering into the Liffey River directly and larger ones berthing at Alexandra Quay. A growing trend in recent years has seen passengers embarking and disembarking at Dublin. This is a new welcome development as previously Dublin was a port of call only.

Dublin Port Company is the pilotage authority for Dublin Bay. A pilot shore station is situated on the Eastern Breakwater and operates direct-boarding fast cutters capable of speeds up to twenty knots. Towage is another service offered by the port, with three powerful diesel tugs. The port also provides a full diving service for hull inspections, video inspections and propellor clearance. Two graving docks are situated to the west of Alexandra Quay, and private companies are licensed by Dublin Port Company to offer stevedoring services in the port.

Expansion Issues

Dublin Port has submitted a request to reclaim fifty-two acres of open sea off the eastern end of the NorseMerchant Ferries Ro Ro Terminal. (To 'reclaim' means to recover something previously owned and restore it to its rightful condition, with the implication that the land somehow 'owns' the sea.)

The request has met fierce opposition from a variety of groups who see the increased industrialisation of what should be the city's prime natural amenity a foolishly short-sighted choice. While it is possible to argue that although the amount of damage done to the bay by this particular 'reclamation' will not be extensive, it is nevertheless damage and therefore wrong. And it is equally reasonable to worry that the port's appetite will not be so easily satisfied, and that the fifty-two acres are a watery version of the camel's nose which, once allowed inside the tent, will soon be followed by the entire camel. Other unpleasant issues include the plan to construct an immense industrial incinerator on Poolbeg Peninsula, which will be taken up in more detail in the chapter 'The Future of the Bay'.

But let us here at least review Dublin Port's request to expand its facilities – facilities that have been remarkably successful. According to the Port, the extension is needed because:

- Dublin Port is the country's principal gateway for the import and export of Irish goods, by virtue of its location close to its principal customers and its modern facilities;

- Economic trends that are driving the rapid growth in the trade of containerised cargo are forecast to continue in the future;

- The increasing size and capacity of vessels and the introduction of new and additional shipping routes demand increased berthing and handling facilities to accommodate this growth in containerised trade and in vessel types.

The port seems concerned only with the economic aspect of the situation, and views economic development strictly in terms of industry and trade, with the bay seen as an asset to be exploited. Trade is important, obviously – one can't subsist on Guinness, turf and Taytos alone. But the transition to a knowledge-based services economy is underway here already; and for Ireland to continue to flourish, a better model might be the regeneration of the Docklands.

This is not to ignore the fact that as an island economy, Ireland is dependent on its seaports for much of its economic activity. Rapid economic growth has resulted in significant increases in imports and exports – the more stuff we get, the more we want. But there is a point when the quality of urban life becomes important. If we aren't there yet we will be soon. The growth of container traffic will surely continue. The question is, does it have to go through the city of Dublin?

In many ways Dublin Bay was a poor choice for a major port when it was developed and is an even poorer choice for one now, trapped as it is at the heart of the country's largest city – a city that is delightfully old with its charmingly narrow streets.

One looks at what has happened to similar port facilities at New York, Sydney, or San Francisco and wonders if Dublin could not learn something from them. Or one can turn to Tokyo Bay to view the complete and utter destruction of what had once been a thriving amenity of historical, social and environmental significance but is now a bleak industrial wasteland.

Sooner or later, we are going to have to choose.

Chapter 21

Ferries on the Bay

Development of the Ferry Services

Ferry services on Dublin Bay date at least as far back as the reign of Queen Elizabeth I. Passengers travelled back and forth between Ireland and other ports well before then of course, but the advent of regularly scheduled dedicated services between two ports found its beginning in the crown's need to communicate regularly with its representatives in Ireland. Ships used for this purpose were called 'pacquets', referring to the mails being bundled up in packets that they carried. Early routes connected Dublin Bay with Liverpool and Chester. A harbour existed at Holyhead, but the roads connecting on to London were poor at the time and travellers avoided that route until improvements were made.

The Restoration established the General Post Office in Britain, and the management of packet ships to carry the mail and other state papers to Ireland was established as a crown monopoly. Contracts were awarded to several ship owners to ensure that a daily service could be maintained. Until the nineteenth century, packet ships were comparatively small sailing vessels and the crossing in foul weather was dangerous, with many delays and difficulties. Small though they may have been, packet ships still had difficulties managing the shallow bay at Dublin or entering Holyhead Bay in foul weather so in 1796 light rowboats called 'wherries' were established at Holyhead and Dublin and used to transport mail and passengers into port when conditions made it impossible for the packet ships to manage.

Packets weren't the only option. Passage boats – so-called because they carried passengers but had no contract with the Royal Mails – also sailed on regular schedules between the ports that were serviced by the packet ships; they were not as well maintained as the packets, however, and abuses finally led to the imposition of stringent regulations at the start of the nineteenth century in order to protect passenger safety, with inspectors appointed by the Dublin Port Authority to ensure compliance.

The Act of Union of 1800 resulted in Irish Members of Parliament being required to make the journey across the Irish Sea, and this led to improvements in the packet service, with larger and more comfortable ships being introduced. Steam-powered vessels had begun to appear, and in 1816 a new ferry company, the Steam Packet Company, was formed in Dublin. The packet station was transferred from Dublin to Howth in 1818, and the new company began to operate two paddle-wheel steamers between Howth and Holyhead as a passenger service. The two paddle steamers – the *Hibernia* and the *Britannia* – were identical and had much improved facilities, with cabin accommodations for thirty people below decks. The new paddle steamers also carried horses and carriages on deck, making them functionally the prototypes for today's modern car ferries. These paddle steamers operated for a number of months, making the crossing to Holyhead in eight hours, about half the time it took the sailing packets; and this success led to the introduction of a second service, 'The New Steam Packet Company', with even faster ships trying to compete for the mail contract between Howth and Holyhead.

The General Post Office had recognised the value of this new technology, and it added its own pair of paddle steamers to the Howth–Holyhead route in 1821. The *Lightning* and the *Meteor* were the largest and fastest ships yet and they quickly monopolised the route, forcing competitors to move to Dublin and shift their regular service to Liverpool. Thus by the third decade of the nineteenth century, the Dublin Bay area supported two regular ferry services linking Ireland to Britain, in addition to the sailing ships which were still in operation, carrying passengers and cargo. Competition increased throughout the nineteenth century with a series of new shipping companies launching services, including The City of Dublin Steam Packet Company and The British and Irish Steam Packet Company (The B&I).

Howth Harbour silted, as had been predicted, and in 1834 the packet station was moved to the new asylum harbour that was being built at Dun Laoghaire. The City of Dublin Steam Packet company won the contract to handle the Royal Mail between Liverpool and Kingstown/Dun Laoghaire, with the British port later being changed back to Holyhead. New, larger steam ships began to cater more to passenger comforts, and crossing times between Dun Laoghaire and Holyhead were cut to slightly under four hours. Each succeeding generation of ships reduced the crossing

The Cambria *leaving port, 1966*

time further; and in 1897, new ships coming into service were making the journey between Dun Laoghaire and Holyhead in about two and a half hours, comparable to some of today's large ferries.

The London North Western Railway company transferred its passengers in Dublin from Dun Laoghaire to the North Wall at the Liffey mouth so that Dublin Bay again had two competing ferry ports. In 1908, LNWR moved back to Dun Laoghaire and operated daily services directly in competition with the City of Dublin company, the two rivals sharing the Carlisle Pier.

The B&I took over the ships and routes of the City of Dublin company after World War I, and by 1919, a number of companies were operating regular services between Ireland and Britain. By the mid-1930s, modern ships were introduced into the Dublin–Liverpool service, and after the ceasing of hostilities in 1945, B&I introduced then replaced a number of ships that continued to sail that route. In 1965, the Irish government bought a controlling interest in B&I, and two years later, the company replaced its conventional passenger ferries with roll-on/roll-off car ferries. The first jetfoil was introduced by B&I in 1980 and was used to make a daylight crossing to Liverpool, taking just over three hours. The service was not popular, however, and was suspended in 1981. In 1992, Irish Ferries took over B&I Line.

A Short History of Ro Ro

Roll-on/roll-off is the conventional description of the fundamental fact of a car ferry. Vehicles did travel by ship before the bow-mounted ramps were incorporated, but they had to be loaded by cranes or perhaps rolled gingerly aboard using ramps, so the experience was hardly comparable. Ro Ro got off to a slow start in Ireland, due to dockers' reluctance to lose their livelihoods. The first Ro Ro ships were serving European ports by the middle of the twentieth century, and the on-shore installation of ramps at Dublin Port was finished in 1956 but not put into operation until years later. The B&I Line's *MV Munster* started sailing between Dublin and Liverpool in 1968 – using a ferry terminal on the far eastern end of the facilities – and was soon joined by a Ro Ro service started by British Railways between Holyhead and Dun Laoghaire.

The *Munster* could carry 220 cars but only seven lorries or buses; but in 1969 it was joined by B&I's *MV Leinster*, with an improved design that allowed it to carry a greater number of trucks and buses. The Isle of Man Steam Packet Company started its first car ferry service between Dublin and Douglas in 1974, and in 1979, The B&I introduced a new generation of car ferries on its Irish Sea routes, capable of carrying 1,500 passengers and 350 cars.

In 1980, B&I's high speed service was inaugurated but was not successful and suspended at the end of 1981. Stena Line bought the Sealink fleet in 1991 and started a Dublin–Holyhead service in 1995.

The year 1995 was a pivotal one for Ro Ro service in Dublin Bay. Merchant Ferries moved to Dublin that year, introducing three vessels – the *Merchant Venture*, the *Merchant Brilliant* and the *Merchant Bravery*, on the Dublin–Heysham route; Irish Ferries brought the *Isle of Inisfree* to the Dublin–Holyhead route

B&I's MV Leinster

– making it at the time the biggest ferry operating out of Dublin. Two years later it was replaced by the *Isle of Inishmore*. Also in 1995, the *SuperSeacat* service commenced between Dublin and Liverpool, reducing travel time to just over three and a half hours.

Irish Ferries' MV Ulysses

In 1999, Irish Ferries introduced the high speed *Jonathan Swift* to the Dublin–Holyhead route. Catering mostly to tourists, the vessel makes four round trips daily. Like 1995, 2001 marked the arrival of new Dublin ferries and greatly improved service. In January, P&O brought the *European Ambassador* to the Dublin–Liverpool route, and in March of that year, the *Ulysses*, the world's largest car ferry, was introduced by Irish Ferries. the *Stena Forwarder* also began service in 2001, and P&O opened a new route between Dublin and Mostyn with two round trips daily, followed a year later by a weekly service to Cherbourg. Finally, the *Stena Adventurer* superferry was launched in Dublin in 2003 and operates twice daily between Dublin and Holyhead.

Roll-on/roll-off is half the story of Dublin Port as a successful shipping facility, with the containerised lift-on/lift-off capability being the other half. (In a sense, Ro Ro is just another form of containerised shipping, with the 'container' – a car or lorry loaded with cargo – being loaded by its driver.) These technologies together have made travel and trade cheaper and faster. It used to take over a day for a crew of stevedores to unload a conventional ship. Now it can be done in a couple of hours.

Ferry Services at Dun Laoghaire

Dublin Port is Ireland's busiest passenger ferry port with up to eighteen sailings daily to the UK and the continent. It is served by five companies and offers a choice between travelling by cruise ferry or high-speed ferry. It competes with Dun Laoghaire where Stena Lines operates the world's largest fast ferry service, crossing to Holyhead in about an hour and a half, and making four round-trips daily.

For over 150 years a regular ferry service has crossed the Irish Sea between Dun Laoghaire and Holyhead. Car ferry vessels were introduced in the early 1960s and operated from St Michael's Pier while the mail boats continued to operate from the Carlisle Pier. The *St Columba*, which was Sealink's flagship on the Irish Sea, was introduced on the route in 1977 and could accommodate 2,400 passengers and 335 cars with a travel time of three and a half hours.

Stena Adventurer *and* Jonathan Swift, *Dublin, 2004*

In 1995, the new terminal was established on St Michael's Pier for a 'high-speed service' and the *HSS Stena Explorer* was introduced on the route. This massive catamaran travels at forty knots and completes the journey in a brief one hour and forty minutes, with a capacity of 1,500 passengers and 350 cars. A long series of tests in Gothenburg resulted in the design of the catamaran hull with concave sides that were extremely narrow at the water line but swelled out again into large pontoons below the water line. Moreover, the angle at which the bows cut through the onrushing water was made as sharp as possible. Thus, the ship's surface area of contact at the water line is very small which results in a remarkably comfortable motion, even at high speeds.

Today, the sight of the *HSS Stena Explorer* entering the harbour and docking is inevitably stirring, although the scale of the 'floating car park' seems somewhat out of place.

Jonathan Swift *on Dublin Bay*

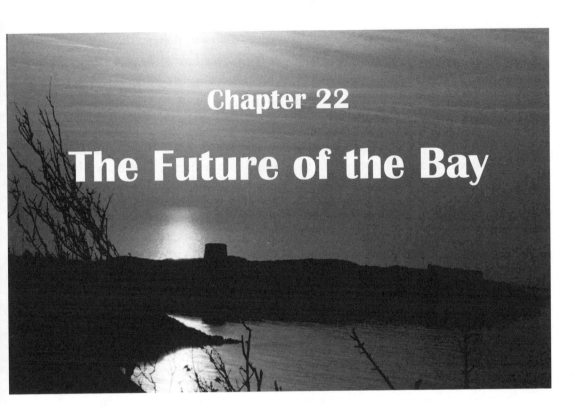

Chapter 22

The Future of the Bay

We can swim in it, or we can dump our trash there. We can fill in the foreshore to 'reclaim' land for yet more apartments, or we can preserve what remains for the pleasure and profit of brent geese and oystercatchers. Whatever Dublin Bay is today, there is no assurance it will be that way tomorrow.

All around the city and country are people who will be making choices regarding the future of Dublin Bay. Some will prevail, others will be disappointed. Who are these people? What do they want? And who finally gets to decide things that determine the future of the bay? Or, rather, the futures of the bay, since no one choice is ever likely to be final.

There is every reason to believe that the future of Dublin Bay will be overseen by well-meaning, thoughtful officials who take into consideration a wide range of variables, weight options carefully then reach conclusions that are farseeing and insightful. Perhaps, as if manna from heaven, good things will sprinkle down on our bay and its foreshore, and all will be well.

On the other hand, there is also every reason to believe that nothing of the sort will happen. Perhaps, whether from greed or ignorance or timidity or sloth, the bay will be reduced – a bit here, a bit there, the degradation metastatic and implacable – until what remains seems lessened by the memory of what was lost.

Perhaps we can entrust this issue to the various statutory bodies that have been elected or appointed to operate in our name. There are about a dozen of them; many if not most will read proposals, hold hearings, make statements, and issue decisions about what should happen to Dublin Bay.

There are also a number of groups who regard conservation of the bay as a right and a duty, and who will respond vividly to proposed depredations, both real and imagined. Good judgement is required from them. Not all development is deleterious, after all, as the renewed docklands area seems to demonstrate.

Then there are the rest of us, users of the bay for sailing on or fishing in or watching skeins of geese fly over; or strolling along beside and pausing occasionally and just gazing out at and feeling blessed by.

Official Groups

The *Department of Environment, Heritage and Local Government* 'promotes sustainable development and improves the quality of life through protection of the environment and heritage, infrastructure provision, balanced regional development and good local government.' Although they make no reference to Dublin Bay in their *Statement of Strategy 2005–2007*; they are in charge of designating Special Areas of Conservation and Special Protection Areas which are important in preserving much of the foreshore around the bay.

The remit of the *Department of Communications, Marine and Natural Resources* covers both communicating and marine resources. They are in charge of coastal zone management which deals with foreshore administration, marine engineering, the fishery harbours, sea fisheries and seafood policy and development. Some bay-related entities, such as the Irish Coast Guard, the Marine Survey Office and Maritime Safety

Division, the Aids to Navigation Section and the Marine Environment Division, and, most importantly, the Dublin Port Company have been moved to the Department of Transport.

Dublin City Council defines itself as delivering 'a wide and complex range of services to a diverse customer base'. That sounds a little ambiguous; it could mean almost anything. Their most direct intervention with the bay has been The Dublin Bay Project, one of their largest infrastructure projects, with three main components: the Ringsend Wastewater Treatment Works, the Sutton Pumping Station, and the submarine pipeline under the bay that links them. The Dublin Port Tunnel is another major undertaking by Dublin City Council; and they are promoting the development of a massive industrial incinerator on the shores of Dublin Bay. Clearly, they are involved.

A lot of people like what the *Dublin Docklands Development Authority* has achieved, and they seem like clever fellows who may need new challenges once the regeneration of the docklands area is completed in 2012. Over the centuries, the port has marched eastward down the quays and into the bay; will urban renewal follow along behind it? Perhaps on a more accelerated schedule? More on the DDDA below.

The *Dublin Transportation Office* concerns itself with transport infrastructure, the expansion of which could certainly have a massive impact on the foreshore; they now also have responsibility over commercial ports, which includes Dublin Port. Although they apparently have no direct concern with Dublin Bay, their recent *Regional Freight Study* confirmed the current heavy use of Dublin Port and repeated hopes that the Dublin Port Tunnel will relieve some of this pressure.

No group has a bigger stake in the bay than the *Dublin Port Company*; they are a self-financing, semi-state organisation whose business it is to facilitate the flow of goods, passengers and attendant tracking information through the port. Port facilities dominate the central portion of the Dublin Bay foreshore. No entity has spent more time, money and energy developing the bay. They will have strong feelings about what happens there, although they might have to learn to share their hopes and dreams with Drogheda Port – if not Bremore at Balbriggan.

Speaking of ports, *The Dun Laoghaire Harbour Company* is a state commercial company charged with the responsibility of maintaining and developing its eponymous harbour as a local marine recreational amenity, as well as promoting investment and commercial development to sustain the value of the historic harbour. Sharing may be appropriate for them too, given the involvement of *Dun Laoghaire/Rathdown County Council*.

The *Environmental Protection Agency* is directly responsible for a wide range of functions. They include the regulation of large or complex activities that have significant polluting potential; monitoring and reporting on environmental quality; and enforcing compliance with environmental protection legislation in Ireland. They will have important things to say.

Other groups may become involved with certain aspects of planning and development, such as *Fingal County Council* who will have a say regarding Sutton and Howth. The *Eastern River Basin District Project* is part of Ireland's implementation of the Water Framework Directive; and the *Three Rivers Project* is to establish monitoring systems and develop management strategies that will restore the waters of the Boyne, Liffey and Suir rivers to good ecological status.

An Bord Pleanála is responsible for the determination of appeals and certain other matters that are related to various planning and development acts. It may not have any direct involvement with Dublin Bay but will certainly be required to make decisions regarding development projects on the foreshore, many of which can be highly contentious.

Ultimately, the biggest single influence on the solution of determining the future of the bay may come from the *Dublin Regional Authority*, a group which promotes co-operation and joint action between local authorities, public authorities and other bodies. More on them below.

It is an indication of how essential Dublin Bay is for our lives that there are so many groups with vested interests. It's a crowd. And things might very likely become a bit cluttered and confused even if there weren't environmentally engaged NGOs involved. But there are. And they care a great deal about what happens to Dublin Bay.

NGOs

An Taisce, the National Trust for Ireland, was established in 1948 and is one of the most influential environmental bodies in the country. An Taisce believes that a high-quality environment is central to Ireland achieving a successful and sustainable economy, as well as a high quality of life. An Taisce is independent of the state, and local authorities are obliged to consult with it on a vast array of development proposals. Consequently, the trust's range of expertise extends across Ireland's natural, built and social heritage.

BirdWatch Ireland is the leading voluntary conservation organisation in Ireland, devoted to the protection of Ireland's birds and their habitats. The group works around Dublin Bay to do survey work with seasonal coastal and breeding bird surveys. The Irish Wetland Bird Survey is the group's principal tool for monitoring wintering waterfowl populations and their wetlands in Ireland. BirdWatch Ireland also runs the Dalkey Island Tern Project which works to create a safe environment for Europe's largest colony of the roseate tern, a globally threatened species.

Coastwatch Ireland is part of Coastwatch Europe, an international network of environmental groups, universities and other educational establishments, who in turn work with local groups and individuals around the coasts of Europe. Common aims are the protection and sustainable use of coastal resources, and the development of informed public participation in environmental planning and management, including Coastal Zone Management (CZM). Over 10,000 volunteers across Europe carry out the annual Coastwatch survey.

ENFO is a public service body which provides easy access to wide-ranging and authoritative information on the environment, including sustainable development. ENFO was established in 1990 as a service of the Department of the Environment and Local Government.

Dublin Bay Watch acts to protect and preserve Dublin Bay as an amenity for future generations. It was founded by Seán Dublin Bay Loftus in response to the Dublin Port Company's attempts to 'reclaim' Dublin Bay and fill in parts of the foreshore. Dublin Bay Watch opposes these plans because any further encroachment into the bay might accelerate the silting-up of the inter-tidal areas of Dublin Bay and the Tolka Estuary.

S2S – '*Sutton to Sandycove*' – is a voluntary group whose sole objective is to promote the construction of a continuous sea-front promenade and cycleway from Sutton to Sandycove, linking and upgrading where appropriate the existing walkways and cycleways and building new ones where necessary.

Friends of the Earth is an environmental campaign group concerned with climate change, waste, water and wildlife issues. It is the world's largest network of environmental groups with over one million supporters and campaigners organised in seventy countries. Friends of the Earth Ireland was launched in October 2004 to promote education and action for environmental sustainability and environmental justice, and to focus on Ireland's response to the big environmental challenges of our time such as climate change and energy, the waste crisis and the spread of GM crops and food.

The Inland Waterways Association of Ireland is a voluntary body of waterways enthusiasts formed to promote the development, use and maintenance of Ireland's navigable rivers and canals. IWAI is a voluntary body founded in 1954 and it successfully fought the threatened closure of the Grand Canal in Dublin and has done much to focus interest and activity on the restoration of the Royal Canal.

The Irish Wildlife Trust aims to conserve Ireland's wildlife and habitats through active campaigning and lobbying, education, and research in order to restore and rehabilitate natural habitats which otherwise would be neglected. The group also provides conservation services and training, and works in co-operation with other environmental organisations towards the common goal of conserving Ireland's natural heritage.

Save Our Seafront works to protect and promote Dublin's public foreshore amenities. They played a leading role in stopping plans to build an exclusive apartment block on the site of Dun Laoghaire Baths and to privatise a major section of the sea front at Scotsman's Bay. They see the campaign over Dun Laoghaire baths as part of a wider battle to protect the public sea front from unwanted developments around Dublin Bay, and are concerned with the planned redevelopment of the Carlisle Pier in Dun Laoghaire Harbour as exclusive apartments.

There are specialised environmental groups that are keenly interested in preserving Dublin Bay. *The Irish Seal Sanctuary* provides shelter, treatment and rehabilitation for rescued marine wildlife found in difficulty around Ireland's coasts; while *The Irish Whale and Dolphin Group* is dedicated to the conservation and better understanding of whales, dolphins and porpoise in Irish waters. Both organisations conduct research and consult on matters directly related to the health of the bay.

There are also huge numbers of bay users who organise themselves differently. Some overlap with the groups mentioned above, some don't. They may not often take the lead but they will have their voices heard if they feel that the ox about to be gored is their own.

Members of yacht clubs and sailing clubs care about the bay, as do wind surfers and kite surfers and board surfers, scuba divers and snorkellers, coastal rowers and kayakers and canoeists, painters and photographers, sea anglers and bait diggers who trudge out at ebb tides in pursuit of the endlessly tempting lug worm. If the bay were threatened with the possibility of oil spills, for example, all of them would have an opinion.

The Dublin Docklands Development Authority

The regeneration of the docklands area was launched in 1997 as a fifteen-year development which will culminate in 2012. Approximately 1300 acres are involved, and total public and private investments are estimated at €7 billion. The project is intended to create well over 30,000 new jobs and result in up to 11,000 new homes being built, of which twenty per cent will be rated as affordable housing.

The former docklands area was substantially derelict or low-value industrial land. The area had severe economic and social problems, exacerbated by the loss of its major source of traditional employment in the port industry. Containerisation resulted in huge layoffs; many families were forced to move out; and at-risk families were often housed in the resulting vacancies. A strong community spirit was retained, however, and is providing a platform upon which future improvements can be based.

In 1997, unemployment in the docklands area was averaging thirty per cent and only thirty-five per cent of local children were still attending school in the Leaving Certificate year. Now only thirteen school at primary level, sixty per cent do their Leaving Certificate and ten per cent go onto third-level education. Around 160 docklands residents are attending university and one female resident is a qualified barrister. The DDDA has certainly been partially responsible for this turnaround in education, thanks to its scholarship programmes and other funding of educational projects and facilities. Employers in the IFSC area have also tried to discourage early school-leaving by ear-marking a number of jobs every year for residents who have completed school.

There are some issues unresolved. Will these improvements be sustainable after the project itself is completed? Will more funding be required? The Docklands Project has already radically changed much of the area, both through property development and the regeneration of a viable local community. But even bigger changes are on the horizon, and not everyone is pleased.

The Watchtower is a hundred-metre tower to be constructed on the north side of the Liffey. It will be joined by the U2 Tower, also an impressive one hundred metres. Together, they will form a dramatic pair of gateway towers connecting Dublin Bay to city centre. Some local residents complain that the towers will be too tall. (It is worth remembering that three castle towers are shown on the Dublin City Coat of Arms, with flames erupting out of them. This does not meant that the towers are on fire but rather symbolises the zeal with which Dubliners defend their city, as can be experienced today on Hill 16. Dublin City Council translates the seal's Latin motto – *Obedienta Civium Urbis Felicitas* – as 'Happy the city where citizens obey'. You have been notified.)

U2 Tower and Britain Quay Development are to be sited at the Grand Canal Dock, taking up slightly less than two acres. Promised to become an 'architectural icon for the skyline of Docklands and the city of Dublin', some householders in Ringsend are complaining that the proposed new tower will overwhelm their neighbourhoods. The thirty-one-floor building will house luxury duplex apartments and other multi-use space, in addition to U2's new recording studios. (U2 is apparently moving much of its actual business to Holland in order to avoid paying Irish taxes.) Once built, the U2 Tower will be the tallest building in Ireland. The adjacent Britain Quay Development will be approximately 11,500 square metres and will contain a mix of uses including leisure, residential, commercial, arts and culture.

The Dublin Docklands Development Authority is mandated to secure 'the social and economic regeneration of the Dublin Docklands Area on a sustainable basis; to improve the physical environment of the Dublin Docklands Area; and to sustain the continued development in the Custom House Docks Area of services of, for, in support of, or ancillary to the financial sector of the economy.' It is guided by the 2003 Master Plan which is based on the 1997 original plan and lays out the strategic approach of the Authority towards realising the sustainable regeneration of the Docklands area.

There are four strategic priorities:

- To maintain the momentum of the roll-out of physical development in the form of buildings and infrastructure.

- To achieve genuine architectural legacy and landmarks.

- To create a sense of place for Docklands, one which reflects the vibrancy, diversity and excellence of Docklands, and most importantly, one which is progressively experienced by the resident, the worker and the visitor.

- To realise the potential of the people of Docklands. This means that all the people of Docklands should be empowered through the project to achieve their full economic and social potential.

An Oil Refinery on Dublin Bay?

The Docklands Project shows what can be done to revitalise what had been allowed to deteriorate and create a valued urban asset. It reflects well what a modern Dublin Bay should feel like, as an amenity that extends and improves modern life.

But it should also be remembered that not all proposals for the Ringsend/Poolbeg area were sensible – or at least they don't seem sensible to us today – and that only an alert citizenry can prevent future depredations.

In 1936, The Irish National Refineries proposed building an oil refinery on Dublin Bay, and the government granted the necessary operating license for it. About fifty-three acres of reclaimed land was available and another seventeen acres would be added, all of it leased by the port to the refinery.

Financing became an issue in 1939, however, and the advent of war delivered the final blow to the project. In 1947, a portion of the reclaimed land along with the refinery facilities was made available to ESB for conversion into a power-generating plant.

In 1972, there was a second attempt at refining oil on the shores of Dublin Bay. This time, the south side of the Liffey was to get the honour. A portion of the foreshore below Pigeon House would be reclaimed and a sparkling new oil refinery built there. Response from residents of Sandymount and Irishtown was furious, not unpredictably. The port defended itself by explaining that it had approved the project provisionally so that formal procedures could be engaged. Critics responded that the project should never have been started in the first place. In the end, planning permission was refused and that attempt died away.

It seems unlikely that the oil refinery will be brought forward again – unlikely, but not impossible.

The Dun Laoghaire Baths at Scotsman's Bay and the Carlisle Pier

The former Dun Laoghaire Baths are located on a rocky escarpment just opposite the People's Park. They were constructed between 1905 and 1911, replacing the Royal Victorian Baths, which dated from 1843. The baths consisted of an entrance building, an open-air pool and a toddler's pool fed by tidal sea water. Heated indoor pools were added in the 1970s, but the facility has long since fallen into disrepair.

In April 2005, the Dun Laoghaire-Rathdown County Council proposed undertaking a massive redevelopment of the Dun Laoghaire Baths site. The core of the proposal would be a 'water world and indoor leisure complex', complete with a twenty-five-metre pool and seaweed baths, a wave pool with sandy beach, a kiddies paddling pool, plus various slides and flumes with their associated pools; and all of it would be safely indoors. There was also to be a splendid new civic plaza – suitable for ice-skating in winter and outdoor concerts in summer – and it would be sheltered from the prevailing north-easterly winds (which can become quite blustery) by a seaward windbreak of 180 apartments (whose inhabitants would provide twenty-four-hour "eyes and ears" security for those ice-skaters and concert-goers below) plus upscale retail space; and all of it anchored on the Sandycove end with a glowing ten-storey glass tower which would also function as a kind of "lighthouse" with a public viewing area on top for the use of those who wished to look at the bay.

In order to provide a large enough site for this development, about five acres of Scotsman's Bay would be 'reclaimed'.

The plan was certainly ambitious. But it soon ran into opposition. Local residents objected to the scale of the development and the fact that it would disrupt the pleasantly low-key ambience of Glasthule and Sandycove. Certainly, the 'footprint' of the proposed structure would have been vastly out of keeping with its neighbourhood.

Another worry was that infilling a significant portion of Scotsman's Bay might lead to increased flooding during storms, so that any 'reclaiming' of wetlands and foreshore should be resisted. Moreover, many people believe the whole of Dublin Bay should be protected under the EU habitat directive as an SAC (Special Area of Conservation). Resistance mounted and the scheme sank under the weight of its own grandiosity.

The derelict Carlisle Pier in the centre of Dun Laoghaire Harbour has also become controversial, for many of the same reasons that enraged opponents of the Dun Laoghaire Baths project. The winning design proposed two long, narrow, glass-fronted blocks with a public space on the side. The scale was prodigious, to say the least, and blazingly modern – a little taste of Hong Kong plopped down in the centre of Victorian Kingstown – with a 127-bedroom hotel and 229 apartments plus retail space and a 'marine life centre'.

Models of the design were made public and can still be found on the Web. The proposed architecture was certainly stunning, but doubts were raised as to whether or not it was appropriate to its surroundings. Well-meaning people can disagree. And certainly if only nineteenth-century designs were to be allowed for Dun Laoghaire, then the place would be well on its way to a kind of Disneyland-esque faux authenticity. Yet, the project seemed to overwhelm its neighbourhood, as would the baths project; and many urban architects argue that new buildings have an obligation to fit in with their surroundings.

The project is currently frozen, the reason given being that the developers failed to meet the timetable for submitting an acceptable planning application. It seems probable that the vociferous public protest against the huge development proposed for the Dun Laoghaire Baths might have influence the decision to go slow. Local residents have made it clear to elected officials that they will fight developments which seem to profit developers unduly, and elected officials have responded accordingly. You cannot do nothing forever, however, and the Carlisle Pier is an eyesore in the midst of a highly valued amenity. Something needs to be done with it.

New plans have been brought forward for the baths, too – one assumes with a certain amount of trepidation. The idea now is to include a public swimming pool and some landscaping of existing walkways. There may also be commercial use but no high-rise developments. At present, it seems certain that there will be no infilling of the foreshore at Scotsman's Bay.

Poolbeg: Apartments or Incinerator or Both?

Responsibility for the Poolbeg peninsula was recently shifted from the Dublin Docklands Development Authority to Dublin City Council who in 2005 published the Poolbeg Framework Plan. This plan visualises major housing, industrial and cultural development within an area that could certainly use some improving.

Still, housing *and* industrial *and* cultural . . .

When the sewage treatment facilities were inaugurated at Poolbeg, Dublin City Council had assured the government that odour would not become an issue. This was a state-of-the-art plant, the only installation of its kind that combined carbon hydrolysis, a process for digesting sludge, with thermal dryers that reached temperatures of 450 degrees Celsius, killing pathogens and producing a pasteurised, organic-based fertiliser marketed under the name 'Biofert' and spread on the green, green fields of Leinster. It was also cost-effective, providing over fifty per cent of its energy requirements itself. (From what? Don't ask.) In any case, at €300 million, it was hardly the kind of place where 'odour' would become a problem.

Now that it has, and all attempts to resolve it have so far failed, Dublin City Council has apparently pinned its hopes on an 'Odour Action Programme'. Relief is promised by summer of 2007. Don't hold your breath. (Actually, holding your breath might be the best option.) In any case, the sewage treatment plant isn't going away – nor should it, obviously – which means locals in Ringsend and Irishtown and Sandymount will just have to learn to live within a kind of heightened acceptance of natural processes.

And there may very well be a lot more of them doing it too.

You would think that the presence of a massive sewage treatment plant would make the Poolbeg area an improbable site for an even more massive housing development. You would be wrong.

In May 2006, Dublin City Council granted property developer Fabrizia permission to build sixteen blocks of seven- to eight-storey apartments and retail space on the foreshore between South Bank Road and Sean Moore Park, bordering the former Irish Glass Bottle plant. The impact of this huge development on an already compromised corner of the bay is hard to imagine. Traffic density alone would seem to make the idea insupportable, but the alteration to the sea front and destruction of what has been set aside as a Special Preservation Area (SPA) for migratory birds is equally dismaying. BirdWatch Ireland has complained that Fabrizia also proposes 'to drain the construction site, used as an illegal dump for contaminated waste from the Gas Company site by the same developers, into the SPA', something that sounds truly unacceptable.

Objections to this proposal include that it will involve substantial encroachment onto lands that are zoned as recreational amenities and open space; that it will be a major change to the existing character of the area; and that a major negative impact on traffic patterns is inevitable from the sheer size and and scale of the immense development. Moreover, a development of this scale so close to the shallow waters of the bay will damage habitats and feeding grounds of wildlife, perhaps increase the risk of coastal flooding throughout adjacent neighbourhoods, and make this corner of Dublin Bay a little more vulnerable.

Yet despite the zoning issues and the impact on Irishtown and Sandymount, it seems likely that the mega-project will be approved.

You would think that the presence of a huge housing development would make the area unsuitable for a huge industrial incinerator. You would be wrong. Again.

Dublin City Council, along with Dun Laoghaire/Rathdown, Fingal and South Dublin County Councils, have applied for approval to build an industrial incinerator on the foreshore of Dublin Bay that will burn 600,000 tonnes of household, commercial and industrial waste per annum. As of the publication of this book, the subject is still under debate.

It is hard to feel very neutral about the idea of an industrial incinerator as big as Croke Park planted on the fragile shores of Dublin Bay, looming over Sandymount Strand like an immense, malevolent . . . there, you see? Lost it already.

Still, there must be something good that can be said about having an industrial incinerator on the shores of Dublin Bay. To begin with, the term 'incinerator' itself sounds a little pejorative, so perhaps switching to 'thermal treatment plant' would be a step in the right direction. It won't be burning wastes, it will be treating them thermally. (I feel better already.) Moreover, incineration technology has – sorry, thermal treatment technology has improved a lot, so that releasing cancer-causing dioxins into the air really isn't all that much of a problem anymore. More dioxins come from domestic burning of common garden rubbish.

We should also keep in mind that burning . . . thermally treating wastes is a good way to produce energy. And in Europe, Ireland is a laggard in the thermal treatment of wastes department, while Denmark tops the table. Surely, if the descendants of those blood-thirsty raiders who pillaged ninth-century Ireland with such fervour like the idea, it can't be all bad. Can it?

The Food Safety Authority of Ireland (FSAI) considers that 'such incineration facilities, if properly managed, will not contribute to dioxin levels in the food supply to any significant extent. The risks to health and sustainable development presented by the continued dependency on landfill as a method of waste disposal far outweigh any possible effects on food safety and quality. As part of an overall waste management strategy, as reflected in the EC Waste Hierarchy, incineration coupled with waste prevention, reduction, recycling and other treatment methods is the preferred option.' If managed properly.

But why build it on Dublin Bay? Is it because Poolbeg seems such a grim wasteland already that making it worse is more or less acceptable?

One of the defining attributes of intelligent life is the ability to adapt from direct experience: the cat who gets her tail caught in a swinging door learns to tread carefully near them. Do we need further proof that creating even more of an industrial wasteland at what by rights should be one of the most attractive parts of the city is a poor idea?

Even if adding an industrial incinerator to the shores of Dublin Bay was a good idea (and it would be hard to find those who would argue as much, other than the plan's supporters, of course) wouldn't the burden of supplying it with wastes to burn become an issue? One estimation is that at least 100 lorry-loads of waste a day would be required to keep it cooking. Does it make sense to add that burden to the narrow streets of Dublin? Aren't we trying to have *less* traffic in the city centre? Wouldn't siting an immense entity such as an industrial incinerator at what is in effect a choke point at the heart of the capital city be a foolish option? Aren't we trying to shift away from industrial manufacturing towards knowledge-based services?

The planning application for the incinerator has been submitted, and the site was chosen presupposing the existence of an Eastern Bypass (a bit of road construction along the south shore that will further reduce the desirability of the foreshore; the kind of destruction of the city-bay union that San Francisco evaded by not rebuilding its version of the road after the earthquake fortuitously levelled it).

Why would we want to bring our garbage from far away and burn it beside our bay? It seems retrograde, primitive, feral. Why would we choose to burn 600,000 tonnes of household, commercial and industrial waste on the shores of Dublin Bay, year in year out, said waste to be trucked in by lorries 24/7, an endless stream of lumbering waste-haulers caravanning through the heart of an already traffic-burdened city and bearing their noxious loads that have been gathered from various corners of the land and transported into the capital city, into the geographical centre of where the city meets its bay . . . solely for the purpose of burning it there? 600,000 tonnes of it a year. Burning.

It really is very hard to feel neutral about it.

The Fifty-two acres or Bremore or Both?

Dublin Port Company has requested permission to fill in an additional fifty-two acres of the bay just off the eastern edge of the current port facilities. They explain that the section would be used to create a deep-water berth for the huge new container ships that are coming into operation. The port argues that without these expanded capabilities, their ability to channel the country's imports and exports through the port will be jeopardised.

The port has reclaimed land on and off over the years, and this fifty-two-acre portion may be the last bit they can take. They seem to feel a sense of urgency – perhaps because opposition has grown to their efforts. In 1980, when what was then the Port Board requested permission to reclaim ninety-four acres of Inner Dublin Bay on the Tolka estuary, complaints from local residents resulted in the plan being scrapped. Then in 1988, the port applied to reclaim the new fifty-two-acre site off their eastern border; and the plan was again met with vociferous objections from those worried that, among other things, it would increase silting in the inner bay. The port's plan was again rejected and the port told to consult with residents' associations.

In 1999, the Port Company published a public notice stating that it had applied to reclaim the same fifty-two acres. Decisions were delayed for various reasons – in May 2000, the Department of the Marine decided that the Environmental Impact Statement (EIS) was "seriously deficient"; but with the transfer of authority over the port shifted from Marine to Transportation, new voices are being heard.

Interestingly, new voices are also speculating on the advantages of moving all or part of Dublin Port to what would be a smaller terminal facility at Bremore Port in Balbriggan. While our current port at the Liffey mouth is shallow and tends to fill with sand, the proposed Bremore Port is a genuine deep-water facility that would make sense as a modern port, well capable of servicing today's huge ships.

The idea of moving the port is not new. ESB suggested something similar in 1990 (*Port Infrastructure in Ireland: Requirements and Proposals*, ESB, June 1990). The current port is basically trapped by the city surrounding it so that great efforts – such as building the Port Tunnel – are required to fit it to its location; while moving to a new port outside urban Dublin would eliminate many of these problems.

Other ports in Europe and America have faced similar problems. Rotterdam, Le Havre, Bilbao, and Copenhagen have all had to move their ports to new facilities. New York and San Francisco were both major ports that exited the business as they moved into a services-based economy, shifting 'their' ports to New Jersey and Oakland, locations better suited to road and rail traffic. The existing terminals at Dublin Port are not easily accessible, and the impact of port-related traffic on the city centre is dire. The Dublin Port Tunnel may grant some relief. Or it may not.

The idea of having a commercial port near the city centre for the benefit of industry and business seems a little quaint. Few products that you can drop on your toe originate in the single-digit 'D' areas; complex financial-services packages are more likely to be assembled there. Today, manufacturing and distribution facilities tend to be found at industrial estates that ring the city, having moved out to the fringes in order to take advantage of the M50 and other segments of our modern road-based distribution network and thus avoid the congestion of the city centre.

The Drogheda Port Company has proposed developing an 'integrated 24-hour, state of the art, deepwater port and logistics centre away from the existing congested hub of Dublin city'. The site of what would become the Drogheda Port Company Bremore Deepwater Port is already rail-linked and adjacent to the M1 motorway, making it about twenty minutes from Dublin.

Obviously, Balbriggan is not on Dublin Bay and so the project lies outside the scope of this book. One wishes them well. Certainly the main impact of the development of a new port there would be to shift a portion of Dublin Port's Lo Lo and Ro Ro traffic (and can we not think of a better pair of terms to express these truly remarkable capabilities?) away from city centre – thus ending the need to 'reclaim' the fifty-two acres?

It seems the request is still before the relevant authorities. Perhaps this is just inertia. Or the hard-deaths old habits seem to need.

Yet, still, it would be a shame if Dublin Port was moved and all that newly reclaimed land was just left lying there, wind-blown and lonely, baking in the sun and growing sodden in the rain. Right out there in the middle of Dublin Bay. A fifty-two-acre parcel with fantastic water views on three sides . . . Close to the vibrant business centre of Dublin . . . An easy walk to the burgeoning Docklands area with its many amenities . . . Surely some other use could be found for it? Apartments perhaps?

The 'Manhattanisation' of Dublin Bay

Those who have lived in Manhattan may wonder if they are really serious.

The PDs have proposed redeveloping Dublin Port as a centre for cruise liner traffic, as part of a major urban regeneration project. 'This has the potential to create a spectacular Manhattan-style approach to Dublin by sea. The plan draws on international experience in cities like Helsinki and Barcelona where run-down port areas have been transformed beyond recognition. It would breath (sic) life into Dublin Bay, which is currently an underused asset.'

The plan depends on moving the bulk of the port's business to the proposed new deep-water port at Bremore, north of Balbriggan. Lo Lo and Ro Ro would be replaced by office accommodation, shops, waterfront promenades, a sprinkling of green spaces, and apartments, lots and lots of apartments.

'The ideas we are putting forward would solve Dublin Port's capacity problem while allowing for the development of "A New Heart for Dublin" in the future'. The idea is intended to spark debate on how best to develop Dublin Bay, although it may be too grandiose to stimulate anything more than open-mouthed wonder at the audacity of it all.

Nevertheless, that changes are in store for Dublin Bay certainly does create a desire that whatever happens is preceded by debate, to say the least.

The Dublin Bay Association

In 2005, the Dublin Regional Authority (DRA) took the initiative to set up a Dublin Bay discussion forum which resulted in the founding of The Dublin Bay Association (DBA). The DRA began with the recognition that there was no overall co-ordination between the many state agencies and organisations whose remit includes the Dublin Bay area. The need was to monitor the development of Dublin Bay and ensure it was being developed as an asset and amenity, with its unique environment taken into account. Three public meetings were held between February and March 2006, and as a result, the DBA was asked to establish terms of reference for a master plan of the Bay. The DRA would seek funding from Government for the DBA project, and a representative council would be established to manage the master planning exercise and ensure it was undertaken on an inclusive basis.

The remit of the DBA is to co-ordinate and facilitate, but not implement, the activities of the public bodies and private entities which operate within the Dublin Bay area. The day-to-day running of the DBA will be the responsibility of the DRA.

Dublin Bay Futures

In April 2006, The Dublin Bay Futures Conference approved a Declaration on the Future of Dublin Bay. A range of representative groups debated the issues and agreed to support the establishment of a Dublin Bay authority that would manage, develop and protect the bay. The group concluded that a statutory body should be set up to co-ordinate, manage, develop and protect the waters and lands surrounding Dublin Bay. It was felt that the public amenities and biodiversity of the bay required greater protection; access for recreational purposes was required; and a building height and land-use master-plan should be drawn up for the lands around Dublin Bay in partnership with the communities, general public and users of the bay, and in conjunction with a Coastal Zone Management Plan for the bay that would protect the foreshore.

So here we are. At Dublin Bay at the end of 2006, with several bad ideas slapped down, at least for now, and several very engaged groups willing to work hard to ensure that Dublin Bay becomes an asset that is treated like an amenity.

Finally . . .

Dublin Bay is a lot of things: a prawn, a rose, an environmentally sensitive politician; a body of water with myriad uses, shared by fish, humans and waterfowl.

Dublin Bay was a bountiful habitat for its Neolithic colonists. It became a fort for Norse raiders, then a port for them as they evolved into Hiberno-Norse residents. It was an important Anglo-Norman asset for controlling medieval sea-borne commerce, and it has continued to be the main gateway for the import and export of Irish goods and passengers down through the centuries.

Now it has become part an amusing hoax which perhaps indicates as well as anything how far we have come and what might lie in store for the bay.

A website created a furore with its announcement of an improbably immense new development on Dublin Bay. Complete with cheesy video and slick graphics, it claimed to be 'The biggest construction project in the history of the state' and went on to propose three man-made islands with a remarkable collection of amenities, including the world's only all-giraffe zoo, a comic touch which would be hard to over-praise. The new artificial development would be visible from space; 42,000 new luxury apartments would become available. (That a real project like this exists in Dubai will not go unnoticed, at least not by those who follow Posh and Beck's every self-indulgence.) Visitors who did not see the site as a hoax can be forgiven. Production values were very high. Perhaps a little too high.

In any case, paranoid types have concluded that the site is nothing more than a piece of viral marketing designed to generate improved search engine optimisation for an entity known as Funda which itself may or may not exist. (The name sounds a little fishy, and nobody wants to be fooled twice.)

What is worth noticing is how far we have come from those sixty Norse warships that sailed threateningly into the bay in 839. Today, a threat to 'develop' Dublin Bay has enough share of mind to function as a convincingly faux ploy that can nevertheless be easily deconstructed (all-giraffe zoo?). Perhaps we have reached the stage where absurdly grandiose property development schemes seem so abhorrent that they can only be viewed as comic, and so comic that we can repurpose them to generate web traffic.

Perhaps Dublin has reached the point where preserving Dublin Bay will become a de-facto stance and greedy pomposity will illicit only mockery. Perhaps.

Index